Inez' blessings
The Lord be
of the Lord be
upon you !!

much Love
and prayers !!

no weapon
is...
formed prosp

Judy J

Will There Be Any Coffee In Heaven?

Will There Be Any Coffee In Heaven?

Jennifer Thomas Hoston

To order additional copies of this book, contact:
Xlibris Corporation
1-888-795-4274
www.Xlibris.com
Orders@Xlibris.com
62112

About the Author

Jennifer would like to think that she is just an ordinary woman that has been irrevocably blessed with an extraordinary opportunity to share with you her life story. What the years have concealed is now being revealed. This riveting autobiography will make an impact, effectuate positive change and challenge each reader to know that in spite of the tumultuous winds of life that blows and incessant punches that life throws you can survive and thrive.

After many years of rigorous deliberation, contemplation, careful reasoning and consultation with my husband I decided to give this project the best that I have.

Jennifer Thomas Hoston originates from South Bend Indiana. She is happily married to her soul mate for life Bishop Ronald Hoston. With unfeigned humility she serves in the capacity of First Lady at the Greater Bethesda Ministries where her husband pastors. She is also the First Lady of the New York Central Jurisdiction where her husband is the prelate. Ron and Jennifer have one son Erike who is married to the lovely Kioya and this union has blessed them with three amazing grandsons. Jennifer is a multifaceted and talented writer, psalmist, musician, recording artist and articulate speaker for conferences and revivals worldwide. Without controversy she functions in these capacities with passion, intensity, humor and clarity. She is the founder of the "Rap-a-round" Ministries which effectuated positive change in their local youth department. Jennifer also served as Executive director of the Bethesda Child Development Center for 10 years. This agency employees 27 people and accommodates over 200 hundred children. Jennifer oversaw a budget of 1.5 million dollars annually and acted as community liaison for the center. She majored in psychology and Christian Education and has received numerous awards and honors of distinction by the mayor of Rochester and elected who's who at the John H. Williams #5 school for her accomplishment as a professional woman making a significant difference in the workforce.

Prepare to cry and laugh. I also suggest that you fasten your seat belts because there will be some turbulence but I assure you of a safe landing. Enjoy!!!!!!

Jennifer

Acknowledgements

After many years of rigorous deliberation, contemplation, careful reasoning and consultation with my husband I decided to give this project the best that I have. I owe appreciation to my best friend and partner for life Ron for his relentless passionate love, encouragement, expertise, tolerance, comfort and joy.... ooops and money for this project. To Bob Geter for conveying the importance of pressing "save" on my computer. To my amazing Greater Bethesda Family especially Valarie Davis Howard who believed in me when this book was in its infancy. A special thanks to my friend Assistant District attorney Loretta Courtney for sharing your knowledge in Law with me. To my grandbabies for understanding that Nana was swamped. To my awesome mother in law Ida Hoston for birthing Ron, a wonderful gift to the world and my father in law Herman who taught Ron how to be a real man in every sense of the word. To my brothers Jimi, Leroy, Wilburd and Tommy. You are the greatest ever. Lenora my sister in law...oops I mean my sister in love, thank you. To Monique Pryce. Words cannot express how you have impacted my life with your genuine allegiance and laughter. To my mom's best friend Louella Spivey for your incredible wisdom and prayers. To Ashawntay, Mary, Crystal and Stacy for holding me up with your love and prayers. To my amazing unforgettable mother. I am all that I am and only half of the phenomenal woman that she was. Mom although you are resting eternally I know that you are proud of me for completing the book that you so very much wanted to write. This one is for you exclusively. And last but certainly not least my daddy. For the brief but full eight years that you were the epitome of a father. Who is like my daddy? NOBODY!!!!! By the way daddy the next time that you visit me in my dreams stay long enough for me to ask you WILL THERE BE ANY COFFEE IN HEAVEN?

Contents

Chapter 1

We're Going to Get that Nigger!

"Mom, why is it so crowded in this car and where are we going and why is it taking *so* long and who are these strange men driving and where is my daddy?" An inquiring young mind just wanted to know. My mom turned her face toward me in the dark and gave me one of those "be not dismayed whatever betide, God will take care of you" smiles and replied, "When morning comes, we will be in South Bend, Indiana, and you will see your daddy."

I was only three years young at that time, and I didn't have a clue where South Bend was. But I was certain that wherever it was, it must have been an amazing place because, after all, the greatest man in the world was there. I also did not have the slightest inkling how long it would take for morning to come. I was not physically or mentally mature enough to process the concept of time. I did not understand that morning was the first or early part of dawn, or that it was the time period between dawn and noon, or that it was the first sign of the breaking of day better known as sunrise, or that it was the interval from midnight to noon. But I was willing to endure the hardship of riding cramped up like sardines because I knew that whenever morning came, I was going to see my daddy.

My mother often complimented me on the ability that I had, even as a small child, to persevere through tough times. She often marveled at the capacity that I had to endure inconvenience, hardship, and difficult situations without excessive complaining and without expressing a great deal of discomfort. I know that you will agree that endurance is not a normal trait or tendency for the average child, but there has always been something . . . something innate, something built within my person that always reassured me that no matter what I was encountering—someway and somehow—everything was going to work out in my favor. Now I fully understand what that something was . . . that something that, in spite of the boisterous waves and the howling winds of life, I always felt an element of safety. I always felt confident that when the storm finally subsided, I would be yet standing and unharmed. That something was having the assurance of a solid foundation.

This level of maturity does not come easily. I stand in amazement at the wisdom . . . the omniscience of God who knows the way that we are going to take in life; and he so graciously places the stamina within us, particularly those of us that have a covenant relationship with him, to weather the inevitable storms of life. He does not charter the course of our lives serendipitously because, before the foundation of the world, he predestined our lives and lovingly and strategically ordered our steps. I can attest to the fact that he gives us tenacity, resilience, elasticity, exuberance, courage, and fortitude to victoriously deal with the tough times. He actually weatherproofs us, which is a process that he implements to protect us from the exposure to life's terrestrial rain, sleet, snow, and wind. And his weatherproofing does not interfere with the success of the process or the lessons and principles that he intends for us to learn and apply.

The waves and currents of life can get pretty fierce, but a good foundation will keep you steadfast and unmovable until the storm is over. That is why it is mandatory that you solidify your foundation!

Little did I know—while taking that long ride from Blytheville, Arkansas, to Indiana—that I was about to become well acquainted with the contrary winds of life so much so that as the saying goes . . . I could write a book.

A building or house will not be able to withstand the weight and pressure that it is designed for, and will inevitably crumble, if the foundation is not sturdy and reliable. The wiring and the plumbing are both essential and time-consuming, but not in comparison to the foundation. The framework, roofing, plumbing, and painting are a piece of cake; but the foundation is crucial, critical, and tedious. And that is what takes time and patience. The foundation is the rock on which the building sits or rests. I will never forget the time that my husband and I had our first house built. I was very anxious to see the frame go up, and I would drive excitedly by the site every day and was very much disappointed because all I saw was the constant digging. I became a bit antsy and frustrated one day, and I asked the contractor when they were going to begin the framework. He responded, "Mrs. Hoston, please be patient. I promise you that we're going to get there." He went on to elaborate that the foundation was taking so long because of the enormous size of our house. He said the bigger the structure, the deeper the foundation. He did not allow my anxiousness to force him into cutting corners that would later compromise the safety and success of his project.

As a matter of fact, when the house was finally completed and the inspectors came to check the house for our certificate of occupancy, they began their inspection in the basement . . . the foundation. The foundation is the greatest of importance and is extremely significant. The foundation is, in fact, paramount. What a revelation I received. I had my anxious moments, but I soon calmed down because I realized that my focus and my concern were about the wrong things. Many times, we place more emphasis and spend more time in making sure that the things that can be visibly seen are impeccable and fail to concentrate on the invisible—the foundation. When the vicissitudes of life are weighing you down, and the turbulent winds of life's nightmares are blowing, it's irrelevant and insignificant how magnificent your frame looks or how ornate and elaborately decked and meticulously arranged your furnishings are. If your foundation is unstable, the building can become a dangerous and hazardous environment; and the city can ultimately declare it unsafe for occupancy and condemn it, thus all of the other labor is in vain.

A firm foundation is integrity. Integrity is the footing upon which everything else is predicated or built upon. Integrity is a learned behavior that has to be properly taught by precept and example. My mom was my example. She taught me that integrity is not optional, negotiable, or debatable and should never be compromised. There are many definitions for the word *integrity*, but the most simple one that comes to mind is that integrity is who you are and what you do when no one else is looking. Those no-one-is-looking situations are the occasions when your integrity will be tested. Anyone can be on their best behavior when they are being critiqued or closely observed or monitored. That would be like the employee that is only diligent when his supervisor is around, or a child that is well behaved only when there are adults observing their actions. That is not integrity; that is simply temporary discipline that is under close scrutiny and governed by external stimuli.

I often use the Statue of Liberty as a perfect example of one that adheres to high principles. I live approximately four hundred miles from that statue, but I can tell you precisely from as far away as I am right now, or even as far away as China, what the Statue of Liberty is doing in New York at any given moment. I promise you that she is standing and holding a torch in her right hand, representing the enlightenment of liberty; a tablet in her left hand engraved with July IV, MDCCLXXVI, representing the Declaration of Independence; broken chains at her feet, representing escape from oppression; and seven points on her crown, representing the seven seas and continents. I am confident and able to do that because of the material that she is made out of. The material has integrity. There is a stubbornness to her credibility and accountability. It has been proven through time that she is durable and dependable and can, in fact, stand the test. And she does it whether you and I are there or not. This is not to say that she has not had oppositions and exposures, which might have created a need for repair. We all have opposing, antagonistic conflicts and make blunders as we are maturing in life, and our integrity sometimes need to be mended or repaired.

I have an amazing beautiful cup that is my favorite to drink out of. I noticed one day, as I was drinking out of it, that it was leaking; and I had to search diligently for the crack because it was so small. And when I found it, I repaired it with superglue. It stopped the leak instantaneously, and I was able to continue using it without losing its contents. The crack was on the bottom of the cup, and it was not visible, and no one was aware of it except me. But if I had not repaired it, eventually someone else would have noticed the leak. It is a beautiful cup, but it just needed to be repaired. Many times, beautiful people are walking around with a small crack in their integrity; and they are losing important contents because honesty is leaking out, justice is leaking out, discretion is leaking out, humility is leaking out, the capacity to forgive is leaking out, and love is leaking out. Right now, they may be the only one that is aware of it or have noticed it; but if it is not repaired, eventually the world will find it out. You repair it by first acknowledging that there is a leak. You cannot be in denial. Secondly, you have to locate the leak and then fix it and maintain it. This can be done by finding yourself a point of reference—which is a good, accountable role model—and allow them to teach you and then practice, practice, practice. Studies show that if you do something twenty-one times in a row, that function should be indelibly ingrained in your psyche and become indigenous to the point of perfection, and you will eventually do it involuntary and automatically without thinking.

I was only three years young in that car, but the process of building a good foundation had begun. It is never too early to start building your integrity (your foundation), and it is never too late to start all over again should there be a need to. There is an inscription on the Statue of Liberty that says,

> "Give me your tired, your poor,
> Your huddled masses yearning to breathe free,
> The wretched refuse of your teeming shore;
> Send these, the homeless, tempest-tost to me,
> I lift my lamp besides the golden door!"

In order for people to bring their tired and their poor, the homeless and the tempest tossed, they certainly would be able to depend on Lady Liberty to be there to welcome them. This inscription is etched in stone, which suggests accountability, dependability, and durability. That's integrity personified.

Getting a firm foundation in my formative years was very essential because my latter years were going to be greater than my beginning. What's to come is going to be greater than what has been. I am appreciative of the amazing mother that took the time to pour principles and the meaning of good character, integrity, and tenacity into me at a young, impressive, and tender age. And more importantly, I am grateful to God that I was thirsty enough to allow her to do so. It's a fact that there can be an ice-cold pitcher of water at your disposal, but if you are not thirsty, you probably will never drink. I concur wholeheartedly with the old cliché that says, "You can lead a horse to water, but you can't make him drink." The horse has to have a strong, uncomfortable, and distressful feeling precipitated by a desire or need for water and characterized generally by a sensation of dryness in the mouth and throat. Now that is what you call thirst, and fortunately I was. The fact that I focused on the basics is why I am able to stand today and face the hostilities of life graciously, without coming apart at the seams and blaming my fate on the world. A firm foundation has enabled me to not flinch in the face of adversity or stagger at the pool of mediocrity. You've got to stand and face it in order to fix it.

There was a time when I would tell people to hang in there when they told me that they were experiencing some difficult times. Wrong answer! Anything that hangs has no foundation. Drapes hang, doors hang, swings hang, you hang a picture, etc. But those are inanimate objects, and they are designed to hang. The reason that they can hang is because they have no foundation. A person that is going to hang himself ties a rope or something similar around his or her neck and then stands up on a chair. As long as he or she is *standing* on the chair, it is difficult to hang him. What he or she has to do is remove the chair; and then the job is done, mission accomplished, because the chair is the foundation. Please do not try this at home or anywhere else for that matter. You are much too valuable for that. My point is in life you are going to encounter challenges and oppositions but don't hang in there. Stand and endure because God has a purpose and a plan for your life, and your foundation is going to bring you safely through. After you have done all that you can . . . just stand. Having God in your life is key along with others that have acquired good principles and stood the test of time. This is unequivocally a prerequisite for developing a solid foundation. It worked for me, and it is yet working. Keep that in mind the next time you are tempted to tell someone to hang in there. Change your advice to stand. My mom always said that if you don't stand for something, you will inevitably fall for anything. The value of a good foundation was one of the principles that I was learning while taking that long ride. I never would have made it and probably would not be here today without it.

My husband and I took a trip to Houston, Texas, to check on some financial investments. I was simply fascinated by the enormously high buildings in the downtown area. I'm talking about some major skyscrapers. We drove around until we found our hotel; and while I was sitting in the lobby, waiting for my husband to check us in to that wonderful hotel, I was passing time by doing what I call people watching. I noticed businessmen talking on their Blackberries and dressed in what appeared to have been Giorgio Armani and Versace suits. They were wearing impeccable crisp white shirts with French cuffs and designer neckties to finish off their professional look. These men looked like either they were on their way up the corporate ladder or they were already at the top and happily reaping the fringe benefits. Some were carrying their Louis Vuitton attaché cases, which I am sure had business proposals and other pertinent transactions tucked neatly inside. Some were walking rather hurriedly, and others were casually browsing, probably because they were early for an appointment. There were also well-dressed women carrying their Coach attaché cases and sending text messages. They were styling their Dolce & Gabbana shoulder bags and dressed in their Yves Saint Laurent, J.Crew, Gucci, Vera Wang, and Marc Jacob attire. Their look was also radiant, polished, and pristine. And you could not help but notice the variety of different intoxicating fragrances filling the air that seemingly were competing with each other. I smelled Chanel, Spellbound, Viva La Juicy, Allure, J'adore, Prada, Versace, and only God knows how many other fragrances were permeating the atmosphere. I was wearing one of my favorites, which is Boucheron, and I wondered if anyone had caught a whiff of that.

There were many couples that were vacationing with their children and just leisurely enjoying the good life. The parents had their gym-inspired attire on; and the children were matching them, casually dressed in their Nike, BCBG, Juicy Couture, Lucky Brand, and Guess. I was simply mesmerized by the soothing décor and the timeless elegant floors that were patterned with absolutely amazing black marble. The interior decorator had lavishly matched the chairs and the window dressings in a sumptuous mixture of velvet and silk. The color scheme was exquisitely done in hues of aqua and gold that was definitely posh and bourgeois. There was an older couple that had a cute little Chihuahua, and I was hoping that my husband would not return in time to witness it because he has a fear of dogs no matter how cute, tiny, and friendly it looked like. He does not believe the owner when they tell him that they won't bite. His philosophy is simply if they have teeth, they will bite. There were stores to shop; a fully equipped state-of-the-art fitness center; business lounge; private event spaces; concierge; several restaurants, including one at the top that overlooked the city; and a huge garage for the valet to park your car. I was just sitting there, taking in all of the ambiance, when my husband walked over to me and handed me my key to our room. He gingerly told me which floor we would be staying on because he knew that I was not fond of heights. The bellman instructed us to go on up to our room, and that our luggage would be delivered shortly. We stepped into the elevator that was faced on one side with oil-rubbed bronze and gold-plated trimmings, and the other side of the elevator was tinted glass designed so that the occupants could visibly capture their surroundings as they rode up to their floor. It was amazing. The elevator was crowded with anxious faces, but no one spoke a word. As we were riding silently to the twenty-third floor, I seemed to have drifted into a trance. I was reflecting on the multiplicity of things that I had observed in this hotel, and then I thought about the infrastructure that had to be underneath to support this humongous building. It had to be a foundation that was incredible. That was another teaching moment for me about the importance of the foundation. What if the contractors that built that five-star extravagant hotel had not concentrated on the foundation? What if they had been negligent and unscrupulous and just focused their attention on the external? That building might not be standing today. And just imagine the impending lawsuits. You see, when your foundation is shaky, it impacts more than you.

Another valuable principle that life was teaching me while riding from Arkansas to Indiana was how to deal with pressure. Pressure is what I was feeling in that car. First of all, the car was crowded with four adults and five children and very uncomfortable to put it bluntly. I definitely felt the squeeze. Secondly, there was a feeling of uncertainty because I was going to a place that I had never been before; and thirdly, it was dark in the car for hours, thus leaving me frightened. Lastly, but certainly not least, I felt deserted because I thought that I had been abandoned by my daddy. You add all four of those components up, and that will equal pressure. And the sobering thing was that there was absolutely nothing else that I could do but deal with it. Life can put the pressure on you. It's easy to say, "Stop the world, I want to get off," but that is a cop-out. Then ultimately, when someone needs you, you would be AWOL or MIA. You are here for a purpose, and your purpose is bigger than you. The definition for pressure is to bear down with a compelling force—a condition of distress, oppression, and sure affliction. Pressure is a force that pushes or urges. Pressure is something that affects thoughts and behavior, usually in a form of several outside influences working together persuasively. Pressure is the atmospheric dominance that you feel when a 747 rises in altitude. That is why your ears become plugged . . . pressure. But there is nothing that you can do but deal with it. Oh, you can chew some gum or yawn a few times, and perhaps there may be a few more options, but the bottom line is you're just going to have to deal with it. But the comfort is in knowing that it is only temporary, and that this too shall pass.

Another perfect example of pressure would be the pressure cooker. A pressure cooker is an airtight metal container that is designed for cooking by means of steam that is under intense pressure. The pressure, combined with the steam, is what gets the job done. Life is filled with sudden, swift, and unexpected transitions and discomforts that can really put the pressure and the squeeze on you. There is not always going to be money in the bank (our economy has already taken a dive); we are facing historic debt, two wars, stumbling health care, a weakened dollar, astronomic gas cost, mortgage crisis, bank failures, trillion-dollar federal bailouts for private corporations; your children are not always going to turn out the way that you had desired; your husband, wife, or significant other might forget your anniversary date; and the sun is not always going to shine. That is *pressure* personified, and that pressure is combined with steam. Life can get crazy. But just remember, that is exactly how good character is developed. Steam and heat are the components that get the job done. It's the driving force. It brings out the flaws so that they can be dealt with, and it also brings out the value, and it brings out the flavor. Pure colorless diamonds, which are the most exquisite, are formed out of carbon that is placed under extreme pressure and extreme heat. Pressure produces principle, and principle produces integrity, and integrity produces character. Character prepares you and enables you to withstand life's vicissitudes and oppositions and then qualifies you to help others. That is really what life is all about. It is bigger than you and involves empowering others, but it all begins with your foundation and how you handle pressure.

It is simply amazing how God charters the course of our lives in order that we may achieve his divine purpose. He providentially orders the steps and the circumstances of our lives that would best prepare us for our destiny. If that were not factual, he would cease to be God. I can emphatically make the declaration that there has been significance to my every experience. It is not my intention, by any means, to paint a picture on the canvas of your mind that my life has only been doom and gloom because—quite frankly—I've had some rather good days. I have tasted the sweet thrill of victory, but I have also shaken hands with the agony of defeat. In other words, as for the storms, I have had my share. But sandwiched in between each line of victory and defeat stood a girl with stubborn determination and integrity.

Little did I know in that car that I was about to ride into one of the storms that was going to impact and revolutionize my life forever. There is a song that my mother taught me; as a matter of fact, it was one of the first songs that I sang when I made my debut in church at the age of three. The title was "If I Ever Needed the Lord." I was so small in stature that they had to stand me up on the offering table (what a sacrifice) in order that I might be seen as well as heard. Wow . . . what a song to teach a little innocent carefree girl. But that was the very song that got me through a multiplicity of nights in my life. A storm can really rock your world. It can rearrange some things that have been meticulously put in place. It can wreak havoc on the best of plans. If you don't believe it, ask the people in New Orleans, and I know that they would attest to these sobering facts. They will tell you that when Katrina struck and FEMA failed, they sure did need divine intervention. I am also sure that the victims of the 2004Tsunami would unequivocally agree as well. Just as a natural storm can rock your world, so can the feelings of abandonment and disappointment.

I suppose that my mom must have been overwhelmed and exasperated in that car. As you well know, young children do not have the capability to conceptualize time or distance while traveling.

We thought that South Bend, Indiana, was right around the corner. A hop, skip, and a jump—or maybe two. I just know that if we asked my mom once, we must have asked her a thousand times . . . Are we there yet? That is one of the annoying questions that children ask rather incessantly while traveling . . . Are we there yet? My brother, Wilburd—who we affectionately called Cricket because of his size—really had pushed my mother's emotional button with that question . . . My mother finally said, out of frustration and desperation, "Boy, if you ask me that one more time, you are going to get *it*." Trust me, *it* was something that you just didn't want to experience from my mom. My mother did not matriculate from any college, but you would have thought that she had a master's degree in *it*. The Bible says, in Proverbs 13:24, that "He that sparest his rod hated his child but he that loves him chastens him quickly." And also, in Proverbs 21:15, it states that "mischief is bound into the heart of a child but the rod of correction will drive it far from them." Believe me, she had several scriptures that gave her convictions validity, but one scripture that was really one of her favorites, which she generally read to us before applying the *it*, was Proverbs 23:13: "Withhold not correction from the child: for if thou beat him with the rod, he shall not die."

My mom was not brutal by any means and certainly did not condone child abuse, but she did firmly believe that the good Lord did design a nice cushiony place on our anatomy—the gluteus maximus, the buttocks, also known as the posterior or the behind—for spanking. It is no coincidence that the English verb *spank* gives reference to a specific part of the body in many punitive traditions. The buttocks were my mom's preferential target for painful lessons, but it was always applied in love. She believed that when verbal communication was not effective, the rod would be. Let the church say amen. That probably would be called child abuse today with this world's system, and the children would be encouraged to call child protective services. But that explains why we have so many young boys looking for a lawyer rather than becoming one and ultimately ending up in prison, on the streets selling drugs, or in a grave rather than in college on the dean's list. It's also why lovely and brilliant young girls see the need to cover up their ambition for greatness rather than cover up their beautiful bodies, thus becoming a mother before they mature into phenomenal women. Pardon this sidebar, but I so vividly remember when our son, Erike, was six years old, and he was having some behavioral problems in school. His teacher immediately recommended Ritalin. Knowing our son the way that we did, we refused her suggestion, and instead we threatened that we would give him a few love taps on his gluteus maximus if he did not start making better choices. We also strongly recommended that his teacher challenge and stimulate his intellect because he was, in fact, a bright kid that was simply bored with her menial, nonchalant, one-size-fits-all preparations and assignments. His brain was functioning more accidentally than hers was on purpose. It worked, and the results were astounding. In addition to that, we saved him from potentially becoming codependent on drugs and becoming a social zombie.

The crowded car struck silence for a few miles; and then Wilburd, very apprehensively and respectfully, said, "Mom, I don't want to ask you are we there yet, but I just want to ask you how old will I be when we get there?" Everybody chuckled in the car, including the two strange men. We all laughed about it later. I was much too young to remember all of the details that transpired while taking that long ride, but my mother said that we played every game, counted every car, and sang every song including "Over the River and Through the Woods." Anything just to pass the time. I suppose that another meaningful lesson that I was learning was the fringe benefits of being patient. Becoming annoyed because of delay is tantamount to throwing in the towel. I didn't mind the roaring of the engine or the reverberating sound of the tires because I had one objective in mind. While traveling, some people anxiously and nervously concentrate on the destination and bite their nails all the way while others just sit back, relax, enjoy, and endure the journey. Probably, being only three, I'm sure that my childlike faith was challenged; but I didn't lose sight of the objective. I knew that the end result would be seeing my daddy. Sometimes, on life's journey, we just have to take the long scenic route before we reach our destination. One thing that is imperative that you should take note of while traveling is the plethora of road signs. There are detours, danger up ahead, construction, road bumps, proceed with caution, slippery when wet, rest stops, traffic merging, and expect delays signs all along the way for the purpose of keeping you informed of the road conditions and accommodations. You'll make it if you observe and comply with the signs. Periodically, you will also see a sign that will give you the amount of miles that you have to travel before you reach your destination. The purpose of this information is incentive and encouragement. It would be disheartening and disconcerting if there were no encouragement in life along the way, letting us know that we are making some progress and getting closer to our destination. Sometimes you are closer than you think. But the most important sign that you should observe is the exit sign. How many of us have passed our exit while traveling? Remember U-turns are illegal on the highway, and this means that you now have to endure *extended stay* on the road to your destination. I am cognizant that on the road of life, you can make U-turns; but if you pay attention to the signs, you avoid delays. Who has time to waste? We only have a minute only sixty seconds in it. Forced upon us we can't refuse it we didn't seek it we didn't choose it but it's up to us how we use it and we will suffer if we lose it give account if we abuse it. It's just a tiny minute but your eternity is in it. Since life is so fleeting, only a minute, it is imperative that we pay attention to the road signs.

The overloaded car finally pulled up in front of the biggest house that I had ever seen in my life; and out piled four exuberant boys—which were my brothers, Leroy, Tommy, Wilburd, and Jimmy—my mom, her sister, those two strange men, and myself. My mom walked hurriedly up to the front door, and before she could knock, a gray-haired, very dark, distinguished-looking man opened the door. It was quite obvious that he had anticipated her coming and had been anxiously awaiting our arrival. They embraced each other, and my mother began weeping while reflecting on all of the things that she had encountered over the last few days. He held her in his arms and began to stroke her hair and comfort her like a father would comfort a frightened child. I soon discovered that that gray-haired man was, in fact, her father—my granddad. They both sat down at the kitchen table and became deeply engrossed in a conversation that was beyond my comprehension, but I remember it being something about a cow and some money. My granddad told her that he had some good news and some bad news. He said that the good news was that immediately, upon my dad's arrival, he did go to that little church that my mom had recommended, and he did meet the pastor, and he also had found a great job at the South Bend Iron and Metal Company. Everything that he had intended to do in order to make a better start for his wife and children had been accomplished in a few days, but the bad news was that the sheriff had located him, and he had been arrested for a felony. There were no words that can convey how devastated my mom was. She felt the weight of the whole world crashing in on her. All she could think about was the last thing that the sheriff had told her that night in Clear Lake County: "We're going to get that nigger!" Her dream was turning into a nightmare.

The two strange men that had driven us to South Bend and my aunt that had accompanied them had removed the boxes of clothes from the trunk of the car and had waved goodbye. As my mom and her father were continuing their conversation inside, my brothers and I were very excitingly and curiously exploring new territory. In and out of the house, banging the doors, kicking some old pop cans that we had found, and saying "Stop, it's my turn" and "I'm gon' tell." In between the bickering and the squabbling, we were having the time of our lives. It's amazing how much fun you could have back in the day—kicking cans, shooting marbles, swinging on a tire that was held up by a rope, playing jacks, and don't forget about making those wonderful mud pies that looked good enough to eat. My brothers and I even had a contest just spitting watermelon seeds to see who could spit them the farthest. There was also a game called hide-and-seek. If you remember any of these games, you are really dating yourself. Entertainment was so creative, innocent, and not even remotely as costly as it is now. Today we have the skyrocketing costs of the Nintendo Wii, Play Station 3, Xbox 360, PSP, Nintendo DSi, and chat rooms to name an astronomical few. Try comparing those games and activities with the cost of kicking cans. There were also some little colored girls next door that were vigorously jumping with two ropes. That was something that we had never witnessed before. It was called double Dutch, and believe me, they had mastered the technique of being able to jump in and out without missing a beat quite skillfully. They had that fascinating synchronized rhythm that they took pride in. It was as if they were jumping to the sound of an orchestra. I was very much engaged in having fun; but I remember, in between making mud pies, periodically going in the house and tugging on my mother's dress. Annoyingly, I was poking her on the arm, asking her over and over again, "Where is my daddy?" I guess you have gathered by now, and it is abundantly clear, that I am a daddy's girl; and I was missing him like crazy. No apologies necessary . . . I only had eyes for him.

Before I proceed any further and give you clarity and the surrounding details on why my dad was arrested, may I pause to say thank you for allowing me to share my life story with you? Out of all the wonderful books that were available for your reading pleasure, you selected this one. You have not only invested your finances, but you are also investing your valuable time and your intellect. I have been candid, open, and transparent. I have shared with you truths that have never been uttered by me before. What the years have concealed is now being revealed. Yes, I am taking a great risk, but I did not cut any corners. I must admit that I am vulnerable because I have left myself exposed and extremely susceptible to be scrutinized and emotionally and psychologically challenged. But I have had to swallow my pride because now I find myself at the point of no return.

However, the flip side of this is that God's amazing grace is covering me, and he has assured me that he has my back, and that the results of your investment will be worth any undue or justifiable assessments of me. This book was not written to make an impression on anyone, but it was written to make an impact. Impressions can be superficial and fleeting, but an impact effectuates positive lasting change. This story is real, and the names *have not* been changed to protect the innocent because none of us were. The real indelible truth is that there is so much bad in the best of us and so much good in the worst of us that it hardly behooves any of us to find fault with the rest of us. And because of that astounding truth, I kept it real. There is something within me that will not allow me to comfortably perpetrate and play masquerades. I must confess that there were times in my life that I have attempted to emulate and duplicate persons that I thought were recognized and validated by the who's-who standards. Individuals that, by our society and especially the religious grading scale, were successfully climbing the slopes of life; but every time that I tried to mimic them, I would get lost in the masquerades. I discovered that slopes are slippery, and that many of them were climbing those slopes while trying to maintain their momentum and status with masks on.

From that rude awakening, I reaffirmed that I would be doing myself a disservice by joining them. In conjunction with that, I would be making a mockery out of the masterful job that God has done when he placed within me an ardent desire to love the skin that I am in. In other words, just be me. So often we can be tried and found guilty of burying the gifts and talents that God has so freely and lavishly given to us, not because we are lackadaisical, lethargic, or unappreciative, but because of—yes, you are so right—*people*. This book is going to paint a vivid picture and show you the danger and the travesty of allowing people to deter, hinder, block, and stop you from giving the world the best that you've got. But I am proof positive that anyone that tries to stop your destiny from happening will ultimately cause it to happen. And on that note, may I pause right now to send a universal thank you to anyone that may have tried to stop my destiny either overtly or covertly. There are several tactics that people will use to throw a wrench into the wheel of your destiny. Intimidation is one of the dreadful tools that is frequently used in most arenas, particularly the religious one. Intimidation is courage turned inside out. Intimidation is showing fear or the lack of confidence in a given situation. When you are intimidated, you are timorous and skittish. This will cause you to stress yourself out over something that has not and probably will not ever occur. If you zero in and take a closer look at the word *intimidation*, you will see another word, *timid*. When you are timid, you are easily frightened. This can cause your day-to-day functioning to become almost impossible.

I will never forget, when I was in the sixth grade at Benjamin Harrison School, there was a girl in my class named Marie that did not like me at all. Marie was very tall for her age and extremely overweight. Nothing personal against the plus size because some exceptionally good things come in large packages also. But Marie had been teased about her size to the point that it had ultimately caused her to develop a complex and become paranoid and even perhaps had developed an emotional disorder. It seemed as if she had mentally shut off any incoming data that would caution her that she was behaving inappropriately. Her bullying behavior was definitely a red flag that she had not learned how to control her aggressiveness. She had absolutely no empathy or sympathy and displayed no understanding in terms of tolerance or sensitivity toward me. She used her size to intimidate, manipulate, and bully people; and I was an easy target. Not because I was guilty of making fun of her, but I am convinced that it was because I was rather thin and petite, and most importantly, it was quite obvious that I was scared to death of her. Quite often, when you are the target of an intimidator, you are just an innocent bystander that just happens to posses something that the intimidator admires and desires. Marie had built up a defense mechanism that she used to protect herself from the psychological pain that she was experiencing from being made fun of.

Marie would threaten everyday that she was going to beat me up after school. She had no problems articulating what part of my anatomy that she was going to injure. I was petrified! First of all, I did not know the first thing about fighting; and even if I had, I was no match for Marie. I mentioned to the teacher what Marie's plans were, and she allowed me to leave a few minutes every day before class dismissed in order to avoid a confrontation with her. What I did not realize was that my fear and timorousness was empowering Marie. There is a saying that goes, "Never let them see you sweat." Well, I had not caught that revelation because I was sweating profusely, and I did not mind Marie or anyone else seeing it. There was no shame to my game. I was skurred (scared)! There were many times that Marie was almost successful at catching up with me while chasing me all the way home. But thank God, there was one thing that I had learned to do very well as far as she was concerned and that was run for my life. I had older brothers, and I shared with them my fear of Marie, and they gave me some advice that I will never forget. They simply said, "Jennifer, if you stop running, she will stop chasing." My brother, Leroy—who is the philosopher and the Einstein of the family—always says that the best way to get a person off your back is to stand up. Somehow I managed to get up enough nerve to take their advice. One day, when Marie told me that she was going to beat me up after school, she got the shock of her life. I stood up and put my hands on my hips and let my backbone slip, and I told her that we didn't have to wait until after school. We could get it on right here and now. I was trembling in my shoes, and my knees were having an intense fellowship with each other, but I did not let her know it. I kid you not. Marie started laughing almost hysterically, and she laughed so hard that I started laughing too. She was probably laughing at the ridiculous thought that little me had the nerve to challenge big her, but I did not care because my adrenaline had me on a roll. The laughter was so contagious that the kids in the classroom joined us along with the teacher. From that day on, Marie's anger seemed to have reduced, and there was a significant improvement in her interpersonal relationship toward me and even others. Marie and I became the best of friends. As a matter of fact, she would defend and protect me if someone else tried to fight me. Imagine that, my bully ended up becoming my bodyguard. Marie, if you are any where out there, "hey, girlfriend"! Most of the time, the intimidators are the one that has fear. Their external behavior is just a façade. They really feel inadequate; and what they are seeking is attention, acceptance, and to be celebrated.

Another tool that is frequently used that can hinder you from maximizing your potential is comparison. I admonish you not to get caught up in the web of this psychological game. Let me serve notice to you just for the record: you will never successfully do what you were designed to do if you waste your time comparing yourself with others. When you do this, you are suffering from the disease that I call *comparisonitis*. Before you put this book down and run to the dictionary to look up that word, let me save you a trip. It will be conspicuously missing because it was invented. However, the root word that you will find is *compare*. Compare means to literally or figuratively put something together in order to note points of resemblance and difference. This can be negative or positive. A positive example would be comparing the advantages and disadvantages of city life with farm life. That is a comparison that would be considered totally acceptable. However, a negative comparison would be if I considered myself to be a cut above you because I live in the city and you live in the country. Or if I compare your house in a demeaning way with mine or my education with yours or my children with yours or my husband with yours in that same manner. I call it the "mine is better than yours" syndrome. Or it could be just the opposite, "mine is not good enough" syndrome. All of those examples of negative comparisons are unhealthy and nonproductive, and create hostility and divisiveness. I suppose that every one of us is guilty of engaging in one of those negative examples at some point and time in our lives, but it is wasted energy. I submit to you that there will always be someone that will surpass you, and there will always be someone that you will surpass. I promise you; it is a wonderful thing when you learn to just compliment rather than compare. A person generally makes a negative comparison when he or she thinks that life has slighted them in some way, and that their best is just not good enough. This mind-set will keep you on a frustrating emotional rollercoaster. God—who is just, immutable, and omniscient—knew before there was a when or a where and a then or a there exactly what it would take for you to successfully complete your earthly assignment. Of course, he leaves something for us to do, and that is to make the necessary preparations that will properly equip and fortify us. And then you've got to know who you are and know your purpose. You must also be cognizant beyond a shadow of doubt that only you can prevent yourself from fulfilling your purpose. Applying these principles, you are unambiguously destined for greatness. Set your eyes upon the top of the mountain and go for it. Don't worry about climbing the mountain; just speak to it with fervor and faith, and I promise you it will move. You've got what it takes; you've just got to work it. I command that you be healed right now from the disease called comparisonitis.

Remember, in the Bible, when David almost got tangled up in that nebulous web when he compared his slingshot and five stones with Saul's armor? When it was time for him to face Goliath, Saul suggested to David that he protect himself by wearing his armor. David became intimidated and skittish and began comparing himself with Saul. He consented and put Saul's armor on. Saul was tall in stature and fully grown while David was just a lad and small in stature, so you can just imagine how awkward and ridiculous David must have looked when he attempted to wear that which was just right for Saul. David and Saul were definitely not in the same height or weight class. Kinda like Marie and me. No matter how David tucked and pulled, it just did not fit. This is not meant to discredit Saul's armor because he had successfully fought many battles with that armor; but God, in his infinite wisdom, chose a different means of victorious outcome for David. He chose for him the simple strategy of a slingshot and five stones. Believe me, he takes the foolish things of this world to confound the wise. David had a flashback of his victorious outcome when he killed the lion and bear with just his hands. Sometimes you have to push the rewind button and recapture the seemingly insurmountable hurdles that you have already successfully come through, then fast forward, square your shoulders back, and proceed with your assignment. After reminiscing and reflecting on his lion-and-bear encounter, David took Saul's armor off and picked up his slingshot and five stones, and the rest is history. It is amazing to think of the incredible things that we can accomplish with a few stones when they are impregnated with the power of God.

So many times, we are guilty of trying to fit into something that was not designed for us. That is like trying to put a round peg in a square hole. Let me help you . . . Take off Saul's armor and pick up what God has equipped you with. You will not be able to successfully or victoriously maneuver in something that was not intended for you. You are robbing the world from experiencing and benefiting from the nuggets that God has given you. In addition to that, you are depriving yourself of maximizing your full potential. Your destiny is waiting, and so is the world. Take off the façade and be your wonderful self. A carbon copy does not have the quality and the sharpness as the original. Anytime you compare yourself with others, you devalue and short-circuit the blueprint that was designed and tailor made by the master architect exclusively for you.

Another tool that is used that can hinder you from maximizing your potential is jealousy. Jealousy is cruel, and people will often use this odious behavior to stop you as well. Jealousy is a painful, resentful, and grudging desire to have what someone else possesses. Remember Joseph in the Bible and the constant conflict and struggle that he had to deal with because his brothers were inebriated with the spirit of jealousy? Jealousy and envy are lethal. They are paralyzing. There were two things that Joseph had that his brothers were jealous of—his coat and his dream. Can you imagine that a coat would create such animosity, hostility, and disturbance? There were probably times that Joseph thought that something was wrong with his coat, but there was absolutely nothing wrong with his coat. The problem was that Joseph's coat just had too many colors, and subsequently it was attracting too much attention. It was unique. But above all of that, I believe that his brothers saw greatness that emanated from his very inner being. When people see greatness in you, they often build up a resistance toward you, and it is designed to distract you from your ultimate goal. Thank God that Joseph realized that his destiny was tied into his coat of many colors and did not allow that green-eyed monster, jealousy, that his brothers had hinder him from embracing his destiny. I, too, have had to take on Joseph's disposition and not allow jealous and envious people to hinder my purpose. They have tried incessantly and are yet trying, but guess what . . . I am wise enough to know that they see greatness in me, and I will not stop on my road to purpose and give attention to someone that doesn't have one.

Not only did Joseph consider his destiny, but he also was cognizant of his legacy. Although your destiny is important, your legacy is crucial.

Destiny is the seemingly inevitable necessary succession of events that prepares us for our intended end. Destiny only takes you to where you are suppose to be, but your legacy transcends your destination, and it continues long after you are gone. And without a pause or an interruption, it continues to perpetually impact the lives of others. Your destiny ends when you end, but your legacy is handed down from generation to generation. Your legacy will extend much further than the brief seventy years (only a minute) that we have been given on this earth and maybe a few more provided we have the strength. I want to leave a legacy! I have learned that the only way that I will be successful at doing that is to celebrate my uniqueness and cancel out and totally ignore the haters. Some people have acquired a taste for *haterade*, but I prefer Gatorade. I have also learned that when there is another person doing exactly the same thing that I am doing and doing it the exact same way I do it, one of us is unnecessary. I can relate with Joseph. I also conscientiously decided from as far back as I can remember to wear my coat in spite of my critics. Wearing my coat simply means stepping out on the stage of life with all of the gifts, talents, and resources that God has given me and say, "Look out world, here I come. Lights, camera, action." I know irrevocably that I am fearfully and wonderfully made and that God created me with a magnificent one-of-a-kind design, and then he threw the mold away. I'm unique, and that's wonderful. Just imagine how boring, dull, and monotonous the world would be if everyone was the same. Variety is the spice of life, and I'm just spicy. Don't hate, just celebrate. And that's my final answer.

I concur with Sammy Davis Jr. when he wrote these meaningful lyrics:

> I've gotta be me, I've gotta be me
> What else can I be but what I am
> I want to live, not merely survive

And I won't give up this dream

Of life that keeps me alive

I've gotta be me, I've gotta be me

The dream that I see makes what I am

That far-away prize, a world of success

Is waiting for me if I heed the call

I won't settle down, won't settle for less

As long as there is a chance that I can have it all

I'll go it alone, that's how it must be

I can't be right for somebody

If I'm not right for me

I've gotta be free, I've gotta be free

Daring to try, to do it or die

I've gotta be me

That's what I'm talking about, Sammy! I couldn't have said it better myself. It's innate. It's in my DNA. It is seared into my genetic makeup. I can't shake it or deny it, so I just embrace it and celebrate it. I would be an impersonator or an impostor. I would be a fraud. I would be lost in the masquerade. Masquerade means to mask. It is a showy false disguise. It is an act of living under false pretenses. In the sixteenth and seventeenth centuries, the aristocrats in England would have balls, and the invited guests would adorn themselves in lavish costumes. The atmosphere that was staged was exotic and very mysterious because everyone wore masks to conceal their true identity. When it first originated, there was absolutely no dialogue permitted the entire time of the ball from the beginning to the end. Can you imagine attending a party and not being permitted to say a word the entire time that you are there? I suppose the reason for that strict rule was your tongue can interpret your head and also your mouth can inevitably expose who you are. The masks were worn to deceive and mislead. A mask camouflages or conceals the real you. Will the real you please stand up? This book was birthed out of the excruciating pain that I have suffered just from being me. Most of the time, people are afraid to be themselves because they fear the lack of acceptance and validation and, ultimately, rejection. Oftentimes, people throw darts of negativity at you in order to draw the attention away from their own inadequacies and idiosyncrasies. After many years of wasted tears and needless sorrows, I have discovered that there was nothing wrong with me after all; it was just my coat all the time . . . It has too many colors. And that's a good thing. I have been ostracized, hated, and criticized beyond what you could ever imagine for wearing the coat that I was born with and for pursuing the dream that God gave me. It's amazing how people can hate you for just looking like your parents (mine just happened to have been pleasant to look upon) and castigate you because you have the will to pull yourself up from the comfortable low place of mediocrity and take your rightful place in mainstream America. As for my dream . . . I can't help it if I had the audacity to dream big and, while at it, dream in Technicolor. I have to smile to myself when I think about all of the things that I have encountered since that long uncomfortable ride from Arkansas to Indiana to where I am today, but take a good look at my face. You'll see my smile looks out of place, and if you look closer, it will be easy to trace the tracks of my tears. Thanks, Smokey Robinson.

The Bible says, in Romans 8:28, "And we know that all things work together for good to them that love God, to them who are the called according to his purpose." Even the hardships and sufferings, the jealousy, the bitter disappointments, and the misunderstandings and even being wrongly treated and isolated were working together for my good. Am I perfect? Of course not! Mistakes? Sit down if you have a week because it would no doubt take that long for me to share some of mine with you. But he that is without fault, let him cast the first stone.

Now doesn't that just make you want to drop those stones in your hand *like it's hot*, which you intended to throw at someone else? I know unequivocally that God worked in the midst of all of those circumstances to fulfill his uncompromising, irrevocable, and inevitable good purpose in me. I've gotta be me!

I would love for this book to find itself in the awesome hands of Bishop T. D. Jakes, Oprah Winfrey, Mel Gibson, Denzel Washington, Spike Lee, or even the phenomenal Tyler Perry. I have closed my eyes and imagined one of them turning this riveting true story into a movie or a play. But if this book can challenge one person to love themselves in spite of the negative bystanders; if I can persuade one person to never quit, never give up, and never throw in the towel; and even if you have already thrown in the towel, if I can convince you to go get that towel and get back in position, then my writing would not have been in vain. You are guaranteed to win if you don't quit. Remember that winners are made up of failures that didn't give up. If I can convince you to take what you have been given and create what you've been promised. If I can convince you to use what you have like Moses used his rod. Use what you have like David used his slingshot. Like Michael Jordan used the basketball when he played for the famous Chicago Bulls or like Venus and Serena Williams use a tennis racket. Like Michelangelo and Picasso who masterfully used their paintbrushes. Like Tiger Woods uses his golf clubs in spite of the envious competitors. Like Ray Charles used his vocal chords and soulfully used his skill to play the piano. And I would be remiss to leave out the amazing Stevie Wonder who, although blind, is able to see better than some people that have 20/20 vision. That is how he could imperiously and expertly demonstrate the exceptional talent to write and compose the song "Isn't She Lovely." I could go on, but I think you've got the idea.

Now put your emotional and psychological seats in upright position and fasten your anticipatory seatbelts securely around you because you are getting ready to ride. Sometimes the ride is going to be smooth sailing, and you may be tempted to unfasten your seatbelt, but I would caution you and suggest that you keep it fastened simply because you may experience some unexpected turbulence. I would love to promise you a smooth ride, but life for me ain't been no crystal stairway. But there is one thing that I will promise, and that is a safe landing. After you have completed this ride, please exercise caution when opening the storage area of your mind because things may have shifted during the turbulence. A shift can be a good thing. I trust that your tendency to have preconceived thoughts about people has shifted. I pray that the propensity to judge a matter or person prematurely has shifted. It is also my sincere desire that the inclination to be jealous and envious of others has shifted. You know the feeling that comes over you when you are boarding a plane and you observe the people that are comfortably seated in first class when you could only afford to ride coach? Stop it! Never be jealous of that. Just tell yourself that the people that are riding in first class are going to arrive at their destination at the same time as you, and they had to pay more to do it. When you are riding on a plane and it is almost time to land, the flight attendant announces that she or he will be coming around one last time to collect any garbage that might need to be discarded. Some things just need to be trashed!

One last thing for your consideration before I continue my life story is to make the observation that we have the propensity to say when we travel by plane that I flew to California or I flew to Atlanta or I flew to Germany when, in all actuality, the only thing that you did was purchase your ticket and board the plane. You didn't fly . . . The plane did. My advice to you is just to board the plane of life and allow God to fly it. He is the one that invented the Global Positioning System (GPS). GPS has unquestionably revolutionized our society and made our travel less complicated and safe. Yet there is controversy and disagreement as to who invented it. Let me settle that dispute right now. God invented it. He has gone before you and me, even before the world began and mapped out, timed out, and measured out the distance in which you and I are destined to travel in life, and he has made our journey less complicated and safe. He knows the way that you are going to take and your boundaries are set, and I am persuaded that he is more than able to see you safely to your destination. Even while riding through the storms of life, he is the great navigator. You are in good hands. Thanks for traveling with Jennifer . . . Enjoy!

Please go back in time with me as I share with you more insight on what precipitated that move from Arkansas to Indiana.

There was a loud knock on the door of that dilapidated shotgun house in Clear Lake County, Blytheville, Arkansas. *It's after eleven o'clock. Who in the world would be out traveling these dark country roads this time of night?* Shivering with fear, my mom wrapped her robe around her and made her way to the door. She pulled back the frayed but clean curtains, and there stood four angry sheriffs with their hands on their guns. They shouted very disrespectfully at my mom, "Girlie, open this door!" My mother knew to obey the white man without any reservation or hesitation. This was in the Deep South in the late '50s, and not following the directives of the white man could result in the loss of your neck or perhaps some other vital body parts. My mom fumbled very nervously at the night latch and finally got the door opened. "Where is Leroy Thomas?" they snapped in an unchivalrous way.

"Sir, he isn't here, and I really don't know where he is," she nervously replied. Although she knew that he was in Indiana, revealing his whereabouts would have been disastrous. My mom was very cautious and respectful with the tone of her response because she knew so well of the potentially life-threatening predicament that she was in. You might say that she was cognizant of her place, and she knew to stay in it. There was a certain way that you had to position your body and carefully monitor your tone in a condescending manner when you spoke to white people. Her kinesics and her nonverbal behavior—such as facial expressions, posture, and gestures—were closely being observed in order to ascertain or determine the veracity of the statements that she was giving.

"I betcha' you betta not be hiding him nowhere in this here house," one of them cynically responded with an idiotic tone. "We have a warrant for his arrest. We are going to get him for grand larceny."

"Grand larceny?" my mother responded with a choking sound.

"Yea, you heard me. Our precinct got a call from the old colored woman that you are renting from. You are rooming here, am I right?"

"Yes, sir."

"Well, she called and reported that her cow was stolen, and upon our investigation, a man that fit your husband's description was seen walking into town with the animal."

Without any warning or search warrant, three of the sheriffs pushed my mom aside as if she was cargo. She had to brace herself to keep her balance. One remained outside, checking around the house with a flashlight. They pulled back the curtains to every room, which was only three not including the kitchen, and searched diligently everywhere for my daddy. One of the sheriffs went out the back door to search the outhouse. We did not have an inside bathroom. We used what they called the outhouse. Thank God that because of environmental concerns and technological advancements, the outhouse is now an endangered commodity. After they were certain that my dad was not there, they very disgustingly said, "Well, we don't know where he has escaped to, but we are going to find him, and when we do, *we are going to get that nigger*. You see, that nigger thinks that he is slick. And you know, girlie, a white man can kill a nigger just like you kill a chicken, and nothing will be done about it."

Nigger, my mom said within herself. The word *nigger* was the most insulting and degrading term that a white man could use. Colored people used it casually and flippantly among themselves, but for a white man to address you as a nigger was not something to be taken lightly. As a matter of fact, it was the epitome of humiliation. Sadly, there was nothing that she could do about it and survive. She also knew quite well that regardless of how they addressed her, it was incumbent upon her to speak to them in an accommodating manner and to keep her true feelings to herself to avoid the consequences. Underneath my mom's gentle and passive demeanor, she had an edge to her that was yearning and chomping at the bit to come out, but she knew better. However, the mind is a powerful thing; and as the sheriff was rambling on and on, my mom was retaliating subconsciously, *You tobacco-spitting, toothpick-chewing, beer-bellied, gun-toting, lily-livered—.*

"Do you hear me talking to you, girlie?"

"Yes, sir, I hear you."

"Well, act like it 'cause it seem to me that your mind had wandered off. I was saying that we know that you are going to be in touch with him, so you make sure that you tell him that the law is looking for him."

"Yes, sir," my mom replied.

On the way out of the door, one of the sheriffs paused and very lasciviously looked my mom slowly up and down with a watering mouth as if she was a delectable piece of meat to be devoured. She was an extremely attractive young woman that weighed an amazing ninety-eight pounds soaking wet, and even after having all of those babies, she had maintained her loveliness and properly resumed her endowments. She quickly clutched her robe with embarrassment to make sure that she was completely covered. My mom was seething and grimacing from the look of his little roving beady eyes. His subtle implications made her nauseous, but her feelings had to be suppressed. Her fortitude and common sense gave her the stamina to stomach his subliminal humiliating sexual gestures. When they were finally gone, my mom sighed with temporary relief. She made her way to the nearest chair and slumped down. She must have sat there for what seemed to have been hours because she was too distraught to move. She finally mustered up enough strength to get up and go check on her children. Miraculously, all of the noise that the sheriffs made had not aroused any of us.

Why hasn't he called me? she thought to herself. *I know that he should have arrived in South Bend by now.* My mother had mentioned to my dad over and over again about how she wanted to move north. Quite frankly, she had not just casually mentioned it to him, but she had become rather adamant about it. She wanted something better for her children, her husband, and herself. My mom and dad had grown weary of being treated like second-class subservient citizens. They had stared social injustice, legalized discrimination, and racism in the face long enough. They had witnessed every form of abuse imaginable. Colored people being lynched, raped, beaten, emasculated, excluded, and exploited was the order of the day in the South during that time. Injustice was commonplace. She remembered vividly that on one very hot Saturday night, three white men were out joyriding in a pickup truck, and they spotted two young colored boys that were walking down the road near our house. My mom was in the front part of the house, ironing our clothes for church on Sunday, when she heard the sound of a noisy truck and ran to the window to peek out. She saw the men stop the truck and jump out and grab the young boys and chain them to the back of their truck. She saw them speed off, driving in a reckless manner, leaving a cloud of dust behind. Rage, hatred, and ignorance kept their engine going at full speed. They were laughing and drinking, throwing beer cans out of the window, while someone's precious boys were on the back of their truck, dangling and strangling with excruciating pain and agony. They had absolutely no remorse! This ruthless recreational crime should have given their conscience a chill; but if you do not have one, you become sedated, callous, and oblivious to any form of animalistic maltreatment. There was a somber hush over that small community in Clear Lake County as they gathered around the radio early that Sunday morning to listen to the despicable news. The young boys' heads were decapitated, leaving pieces of their brains splattered all over the road. Their bodies were found dumped in a ditch miles from their severed heads. All of the colored people discussed this hideous, brutal crime quietly among themselves because they knew so well the consequences of taking it any further. In addition to that, they knew that this was a notorious common offense and that it would be nonproductive and an exercise of futility because justice had never been appropriately executed before. I believe that this was a premeditated act because those white men were joyriding in our neck of the woods, and they just happened to have had a chain. Go figure! Over seven decades have passed since that particular gruesome night, but my mom never emotionally or psychologically got over it. I must commend her though because she did not become victimized or paralyzed by it. As far as I know, those men got away squeaky clean; but if there be a just God in heaven (and there is), they may have gotten by, but they certainly did not get away. Galatians 6:7 says, "Be not deceived; God is not mocked: for whatsoever a man sow, THAT shall he also reap."

"We have to go north," my mom continued to reiterate to my dad. "Life has to be better up north." My dad pondered on how he could get the money to get his bus fare to Indiana so that he could make provisions for his family to join him later. He barely had the means just to keep food on the table and a roof over our heads. He had become drained of much of his energy and strength through boredom, exertion, and impatience. Such depletion of interest, energy, and patience would cause one to become both unable and unwilling to continue. The lady that we were rooming from had grown older and had very little dexterity remaining in her hands to graze and milk the cow. Long years of picking cotton and peas and milking and grazing the cow had contributed to her debilitating arthritic condition. She made a deal with my dad that if he would assume the responsibility of taking care of the cow, she would deduct half of the rent. That was my dad's motivation and incentive for taking on this additional laborious task. He always had the welfare of his family at the forefront of his mind. My dad did not mind rolling up his sleeves and making things happen for his wife and children. One morning, while he was milking old Betsy, he thought to himself, *This is the last time that I am going to do this.*

Needless to say, both my dad and my mom were tired. I have discovered that you will never move to another place mentally or physically until you grow tired of where you are. My brothers told me later that they were tired also because they had to take turns getting up early before going to school to graze and milk the cow. One night, after all of the children were in bed, my dad told my mom that he had finally made up his mind and that he would be leaving for South Bend, Indiana. He told her that she should secretly pack all of our clothes and wait for instructions to join him in a few days, and that she should not breathe a word to anyone. She was not aware that he was going to steal Aunt Mae's cow and sell it in order to get his fare. We affectionately called the old lady that we roomed from Aunt Mae not because we were related, but it was simply a term of endearment and respect. I am not condoning, nor am I justifying, what my dad did in order to facilitate that move; but I will be eternally grateful that he did. That enormously risky and brave move that he made started the wheels of my destiny spinning, spinning, spinning. My dad was restless in bed that night, tossing and turning.

"What's the matter, honey?" my mom said.

"Oh nothing, go on back to sleep," he said.

There was a lot on my dad's mind because he knew what he had to do in the morning, and nothing was going to deter or hinder him from bringing it into fruition. Daybreak did not come fast enough. My dad slid quietly out of bed, bathed, and got himself dressed and made his breakfast. My dad always cooked his own breakfast, and he always perked his own coffee. My mom was not lackadaisical by any means, but my dad always got up much earlier for work, and he would insist that my mom stay in bed and rest as long as she could. With all of those children, trust me, she had her chores cut out for her from the time that her feet hit the floor until late at night when she finally called it a day. As for the coffee that my dad made every morning, it was none of that instant stuff. It was that fresh Hills Brothers brewed coffee that permeated the entire house with its inviting aroma. He was a real coffee connoisseur. I have been awakened by the smell of his coffee every morning since the day that I was in the world. My dad would always quietly take me out of my crib when I was an infant and cuddle me up on his lap while he ate his breakfast and drank his coffee. Lots of cream and a little sugar. I was about one year old when my dad first introduced me to coffee. He would always save some for me in his cup. My mom was not aware that he was sharing his coffee with me at such a young age until one morning she got up and caught us in the act.

"Honey, are you giving that baby coffee?"

"Yea, it's not going to hurt her," he responded.

"But, honey, her little system might not be able to handle that strong coffee."

"Yea, yea, yea," he said while smiling and winking at me.

Nothing on this planet could stop my dad and me from having our coffee time. When I became a little older, I remembered him always reminding me to stop drinking the coffee when I got to the grounds at the bottom of the cup. My dad took great pride in making a nice fresh pot of hot coffee, but every once in a while, a few grounds would escape through the filter. This was back in the day, before they perfected the brewing process. I did not understand why I had to stop drinking the coffee before I got to the grounds, and just between you and me, there were many times that I swallowed some of them. But even the grounds were hmmm, hmmm good. Probably because it came from my daddy's cup. That coffee was "off the hezee" as the young people put it colloquially when they are making reference to something that is exceptional. I was definitely hooked. I had become a coffeeholic. It tasted better to me than milk. I preferred it over juice or soda water (that's what they called pop back in the day)! Early every morning, while everyone else was asleep and the world was quiet, my dad and I would faithfully share a cup of coffee together. Lots of cream and a little sugar. Spending precious affectionate bonding time with my daddy as I babbled with the English language over coffee was the best part of waking up. He would smile and respond to me as if he understood every word that I was trying to articulate. My daddy!

One morning, just as the sun was coming up, my dad kissed my mom and whispered to her, "Kid, I am leaving today for Indiana, and I will call you as soon as I get there." My dad called my mom Kid, and I will elaborate on the reason why within the next few chapters. My mom was elated that my dad had made up his mind, and that we were finally all going to the land of opportunity. She was quite busy and preoccupied preparing our things and did not see my dad ease the cow out of the backyard. My dad walked for miles with that cow until he got into town. Because of the great demand for that commodity, he had no problems making the transaction. The average cow could produce as much as thirty-two liters of milk a day, and some of that milk could be churned into butter or made into cheese. Or the cow could be butchered and produce steaks, roasts, ribs, briskets, and ground beef. It really would depend upon whether the buyer wanted the cow to make a continual contribution or a final sacrifice.

My dad had no idea of the plans that the merchant had for Aunt Mae's cow, but he made the financial transaction hurriedly and left by way of the bus to South Bend, Indiana. He boarded the bus taking nothing with him but the clothes on his back, a few items of clothing in his knapsack, and a couple of dollars in his pocket. I can just imagine the thoughts that must have bombarded his mind while taking that long ride. He must have thought about the safety of his small children and his beautiful young wife. And I know that he thought about the crime that he had just committed, wondering if or when he would ever get caught. I think that the consolation and justification that he had was that Aunt Mae was too old to maintain the cow, and he also considered all of the years that he had taken care of the cow and received only meager compensation. Most importantly, he wanted to do what was best for him and his family. For the next few days, those same sheriffs were continuously back and forth at our house interrogating and harassing my mom about the whereabouts of my dad. By then, Aunt Mae had come to the resolve that my dad had something to do with her missing cow, especially since both of them had conspicuously disappeared. This had created an antagonistic atmosphere in the house that was thick enough to cut with a knife. The next few days were filled with anxiety, frustration, and anticipation as my mom waited for that phone call. Finally, just as he promised, my dad contacted my mom and gave her some explicit but brief instructions. "There will be two men and your sister, Pearl, that will be picking you up," my dad whispered. My mom's sister was coming along because she had visited us before, and she was familiar with the exact directions without getting lost since time was of the essence. My dad had strategically arranged the time of their arrival to be in the middle of the night because that would be less conspicuous. The plan was that the car would arrive on the outskirts of Blytheville, and they would stop at a designated place and give my mom a call. My mom was to then call a cab and meet the car away from the house to avoid anyone from spotting the license plate of an Indiana car. She did not breathe a word over the phone about the sheriffs that were looking for him because she didn't want to alarm him. My dad hung up the phone precipitously, but my mom continued to grip the receiver tightly, as if she was holding on to him, and just listened to the silence on the other end. After coming out of her trance, she placed the telephone back on the cradle and excitedly but secretively told my brothers the plan. It was bittersweet for them because they would be leaving their school and also their playmates. They were older than me and were better able to understand the concept of separation anxiety. They certainly were not going to miss Aunt Mae very much though because I was told that she was a bit cantankerous, and I do remember her pinching me occasionally with those old wrinkled arthritic fingers when she thought that no one was looking. Aunt Mae had that aristocratic but sneaky look. She was a feisty little old lady. She had long pretty silver hair that she always wore parted in the middle and plaited in two long thick braids. Her head was always tied up with a scarf that was proudly worn in an Aunt Jemima style. She wore long cotton dresses all the way to her ankles with thick stockings and a plaid apron with two big pockets that were always filled with some of everything from clothes pens to Double Mint chewing gum for the boys. She always kept a little tin can close by because she dipped snuff, and she used it to spit in all the time. YUCK! She must have had a little money because she owned her own home and a cow. She also supplemented her income by renting a portion of her house out to us; and she sold milk, cheese, and butter to all of the neighbors in that little community. I must give Aunt Mae kudos because she was a very smart and industrious woman and had the nerve to have some entrepreneurial potential. In addition to that, she was about the only one that had a telephone for miles. Needless to say, the environment had gotten to be a hostile one, and she made it quite clear that she wanted us all out. She was livid because she was convinced by then that my dad had stolen her cow, and that my mom was an accessory to the crime, which exacerbated the situation and had left a bitter taste of revenge in her mouth. What she did not know was that a car was on the way.

Finally, we were all packed, and my mom was anxiously waiting for the phone call. A few days had passed when my mom was awakened by the ringing of the telephone at a little past one in the morning. The voice on the other end sounded muffled but familiar.

"Beatrice," she said.

"Yes," my mom responded in a tone that was a little above a whisper.

"We just got here and you are to get a cab right away. We will be looking out for you. Please hurry," her sister added, "because it is dark and very scary out here."

My mom did not even say goodbye; but she quickly hung the phone up, called a cab, and very quietly got us all up. We kept our pajamas on because time would not allow my mom to get us all dressed. Surprisingly, the cab did not take very long probably because of the time of night. My brothers helped the cab driver put the boxes in the trunk while my mom was inside making sure that she had not forgotten anything of importance. As she was about to leave, she passed by Aunt Mae's room. You could hear her snoring all over that little shotgun house. My mother gently pulled back the curtain to the doorway of her bedroom, and she saw Aunt Mae dead to the world. For some reason, she wanted to get one last look at her. Aunt Mae had her contentious ways, but she was the one that took all seven of us in when we needed a place to stay. She pinched me occasionally, but it didn't kill me. I promise you that I probably deserved a pinch every now and then or perhaps two. When my mom had to go to town, she was our babysitter. She baked us delicious treats on that wood-burning potbellied stove and made us her favorite French toast that was smothered with hot glazed apples. Yummy, I can just taste them now. She taught my brothers how to make delicious homemade ice cream, which was a very interesting, fun, and tedious process. She also played with us and would have so much fun tickling us in our rib cages and on the bottom of our feet until she was exhausted. When my dad was running short of money and could not pay the rent, in other words, when it was time to pay up but he had nothing to pay down, she would wait on the money without too much resistance. My mom and Aunt Mae had bonded and really had developed a mother-and-daughter relationship because my mom's mother died when she was eight years old, and that intricate, very important part of her life was missing. Aunt Mae filled that void as best as she could. Aunt Mae never had children; so when her husband died, she was alone and all seven of us turned that dreary, lonely, small, shotgun house into a lively home. Those houses were called shotgun houses because you could look straight through them from the front door to the back door. My mom stood there, watching Aunt Mae snore, and was reminiscing about all of the pleasant and difficult times that we had experienced there. She was tempted to quietly kiss her on the forehead, but she did not want to risk the chance of awakening her. That would have been a travesty. Her eyes filled up with tears as she gently closed the door behind her. There was no way that she could lock the door from the outside without a key, so she just closed the door and prayed for her safety as she made her way to the waiting cab. My mom blurted out the directions to the cab driver, and we were on our way.

We have often thought about how Aunt Mae might have reacted when she awakened and discovered that we had mysteriously left in the night. Our escape reminds me of Harriet Tubman, the heroine of the Underground Railroad. When she grew weary of the racial dysfunction, she also made her break in the middle of the night. She escaped as a slave for freedom and brought her family and others with her, and they traveled by night in extreme secrecy just as we did. She heard the resounding voice of destiny calling her, and our destiny was calling us also, and we had to answer. "Keep going" was the directive that Harriet Tubman gave the slaves as they left. It has been said that Harriet gave the slaves explicit instructions that "if you hear the ferocious dogs gaining on you, keep going. If you see the torches in the dark woods, keep going. If there's a shouting after you, keep going. Don't ever stop, keep going. If you want a taste of freedom, keep going." There has been some controversy as to whether or not she spoke those specific words, but that is irrelevant. It is not profitable for me or anyone else for that matter to argue that point. That would be what I call majoring in the minors. But the thing of significance is that their successful escape affirms the directive, and her life and legacy give credence to those words, "don't stop, keep going."

My mom left with that same fervor, quest, and tenacity. In essence, she told those two strange men that picked us up to drive and go forward and don't stop. My mom left with determination on her mind, hope in her heart, and a feeling of emancipation and joy deep down in her soul. She was not basing her feelings of determination, hope, and joy upon what she could see with the physical eye, for if that was the case, she did not have very much to focus on. With the physical eye, when she looked out, all she saw was racism pervading in a nonsensical way and doing undeniably well. When she looked around, she saw social injustice interwoven deeply into the fabric of this world's system, so much so that it had become a normal way of life. When she looked down, she saw her race chocking to death from the blatant manifestation of economic deprivation, but she remembered that there was one other direction in which to focus, and that was up. When she looked up, thank God, she saw justice peeking its head out at a culture that had the potential of transformation, change, and a consciousness of the powers that be to acknowledge the dire need of an extreme social makeover. You can only see justice when you look to the hills from which cometh your help. She was not oblivious to the fact that she had to do more than just look up in order to bring about such a transformation, but looking up was a good direction in which to start because it suggested a mind-set. You cannot really get up until you think up.

It was approximately a forty-five-minute drive before the car from Indiana was spotted, parked inconspicuously off to the side of the dark road. My mom rushed us all out of the cab, almost pushing us into the waiting car. Both of the strange men had gotten out of the car—one helped transfer the boxes and the other one reached into his pocket and pulled out some money to pay the cab driver—and within minutes we were on our way. The cab driver swiftly made a u-turn and headed back toward Blytheville, gradually disappearing in the night, leaving a trail of dust behind him. My brothers inquisitively continued looking back and watched the taillights until they grew dim in the distance. I had just turned three, and it is amazing the things that I can remember. I think that you tend to remember the traumatic or meaningful events that happen during your formative years better. We were packed like sardines in that car, and the ride was long and uncomfortable. We had to go the long route through the cities because the four- and six-lane interstate highways had not been constructed. The only time that we stopped was to purchase gas. When it was necessary to relieve ourselves (I am sure that was quite often with five little children), we had to stop and take a nature walk because it was very dangerous, forbidden, and against the Jim Crow law for colored people to use public facilities while passing through those Southern cities and states. The socially accepted behavior was racist. My mom packed sandwiches and water for us because she was aware of the *white only* and *colored only* placards. The restaurants that did serve colored people had a sign that directed us to the back door where we had to wait outside for the food, and it was handed to us through the door.

My mom said that as we were nearing the Indiana line, she had a taste for one of those big juicy delicious hamburgers with lettuce, tomato, mustard, ketchup, pickles, and onions. She thought that it would be permissible for her to go to the front entrance of the restaurant, but the waitress met her at the door and said in an indignant Southern dialect, "I'm sorry, but we don't serve 'nigrees.'" And without thinking, my mom responded very flippantly, "Good, because I don't eat them. I just wanted a hamburger, not a 'nigree.'" She put her head up in the air, squared her shoulders, and strutted her proud good-looking self back to the car. After she sat down, she had a flashback of what could have happened to her and broke out in a heart-attack sweat. Thank God for his mercy and his grace. I really do not remember everything about that trip, but I do recall that the car was crowded, and I definitely remember asking my mom incessantly why it was taking so long and if we were there yet. My primary focus was getting to South Bend, Indiana, so that I could see my daddy. I was the apple of his eye, and my small world revolved around him. I missed our intimate times together in the morning, drinking coffee. Lots of cream and a little sugar. I missed being awakened by that familiar distinct aroma. That was the best part of waking up. No one in Aunt Mae's house drank coffee except my daddy and me, his little baby girl.

We finally arrived in South Bend at 3809 West Washington Street. That address is indelibly etched in my mind. This was the biggest house that we had ever seen in our lives. The two strange men—that had driven us and my aunt Pearl—had waved goodbye. My brothers were having the time of their lives running in and out of that big house. I was having fun also, but my fun was intermingled with agony because the desire to see my daddy had intensified. My mom and her dad were sitting at the kitchen table, having an impassioned conversation about a cow and some money. I could sense by the look on my mom's face that something was dreadfully wrong. The tears that she was shedding were because her dad had broken the devastating and painful news to her that her husband had been arrested and charged with a felony. How could this have possibly happened? How could they have tracked him down? He was over five hundred miles from Blytheville where the crime had allegedly taken place. During the sheriff's thorough investigation, it was discovered that a cab had picked up this colored family and dropped them off just outside of the city limits, and that a car was there waiting for them. It had slipped my mom's mind that there was one person that probably had noticed the out-of-town license plate . . . the cab driver. He had sensed that there was something clandestine and quite secretive and unusual about the arrangement. In addition to this, the news was circulating in that small community about my dad and Aunt Mae's cow. Needless to say, the cab driver had, in fact, reported the information to the police; and he had also reported that the car had an Indiana license plate. My mom shivered as she rehearsed in her mind the last thing that those four sheriffs had emphatically said to her before they left Aunt Mae's house: *"We are going to get that nigger."* Their plan was to find that slick nigger by any means necessary if it was the last thing that they did. They did not care anything about Aunt Mae or her cow. They wanted to get their hands on Leroy Thomas. I will always believe that Aunt Mae collaborated with the police and the cab driver. They surmised that my dad was somewhere in Indiana, and during their further investigation, they discovered that my mom's dad resided in South Bend. They put all of their information together, and within approximately four days from the time that my mom received the phone call from my dad, he had been located and arrested. This was a major crime for a colored man to have committed back in that day. It was not so much the felony, but it was the fact that my dad had the mitigated gall, the nerve, and the skill to mix practicality, bravery, and cleverness together and escape without getting caught. Again, please do not see this as an attempt to excuse or justify my dad's insurgent behavior because I assure you it is not. I am not by any means condoning the crime, but sometimes a man has to do what a man has to do. It is painful telling this true story, but I humbly submit to you that I need to tell it more than you need to hear it. It is actually going to be therapeutic and cathartic. It is going to allow me to deal with, turn the page, and bring closure to this particular chapter in my life. Furthermore, and most importantly, it is going to bring about a long-overdue healing for me and perhaps even you. You see, we all have a story whether we tell it or not.

Chapter 2

Locked in the Position of Hopelessness

*B*ang! *Click!* The jailor very angrily slammed the cell door shut and then pulled on it forcibly to be certain that it was securely locked. He peered at my dad from between the bars and sneered, "We finally gotcha, nigger. Now what are you going to do?" He then very arrogantly gave the cell door another pull for effect, and walked slowly away with the keys to my dad's hopes, dreams, and aspirations dangling from his side. You could hear him whistling as he disappeared out of sight. "Oh god," my dad said as he glanced around at the smelly toilet, the basin, and the dingy cot. "What in the world am I going to do now?" My dad stood over six feet tall and weighed nearly 225 pounds. He was a strong, rugged, dignified, and very self-sufficient handsome man that had never cried a day in his adult life. I suppose that he had taken that old cliché seriously that said men aren't suppose to cry. My dad laid his very tired body on the cot and stared up at the ceiling. He was tired, not sleepy tired, but it was the kind of tiredness that drains you emotionally and psychologically. The kind of tiredness that a colored man felt when he looked back retrospectively on how he had been treated for as long as he could remember, like a person undeserving of dignity, equality, and respect. As he lay there, some murky memories began to resurrect. He began to remember things that he thought had been deleted, only to find out that they had just been downloaded on his mental hard drive and saved in the recesses of his mind just waiting to be called up. He thought about the times that he was addressed as *boy* when he was, in fact, a grown man that had four boys of his own. Back then, the Jim Crow customs took advantage of every opportunity that it had to disparage, humiliate, and dehumanize a colored man. They reserved the right to address white men, women, and children as miss and mister and addressed colored people as boy and gal regardless of how old they were or either they would just simply call them nigger. He reflected on the white and colored bathroom and water fountain signs. One of the signs that left an indelible mark in his mind was a demeaning sign that read, No Coloreds or Dogs Allowed. That sign seemed to have had an overt comparison.

He remembered the times that he wanted to go to school, but instead he had to help his parents pick and chop cotton from sunup to sundown for fifty cents a day. He anxiously looked forward to the cold months because that was the only time he was permitted to go to school. He thought about the times that he was forced to walk to school for miles in the cold, and sometimes even without shoes, while passing a white segregated school that was only a few blocks away. He remembered the many times that his brown greasy lunch bag was snatched out his hand by little white boys and tossed into the creek. He remembered the old dilapidated bridge that he had to cross to get to school, and if there were white ladies standing on the bridge talking, he had to get off the bridge and patiently wait until they were finished. Whites always had the right-of-way, and they were always next in line even though coloreds were first. After they finally made up their mind to finish their conversation, he could hear them snickering and saying, "I guess we should let this darkie get on to school." The racial hatred was so intense that he imagined sometimes that they purposefully or intentionally prolonged their conversation just to detain him.

He thought about the day that he and his best friend were walking down the road and a white girl was approaching them, and his friend looked at her. She immediately got a white man's attention and franticly told him that my dad and his friend had gotten out of their place with her. Fortunately, my dad was quick on his feet and he managed to get away, but the man grabbed my dad's friend and he mysteriously disappeared, never to be heard of again. It was said that his remains were later washed up by the river, but the body was so decomposed that it could not be proven. He should have known better, my dad thought as he laid there on the cot. A colored man just could not look at a white woman, period. The white people called it reckless eyeballing. If a colored man met a white woman on the street, he had to either cross over to the other side or he had to look down at the ground. But a white man could not only look at a colored girl, but he could also rape her and even impregnate her, and nothing would be done about it. The injustice was blatant.

He thought about the times that he wanted to purchase shoes for himself and his family, and he knew that coloreds were not permitted to try them on, so he would have us all place our feet on paper and he would trace them and take the paper to the store so that he could get the correct sizes. And after getting to the store, if there were white customers already in the store, he had to wait until after they all were accommodated before he was served. And he remembered when he could not buy something as simple as a Coke. At the little country store by our house, colored people could only purchase a Pepsi. The Coke was more expensive (six cents) and considered an upgrade, and they thought that coloreds didn't deserve such quality.

The grim reality of all of the social, economical, emotional, and physical exploitation was weighing heavily upon his mind, but the one thing that set his emotions in a tailspin was when he remembered the time that he forgot to say "no, sir" to a young white boy that was even younger than he was and he spit on him. My dad asked him why he did it, and he responded, "'Cause you think you something. You are one of those light-skinned uppity niggers." That capricious act almost caused him to lose his life. He could just imagine himself rearranging that boy's nose, but he thought about the extreme violent consequences that could possibly happen to him. He quickly convinced himself that the time would not fit the crime, and he wiped the spit off and reluctantly walked away. Out of all of the degrading, demeaning, unethical, and unlawful things that he recalled, that was the one thing that caused something to happen to him on that cot that had never transpired since he was a full-grown man. I am sure that it was a culmination of all of the above, but the catalyst was the humiliation of being spat on. My dad was always told by his father when he was growing up that only girls cried. Whenever he fell down and skinned his knee or experienced other mishaps that were common for adventurous boys, he was always told to not behave as a sissy but to "take it like a man, son." What a misnomer. Weeping is the most human and the most universal antidote of all relief measures, and it is not gender specific. Unfortunately, his father was associating that emotional trait with the female gender. Society tells us that females are soft and caring while males are hard and stoic. Society also says that females are compassionate while males are aloof. But males are human beings that are complete with feelings, hopes, desires, apprehensions, fears, anger, loss, the need to be loved, and the need to be successful. They are human, and human beings are the only animals that can cry emotional tears when they are overwhelmed. A man does not always have to be the rock in the middle of the storm. That is an unfair, outlandish expectation. It was, in fact, unhealthy for my dad to bottle up all of those emotions and shove them deep down inside just to prove his masculinity. The unshed tears of his many traumatic experiences as a boy and a man, and a black man at that, no doubt was eating away at the core of him and it had had a devastating effect on him mentally, physically, and emotionally. Tears come from the inability to articulate or tell our story. Sometimes words just get in the way, and that is when we allow tears to speak for us. My advice to all men, regardless of their race, creed, or color is that it's okay to tell your story through tears. Telling your story through tears can be cathartic and bring a release.

My dad slowly glanced around his jail cell again at the dingy basin, the smelly toilet, and his dingy cot and he thought to himself, *I am locked in the position of hopelessness.* His strong ambitions and intense desire to achieve the things for himself and his family that he knew he was entitled to were enclosed, fastened up, and confined within this four-by-four jail cell. His dreams, expectations, chances, hopes, and promises were gone. My six-foot 225-pound dad, my mom's rock of Gibraltar, my four little brothers' hero, and my everything began to experience an emotion that was aroused by agony; and he had no willpower or inclination to stop it. When we are emotionally upset to the point of tears, our bodies and brains react and work overtime producing high levels of hormones. These chemicals are designed to be released. It's nature's way of saying let it go. Finally, the tears came. My dad's eyes became a fountain of tears. His first inclination was to suppress them. His ego—the superimposed egotistical part of his consciousness initially felt that crying was inappropriate. And although he was alone he yet felt embarrassed, but it was too late. The tears began to fall. Quite frankly, I hate to see a man cry, but that was the best thing that my dad could have done. It facilitated a cleansing and a release of stress. He told us that he cried for what seemed like an eternity, but those tears were carthartic because they gave him permission to tap into some old devestations that needed to be dealt with. By now, his pillow was soaked and finally, somehow, tranquility engulfed him, and he drifted off into a deep sleep and actually slept through the night. That is what a good cry can do.

Early the next morning, he was awakened by this belligerent rough voice saying, "Boy, I've been calling you for the last five minutes, and I was only gon' call out to you one last time . . . Here is your breakfast. You can take it or leave it." The guard shoved my dad's plate under the cell door. The food was not the best, bordering disgusting, and certainly the coffee was not remotely close to the delicious Hills Brothers coffee that he was accustomed to, but he was so hungry and thirsty that he cleaned his plate and swallowed down the cold coffee and lay back down on his cot. All he could think about was his wife and his children. Fear gripped his heart when he considered where he was, why he was there, and how his life was in the hands of a system that was anticolored and entrenched in institutionalized racism. *God, please help me! God, please help me!* He said those words repetitiously to himself until he drifted back off to sleep. He slept off and on that entire day just to escape from the thoughts of his impending doom. The next morning, he was awakened again by that same rough voice, but this time it was not to eat. Instead the jailor said, "Boy, get up! You got a visitor." The jailor unlocked his cell door, mumbling under his breath, "You lazy, shiftless, good-for-nothing . . . nigger!" My dad quickly stood to his feet when he recognized that it was the pastor from Saints Memorial Church of God in Christ, Bishop J. B. Davis. The jailor closed the cell door behind him with a smirk on his face and walked away from the door but, intentionally, remained close enough so that he could monitor their conversation.

Although my mom's father was a Baptist minister, he knew that she had devoutly embraced the Pentecostal faith, and he had informed her about a little church that he knew she would love when we moved to South Bend. Immediately upon my dad's arrival, the first two things that he did were seek employment and visit that little church. I am sure that the crime he had committed had much to do with him going to church right away because at that point in his life he definitely needed solace.

After a very moving, hand-clapping, tambourine-beating, foot-stomping, and electrifying church experience, he waited to shake hands with the pastor and asked him if he could speak with him privately in his office pertaining to a dire situation. The pastor kindly acquiesced, and my dad sat down with him and explained in detail what he had done to create his dilemma. He also informed him that he only had a few dollars, but that he had a wife and family that were in Blytheville, Arkansas, waiting for him to send for them. I am so proud of my dad because he could have shirked his responsibilities as a father and become just a sperm donor as many men are today. He could have attempted to remain a fugitive for the rest of his life. But because of the ardent love for his wife and children, he refused. The pastor was tremendously moved with compassion by my dad's predicament and his candidness. He told my dad that his family was in imminent danger and that it was imperative that we be expeditiously brought to South Bend, Indiana, and that he would assist him in doing so. He immediately asked two of the deacons from the church to prepare to drive to Blytheville that next day and warned them that time was of the essence, and that the trip should be done in secrecy. He gave them money to cover what he thought would be their expenses and assured them that he would reimburse them should the trip exceed the amount that he had given to them. My dad was not aware that the police were looking for him at that time, but within a day or so they had located him, and before our arrival in South Bend he had been captured and arrested.

The morning that the pastor stepped into that jail cell, he was well aware that he had entered into a devastating situation that could be compared to him stepping into the lion's den to rescue Daniel from the ferocious hungry lions. My dad being Daniel, and the ferocious hungry lions being the powers that be. He knew that the potential demise of my dad was probably inevitable. The governor from Arkansas had already been informed of his arrest, and they had ordered that my dad be extradited back to Blytheville. Those of you that are familiar with the extradition process, please indulge me as I attempt to explain it to those of you that are not. Because of the value of the cow, my dad was automatically charged with a felony. And being that he had fled from the jurisdiction had added insult to injury. The Blytheville prosecutors had taken the court's arrest warrant and accompanying documents, showing that the fugitive had committed a crime, and sent those documents to the governor of Arkansas. At this point, a request for extradition is ordered, and it must be in writing and it must allege that: (1) my dad was in Arkansas at the time that the crime was committed, and (2) after committing the crime, that the fugitive (my dad) fled the jurisdiction. Along with these claims must be a copy of the indictment that is supported by affidavits. All of this, together with a copy of the arrest warrant, is sent to the Arkansas governor. The Arkansas governor closely examines the documents that have been sent to him and if everything is in order, he places a demand on the Indiana governor to return the fugitive to Arkansas. The Arkansas governor files a stack of documents with the Indiana governor, legally showing why the fugitive must be immediately returned to Arkansas. In the meantime, while the governors are sorting out their warrants of extraditions, the prosecutor sends the police in Indiana a copy of the arrest warrant, which is an indication that the fugitive committed a crime in Arkansas. This allows the Indiana authorities to arrest the fugitive and hold him up to ninety days while waiting for the governor's warrant of extraditions. During the time that the fugitive is being held on the arrest warrant, the court can allow the defendant to be free on bail. Needless to say, they set my dad's bail astronomically high, knowing that he was poverty stricken and would not be able to pay it; but what they didn't know was that the pastor, Bishop J. B. Davis, was well fortified. But unfortunately, when he offered to pay his bail, they refused the request stating that my dad was a high risk because he had fled before; and the chances of him doing it again were highly probable. My dad was in a catch-22 situation because the system was deliberately working against him. Their intent was to do exactly what those belligerent sheriffs that invaded Aunt Mae's house said they were going to do, and that was *get that nigger*. The next step is a waiting process while the governors from both states are processing more documents. During this time, the fugitive, his attorney, or a person representing him may petition the Indiana governor to allow him or her to appear on the fugitive's behalf.

My dad was not the only one that was weary because the pastor was deeply concerned as well. Although he was cognizant of a multiplicity of challenges ahead, he did not flinch because he knew that challenges open the door to opportunities. He was very much aware of the unprecedented *hurdles* that he was facing should he be granted the opportunity to represent my dad. First of all, it was incumbent upon him to present a justifiable, convincing argument as to why a colored man that was guilty of committing a crime in the South and fleeing to the North should not be extradited but instead exonerated. Please understand that exoneration means to be relieved of the burden of guilt or obligation. It means to be freed from the charge or the imputation of guilt. It means to be declared or proven blameless or innocent of the said charges.

Bishop Davis had his work cut out for him and it had to be done skillfully, tactfully, diplomatically, and respectfully. And he had to do it in an adverse, antagonistic, and racially motivated environment. In the '50s, a colored person was not innocent until proven guilty, but he was guilty until proven guilty. My parents had moved to the North to get away from the injustice and the degrading acts that were subsequently imposed upon them, but what they were ignorant of was that systematic racial discrimination was prevalent everywhere, just in a different zip code. It was the same ugliness just dressed up in a different suit. The differentiation being that in the South, racism was overt while in the North it was covert. Overt racism is public and obvious. Overt racism can be defined as racism that is blatantly deliberate and explicit. For example, if a colored person came into a department store in the North, the clerk would stare at him or her sarcastically, and deliberately ignore them. That would be covert. But in the South, where racism was overt, the clerk would explicitly tell them to their face that "we don't serve coloreds here." It would not be concealed and would be clearly observable. In the North, there were no visible "white only" signs, but there were signs that were invisibly and deceitfully hidden in the fabric of their minds and subliminally acted out. It was subtle, disguised, and suppressed. It was masked, perpetuated injustice. On the other hand, covert racism was less public and obvious. Look closely at the word *covert* and you will see another word, *cover*. Cover means to hide; to camouflage one's flaws or real intention or activities. Covert behavior was designed to methodically disable, suppress, and oppress. I know that you have heard the saying "my best friend is black." That is a perfect way to talk, skip, and skirt around racism without addressing the issue. Please believe me; this is not to suggest that whites have not ever genuinely befriended blacks. That would be preposterous of me to come to such a conclusion, but I am inclined to believe that that would be the exception rather than the rule. Covert and overt racism is systemic and its function is to empower the suppressor while diminishing the legal rights and powers of the oppressed. Bishop Davis's work was cut out for him.

Another *hurdle* that he had to deal with was Jim Crow, which was alive and well in the '50s. The term Jim Crow originated in 1828 when Thomas "Daddy" Rice, a white minstrel, saw a crippled colored stable hand named Jim Crow doing a song and dance called Jumping Jim Crow. Rice bought the man's clothes right off his back and stole his act and made it his stage routine. Rice would cover his face with charcoal or burnt cork to resemble a colored man, and then he would sing and dance a routine mimicking the silly stereotypical behavior of coloreds in the name of comedy. This was just a precursor to the real meaning of the name. Jim Crow was not only a person, but it was a system that was undergirded by the dehumanizing beliefs or rationalization that whites were superior to blacks.

Jim Crow was the name of the racial system which was operated primarily in Southern states between 1877 and the mid-1960s. And although the system originated in the South and was strictly enforced, its philosophy and its tactics had full reign and was practiced in the North as well. It relegated the status of colored people as second-class citizens. It was indeed power out of proportion and out of control. Jim Crow sanctioned racial oppression and segregation. Coloreds were hanged, shot, burned, castrated, and dismembered sadistically, and public lynching was done purposefully to frighten or intimidate them and to keep them in their place. These acts were inflicted upon innocent human beings, so you can just imagine the punishment that they suffered if they were guilty. Although these gruesome, animalistic acts were more prevalent in the South, the concept was pervasive in the North. Its larger goal was to maintain at all costs white supremacy throughout the United States. Jim Crow passed statutes that severely regulated any social interactions and intermingling between races. This permitted "white only" signs to be placed above water fountains, door entrances, and exits. There were separate schools, transportation, restaurants, churches, restrooms, hospitals, prisons, and cemeteries. The need for segregated cemeteries really baffled me because death is an equalizer. What harm could the dead do? At the time that my dad committed this crime, the Jim Crow system was in full effect, at an all time high, and was supported by the powers that be. Bishop Davis's work was cut out for him.

To add insult to injury, Indiana was one of the northern states that were notoriously known as Ku Klux Klan country, which was another *hurdle*. Their abbreviated name was KKK or the Klan. The KKK was an illegal organization that was established in May of 1866 and its primary purpose was to reinforce white supremacy through intimidation. The KKK was alive and moving at the peak of its strength in an unprecedented way. They believed in the innate inferiority of blacks and therefore resented and despised them with a passion. They worked to curb their education, economic and social advancement, and voting rights, and they cowardly hid their identity behind masks and white cardboard pointed hats, and draped themselves in white sheets to accomplish it. Their attack was at night, and they usually rode on horses and held burning crosses in their hands to add to the drama. Many coloreds were superstitious and scared out of their wits of ghosts, and the KKK's attire reminded them of such. They were petrified. The Klan's first tactic was to go into the area near the homes of those that they wished to frighten in large groups and verbally warn them that they must respect the rights of the white race in whose country they were permitted to reside. Often they would select one victim and lynch him as a method to terrorize and place emphasis on their command. When this method failed to produce the desired results, they would return in the middle of the night and throw burning crosses through the windows, burning many of them to death. They would also break into their homes at night and rape the women and drag others out of their beds, torturing them in the most inhuman manner by mutilation and murder. These acts were justified by the powers that be as necessary measures in defense of white supremacy. Many murders were unreported and unpunished. There was no one to blow the whistle on them, and even if there were, there was no one to listen. The dreadful truth is behind those masks were the faces of civic leaders, politicians, illegal whiskey distillers, rapists, employers trying to reinforce labor discipline, white workmen that were fearful of colored competition, common thieves, neighbors with decades-old grudges, and the *law*. This behavior was socially accepted by the white majority community. At the time that my dad was arrested, governors, senators, sheriffs, local politicians, congressmen, and people that served on the jury were active Klan leaders and/or participants, and they condoned the disenfranchisement of blacks everywhere. My dad was smack dab in the middle of this racial stalemate, and Bishop Davis's work was seriously cut out for him.

My dad slumped back down on the cot with his head in his hands and said, "Oh god, what are we going to do?"

"Well, son," the pastor said with grave concern in his voice, "it is not so much the crime that you have committed that worries me, but our challenge is going to be the system. I believe that they are going to diametrically oppose my request for your exoneration and demand that you be extradited back to Arkansas. Quite frankly, it seems insurmountable, but I am up for the challenge, and we are going to take it one step at a time. You see, it will be hard by the yard, but it will be a cinch by the inch. Just trust that I am going to do all that I can, and then we're going to let God do the rest."

My dad looked up at him through bloodshot eyes and said, "I want to trust you, Pastor, but I just don't trust the white man because he is not afraid of you or God."

"Now, son, that is where you are wrong. They are afraid of us because what you fear, you *devour* rather than *empower*. You just try to get a good night's rest, and I am going to place a call into the governor's office the first thing in the morning to request a meeting with him. He is the one that has the authority to exonerate you, but God has the power. I'll be in touch with you." He cleared his throat as he was preparing to leave and he turned to say, "Oh, by the way, your family arrived safely from Blytheville. I went by your father-in-law's house yesterday evening, and I met your beautiful wife and children. You've got something to be mighty proud of, son."

"Yes, sir, I sure do, Pastor."

"And that baby girl of yours is as cute as she can be. She's the spitting image of you."

"Yes, sir, she is, Pastor. Thank you so much, Pastor, for all that you have done for my family and I, and now I just want to get out of this place so that I can take care of them like a real man should."

The pastor stood up and walked slowly to the cell door, deliberately adjusting his Stetson hat. "I'm going to do my level best you hear?"

"Yes, sir, Pastor."

Bishop Davis said a mouthful, and was definitely on point when he stated that "*what you fear, you devour rather than empower.*" This system is strategically designed to hinder the black man's progress because it fears or has the sneaking suspicion that, if given the slightest ghost of a chance, we will transcend any—and everything that we set our minds to do. Consider the oratory prowess of Fredrick Douglas and the skillful, tactful leadership of Harriet Tubman, Cicely Tyson, Jessie Owens, Jackie Robinson, Ernie Davis, Bill Russell, Tiger Woods, and—last but certainly not least—our new black president, Barack Obama, who broke the biggest glass ceiling in American politics today. Never in my lifetime did I ever think that I would see a black president. His election has definitely changed the political landscape of our nation. Their suspicion that we would succeed if given half of a chance was right. Although Obama has inherited two wars, one in Iraq and the other in Afghanistan, and the worst economic conditions in three generations, and although he is facing daunting domestic and international challenges, it is a blessing in disguise because unemployment is so high and consumer confidence is so low that even modest improvements will allow him to claim progress. With prayers, patience, and perseverance he will lead this country to heights never known. We have made history, so we might as well make progress. This is indeed a special moment in time. His achievement, along with the others previously mentioned, is proof positive that we were capable of doing more than picking cotton, shining shoes, carrying luggage, and cleaning toilets. This list of names just skims the surface. There are a plethora of others that have successfully defied the system and have made an outstanding contribution to society, and they accomplished it while going against the grain.

The pastor, Bishop J. B. Davis—knowing that my dad needed an attorney (and a good one at that) but could not afford one—petitioned to the Indiana governor by letter to allow him to represent my dad. This amazing man that had only known my dad for a few days was willing to invest his money, time, and energy—and in this serious case, I must add, his blood, sweat, and tears—on my dad's defense. Again, time was of the essence because once the governor from the state of Arkansas sends the final warrant of extradition to Indiana, there is a very slim chance that they would recant. The fugitive does have a right to the writ of habeas corpus, which is a civil procedure in which a court demands that inquiries are made as to the legitimacy of a prisoner's custody. The function of the habeas corpus proceedings are to determine whether the courts that ordered the arrest had the jurisdiction to do so. It is a legal action, and the prerogative that the prisoner can take to free himself from unlawful retention. But at this juncture, a writ is seldom granted, particularly in my dad's case in the '50s.

The wait was on! The waiting period to hear from the governor was not like waiting for a bus or a cab because when you are waiting for a bus, there is a schedule that they generally adhere to. And when you call a cab, they give you an approximate time that the cab should arrive, but most importantly, you know for certain that your means of transportation is coming. However, this wait might possibly have been with anxiety and apprehension because there was no way of knowing whether or not the governor's office was really going to respond to his letter, and if he did, the chances of it being in my dad's favor were slim. When waiting is inevitable, there are two ways that you can do it. You can wait agitated, frustrated, and with fear of the negative results or you can wait with composure, tranquility, and a certainty that God is in complete control of your destiny, and that he is well able to make good come out of the worst catastrophe. This wait should be done with patience.

Patience is a virtue that implies that you have self-control and self-discipline. It means that you have acquired the capacity to endure delays without becoming indifferent. If you take the letters *c* and *e* off *patience* and add the letter *t*, you get another word, *patient*. And *patient* can either be a noun or an adjective. An adjective meaning to endure difficulties without complaining, or it can be a noun meaning one that is under medical care. I have given an excellent definition of the adjective patient, but the patient, which is a noun, has to have patience also. Have you ever seen a clock in the waiting room of your doctor's office? Not likely! What you will see is a table of magazines for your reading or perusal pleasure. This is a psychological overture that is designed to take your mind off the waiting time. Even though most of the magazines are outdated, you take a seat, select one, and wait. Who are you waiting for? You are waiting for the one that has fulfilled certain academic requirements and has received a license to practice medicine, and his or her objective is to maintain or restore human health through diagnosis and treatment. Well, in a real sense, my dad was a patient that had to patiently wait, not for a doctor per se, but then again, he did need a doctor because he was emotionally sick. Although this doctor that he was waiting for has never attended medical school, he nevertheless has the medical knowledge that supersedes any physician on the planet, and he has the power to heal you wherever you hurt. Isaiah 53:5 says that he was wounded for our transgressions and he was bruised for our iniquities, and the chastisement of our peace was upon him, and with his stripes we are healed. That unconditional act of love on the cross qualified him, Jesus Christ, to be a doctor extraordinaire. My dad not only needed an emotional healing, but he also needed an advocate. My dad desperately needed consent from the governor to allow a representative to advocate or plead his case. He was irrevocably locked in the position of hopelessness and it was going to take nothing less than a divine intervention to unloose the chains. Sometimes you don't know that God is all that you need until God is all that you have, but the patient has to patiently wait!

Bishop Davis placed a follow-up call to the governor's office within a few days, but he was not available. He explained the nature of his call to the governor's administrator, and her response was that he would receive a letter of consent or denial from the governor's office within the next few days. She hung up abruptly, and her tone was brusque and unceremonious. Her disposition precluded nothing more than guesswork and left him in a quandary.

The wait was a tedious one, but Bishop Davis finally received a letter from Indianapolis, from the governor's office. With trembling hands, he anxiously opened the letter and it read,_

TO ALL WHOM THESE PRESENTS MAY COME, GREETING:

WHEREAS the Bishop J. B. Davis has requested to represent Leroy Thomas before the Honorable Governor Henry F. Schricker and WHEREAS Leroy Thomas is an accused fugitive from the state of Arkansas, the governor has hereby granted your request, and you have been summoned to appear before him in Indianapolis, Indiana, in the county of Marion at his chamber.

This was some incredible and almost inconceivable news, and Bishop Davis read the letter over and over before the reality set in that he had actually received a favorable response. He rechecked the date and time of the meeting, and he spent the next few days in preparation and prayer.

The drive to Indianapolis was tense and seemingly endless, and he had to constantly dismiss all of the negative thoughts that were trying to bombard his mind all the way there. He arrived twenty minutes early because he knew that it would be inconsiderate and disrespectful to be late. After all, he had an appointment with the commander and chief of Indiana.

"The governor will see you now, sir."

"Thank you very much, madam." Bishop Davis reverently entered the governor's chamber, and he stood until the governor motioned for him to be seated.

"Well, what can I do for you?" the governor said while looking at him over his bifocals.

"First of all, Honorable Governor Schricker, I want to express my sincere appreciation to you for taking the time out of your busy schedule to meet with me. I am Bishop J. B. Davis, the pastor of Saints Memorial Church of God in Christ in South Bend, Indiana, and I am the jurisdictional prelate of Wisconsin under the leadership of Bishop C. H. Mason who founded this organization in 1907. Your Honor, I am here on behalf of Leroy Thomas who committed a felony in the state of Arkansas and then fled to South Bend, Indiana, where he was arrested."

There was a moment of cold silence as he waited for the governor to make a comment, but he just looked at him with piercing eyes and made a gesture with his hand and nodded for him to continue. "Your Honor, Leroy Thomas and his family roomed with an elderly lady in Blytheville, Arkansas, and she made a deal with him that if he would maintain her cow she would reduce his rent so that his housing would be more affordable for him and his family. Your Honor, he took good care of her cow for years until he decided that he wanted to come north because they were tired of being treated . . . I mean, so that he could . . ." He swallowed and hesitated because he did not want to say anything that would be incriminating. "Your Honor, what I am really trying to convey to you is that Leroy Thomas's wife's father was getting up in age and having some physical challenges, and she wanted to move to South Bend so that she could be closer to him in the time that he had left." He told as much truth as he thought that he should and waited again for a response from the governor. But he gave him that same look again of consternation that just penetrated as if he had X-ray vision, and then he nodded for him to continue. "Your Honor, this is a very poor family, and Leroy Thomas just did not have the money to move his family up north. So, Your Honor, since his landlord was about seventy-six years old and had developed arthritis in her hands, he knew that she could not physically take care of her cow, so he sold it in order to get his bus fare. Your Honor, he applied for a job at the South Bend Iron and Metal Company the day after he arrived, and he visited my church that Sunday morning. Your Honor, this man has integrity because he told me exactly what he had done and asked me if I would help him get his family to Indiana. Your honor—"

"Ah!" The governor interrupted him by clearing his throat and said with loud indignation, "*Integrity*! Did I hear you say that you are a preacher?"

"Yes, sir, Your Honor, you did and I am."

"Well, how in the tarnation do you equate stealing with integrity? I heard you say that Leroy sold the cow, but you deliberately and conveniently left out one significant detail. He stole it before he sold it." The governor shifted his position in his plush leather chair and said, "Are you familiar with the Ten Commandments?"

"Yes, Your Honor, I am."

"Well, you must have conveniently skipped right over the fourth one."

"No, Your Honor, I didn't skip over it. I know just where it is found in the Bible. It's in Exodus 20:15."

"Well, what gives you the right to think that it does not apply to you people?" the governor asked rather arrogantly. Bishop Davis really did

JENNIFER THOMAS HOSTON   78

not like being addressed as "you people," but he did not want to rock the boat.

"Your Honor, it does apply to us, and I am in no way condoning what Leroy Thomas has done. Your Honor, Leroy Thomas was wrong but, Your Honor, there is another scripture in Proverbs thirtieth chapter round about the sixth through the ninth verses that I didn't skip over either, and it says,

Two things have I required of thee;
Deny me not them before I die
Remove far from me vanity and lies
Give me neither *poverty* or *riches*
Feed me with food convenient for me
Lest I be full and deny thee and say
Who is the Lord? Or lest I be *poor* and *steal*
And take the name of my God in vain

Bishop Davis attempted to explain the meaning of those verses, and the governor gave him a look that meant that an explanation would not be necessary because it's really irrelevant.

Silence pervaded the chamber. Bishop Davis did not say another word for fear that he had already said too much.

The governor cleared his throat again and said, "By virtue of the authority that is vested in me, I am the governor of Indiana and I have wide-ranging authority to manage the government of the state, and I am the executive of the executive branch of the state government. These powers are established in the Constitution of Indiana. I work in concert with the Indiana General Assembly and the Supreme Court of Indiana to govern this state. Among my other duties, I am also charged with the enforcement of all the state's laws and the Indiana Code, which is carried out through the Indiana State Police. I also have the ability to pardon or commute the sentence of any criminal offenders except in cases of treason or impeachment. But I will not stand the constant companionship of an accusing conscience, which would incessantly remind me in every thought that I, as the governor of Indiana, failed to do what I thought to be right. The responsibility is upon me to maintain the dignity and the integrity of the law." The governor leaned forward and removed his reading glasses and said, "It is important that you understand clearly that Leroy Thomas indulged in insurgent behavior. Be it further understood that it is against the law of Indiana to steal and it is against the law in Arkansas to steal as well. And furthermore, be it resolved that the extradition papers from the governor of Arkansas have already been processed, and I am certain that they are somewhere in the mail as I speak. Those documents are going to command me to send Leroy Thomas back to the state where the crime was committed. He not only stole the cow, but he is also a fugitive. It is out of my jurisdiction, and he must go back to Arkansas."

"But, Your Honor, if you send him back, they are going to kill him. They are going to kill Leroy Thomas for a cow. Your Honor, he may not have value to the powers that be down there in Arkansas, but he certainly does have value to a young wife that loves him and four boys that desperately need him and a beautiful little girl whose world revolves around him. Honorable Schricker, I beg of you. Please, in the name of God, have mercy on this family and do not send Leroy Thomas back to Arkansas."

The governor stood up and glanced at his watch and turned his back toward Bishop Davis while looking out of his picture window over the city of Indianapolis. "He has to go back," he reiterated. "He has to."

"Your Honor, may I ask of you one last favor before you send him back?"

While yet looking out of the window, he responded, "What is that?"

"I would love for you to meet his wife before you send him back. I will bring her here tomorrow morning."

The governor responded rather matter-of-factly while turning to look at his desk calendar, "I have a full schedule on tomorrow, so that will be impossible."

"Well, Your Honor, could I bring her the day after tomorrow?"

"I must not have made myself very clear to you, Bishop Davis," the governor responded.

"Yes, sir, Your Honor, you have made yourself perfectly clear, but I sure would like for you to meet his wife before you send him back."

Glancing at his watch again, he quickly said, "All right, all right. I'll meet the woman. I will tell my administrative assistant to schedule you in. Be here around 10:00 a.m. day after tomorrow, but keep in mind that the law is the law."

"Thank you, thank you, Governor Schricker. We will see you then." Bishop Davis extended his hand to shake his, and the governor cautiously reciprocated the gesture.

Bishop Davis was filled with mixed emotions as he began his drive back to South Bend. His feelings vacillated from extreme joy and satisfaction to a feeling of apprehension and uneasiness. It was disconcerting and grievous to know that within a few days, Leroy Thomas would be on his way back to the misery that he thought he had left far behind. But the fact that the governor had consented to meet his wife gave him a gleam of hope. He leaned hard toward the emotion of hope because of his faith in God and his great expectations for a positive outcome. That's what faith is. Faith is unquestionable, unequivocal belief that does not require proof. It is complete trust, confidence, reliance, credence, assuredness, and staunch belief that something is going to happen in spite of the odds. With faith, there is no reservation, hesitation, and no second thoughts. When you have faith in something, you rest on it, lean on it, count on it, and stand on it. Faith is the unwavering confidence that something is there even though you cannot see it with the natural eye. You've got to have the capacity to see it before you see it or you will never see it. Faith motivates you to purchase that business suit before you are hired as CEO. Faith allows you to apply for college without the tuition. And single ladies, faith nudges you to get that hope chest even before you meet Mr. Right. Now that's faith, and Bishop Davis left the governor's office with that kind of assurance.

But somewhere between Indianapolis and South Bend, he began to tremble with apprehension. He had to get himself together and apologize to God for doubting his ability to do the miraculous, but he was basing his assumptions and conclusions on facts rather than the truth. *As a man of God, I have to base Leroy Thomas's clemency on the truth and not facts*, he thought to himself. It is a fact that Daniel was thrown into the ferocious hungry lions' den, but the truth is God stepped in the den as a zookeeper, took their appetite, and they were as gentle as lambs and Daniel came out unharmed. It is a fact that Shadrach, Meshach, and Abednego were cast into the fiery furnace that was seven times hotter than it should have been; but the truth is God stepped in the furnace as a fire chief and took the heat out of the flame. It is a fact that you cannot part the Red Sea by merely stretching out a rod, but the truth is if God supernaturally empowers the rod, the sea will open up like a highway. It is a fact that Peter could not walk the water, but the truth is if God bids you to step out of the boat, the water instantaneously becomes a sidewalk. *Now, it is a fact that Leroy Thomas and I are facing an uphill battle with this racist system, but the truth is the battle is not ours. The battle is the Lord's, and he has never lost a battle yet.* Bishop Davis preached to himself all the way home. He preached himself happy.

Bishop Davis wanted to go and visit my dad in jail again, but he decided that he should wait until after he had made his final plea with the governor.

"My, you are looking mighty nice and spiffy," the bishop said as my mom sat down in the car. She wasn't dressed in an elaborate manner because she could not afford all of the frocks and frills. Sometimes less is more. The night before, she had washed out her favorite cute navy blue dress and starched it just right with Argo. She took her time and ironed it to perfection. In the '50s, it was still considered a luxury to have a washing machine and running hot water for some colored people. The laundry was washed by hand after the water was heated in a no. 2 tub. And I remember my mother telling me that before they could afford to purchase soap, she actually made her own out of lye. Don't ask me how. All I know is that our clothes were the whitest white, and the colored clothes were the brightest bright. She was a woman phenomenally as Maya Angelou says.

My mom was petite and shapely, and whatever she wore looked fashionable and appropriate. She was a beautiful, shy woman with a set of perfectly white teeth and a smile so bright that they could have been candles to warm the coldest heart. She never wore makeup, but just a little face powder that she mixed together herself because she could never find the right shade for her complexion. You know colored people come in all shades. There is pecan, cocoa, honey, light brown, chocolate, high yellow, and some of us are as black as a blackberry, but they say the blacker the berry, the sweeter the juice. So any shade that is selected is a winner. My mom's skin tone was a mellow radiant cocoa that was impeccably flawless. I remember her using that big spongy powder puff to keep the shine off her nose. She looked lovely sitting in that car and smelled as sweet as a rose, but there was sadness in her eyes. She missed her man.

"The governor will see you now, sir and madam."

"Thank you very kindly," Bishop Davis responded. My mom managed to smile as they entered the governor's chamber. She remembered that Bishop Davis had given her explicit instructions not to sit until the governor invited them to and to always say "Your Honor." Governor Schricker had the same demeanor as he had before, but this time he seemed a bit more preoccupied. He greeted them with a salutation, but it seemed as if he had forgotten that they were standing. He finally motioned for them to be seated. The chamber was quiet until he commented about the gloomy weather.

"Yes, sir, it looks like rain, and we are going to be heading back before too long," the bishop replied.

"Well, what can I do for you?" the governor finally asked.

"Your Honor, I just want to thank you again for taking the time out of your busy schedule to see us. This is Leroy Thomas's wife, Beatrice."

"It is an honor to meet you, Governor," my mom said with a smile. The governor acknowledged my mom's salutation, but he avoided eye contact with her. It was quite obvious that he was a bit intimidated by her persona. I don't think that he expected to see such a pleasant, elegant, and charming Southern colored gal.

"Governor, it is my sincere plea that you reconsider your decision to extradite Leroy Thomas back to Arkansas." Before the governor could respond, Bishop Davis continued. "And if there is anything that I can do to make restitution, I will be more than happy to do it." Before the governor could respond, he again added. "And, Your Honor, I know that it was wrong for Leroy Thomas to have committed that crime and then flee from the state. But, Your Honor, he was under great duress and pressure. His wife wanted to be with her dad that was getting up in age and, Governor, to be honest with you, he just simply wanted something better for his family. Your Honor, this is a very poor family, and he just did not have the money to move his family up north. You remember that scripture that I gave you the last time that I was here that said don't make me so poor that I will steal?" He had not allowed the governor to get a word in edgewise, but this time, he wished for the governor to say something—anything. But he said absolutely nothing. "Your Honor, I am not condoning, neither am I justifying, the crime that was committed by Leroy Thomas. But I am pleading that you not send this poor woman's husband back to Arkansas. Your Honor, I do believe that they are going to kill him."

My mom tried to hold back the tears, but she couldn't, and surprisingly, the governor reached over and pulled out a few Kleenex from the box that was on his desk and handed them to Bishop Davis to give to her.

"Your Honor, this man has five children, and he has already found a job and has been hired at the South Bend Iron and Metal Company. Your Honor, they are holding that job for him. For God's sake, please have mercy on this family."

Governor Schricker cleared his throat to speak, and Bishop Davis felt faint and just inhaled and exhaled. It was a nail-biting predicament. He saw no signs of negotiation on the governor's face. After a few minutes, the governor spoke.

"I thought that I made it succinctly clear to you what my position on this matter was. I told you that it is my responsibility as governor of Indiana to maintain the integrity and dignity of the law. Leroy Thomas trespassed the law. It is against the law to take or misappropriate another person's property without their permission. It is dishonest, unfair, and unlawful. And what about that poor woman that lost her means of supporting herself?"

"I do understand that, Your Honor, and I am willing to make restitution to her."

"Well, that might be possible, but you cannot do it from the state of Indiana. You are going to have to make your plea to the governor of Arkansas."

My mom has told us this story over and over, and each time it has moved me to tears. She said that Bishop Davis pleaded and pleaded and became so emotionally involved that sweat literally poured off him profusely but to no avail. The governor refused to recant his decision. The governor stood up—which was an indication that the meeting was over—but for the first time, he glanced at my mom, and there was empathy in his eyes.

"Beatrice, I am sorry. The law is the law, but it may not be as bad as you think. The governor of Arkansas's name is the Honorable Sidney Sanders McMath. I hear that he is a fair and considerate governor. He has set a progressive tone in race relations by supporting a state antilynching law. He has sought repeal of the poll tax and appointed a number of coloreds to previously all-white boards and commissions. It just might be that he will consider that your husband is a first-time offender and give him a light sentence."

My mom tried to hold her peace, but she blurted out, "But, Your Honor, my husband will probably never arrive in Arkansas alive. The sheriffs told me when they came to my house while looking for him in Blytheville that they were going to 'get that nigger.' Your Honor, they said that a white man can kill a nigger, and nothing will be done about it. You don't know how it is in the South, Your Honor. Your Honor, please have mercy on me and my five little children. They need their father and I need my husband. A cow is not worth him losing his life over. I don't want my husband to be killed over a cow, Your Honor."

Surprisingly the governor sat back down in his plush leather swivel chair. He looked deeply into my mom's eyes and said, "Beatrice, tell me a little about that cow."

My mom was surprised and did not understand the reason for his request, but she gladly accommodated him. "Well, Your Honor, we roomed from an elderly lady, and she owned a cow. Your Honor, she was getting arthritis in her fingers so bad that she could no longer maintain old Betsy. My husband, my boys, and I milked that cow, grazed her, and made sure that she received the proper care that she needed. We churned the milk to make butter. There is an old saying, Your Honor, 'milk the cow, churn your own butter.' We also bottled the milk and helped her distribute it to her customers. We did this for a few years, Your Honor. We took good care of that cow for meager compensation. Your Honor, my husband did not consider what he did as stealing. He knew that we would be going north and that our landlord would not be able to properly care for the cow. He should have gotten her permission, Your Honor, but he thought that she would say no. He's a good man, Your Honor. A real good man."

For the first time, the governor relaxed, and a smile came over his countenance. He casually placed both hands behind his head and began to lean back in his chair. And then, he pointed to his wife's picture on his desk and said proudly, "That's Maude Brown Schricker. The love of my life. That lovely gal and I have been married since October 21, 1914, before you were even born. I will never forget the first time that I laid eyes on her. Her parents had a farm, and she was taking their cow out to graze in their pasture at the edge of Knox, Indiana. I was walking on the railroad tracks to my job at the county clerk's office when I looked up and saw her. Boy, she was a pretty thing. She was a schoolteacher, and before she went to class every morning, that was one of her chores. I introduced myself to her, and I tell you, it was love at first sight. While we were courting, we spent a lot of time together milking and grazing that old cow. Yes, sir, by golly, those were the good old days."

My mom and the governor began laughing and exchanging pleasantries about farm life for quite some time as if Bishop Davis was not even there. They had a common connection or denominator . . . a cow. She had captivated his heart with her charm and beauty; her shyness, sincerity, and authentic love for God; her husband and family; and . . . old Betsy, the cow. This reminded me of when Esther went before the king on behalf of her family and received favor. Esther's beauty got her in the door, and her sincerity and her die-hard love for her God and her family allowed her to not only to save her family and the rest of the Jews, but she also became the queen.

Suddenly the governor looked at his watch and said, "Oh good heavens, I am going to be late for my next meeting with the executive board." His face was flushed from blushing, and he seemed to have been embarrassed that he had condescended and lost his stately composure by becoming so congenial with my mom. He stood up and adjusted his suit jacket and tie and said, "Bishop Davis, give me a day or two to sleep on this, and you will hear from me as to what I am going to do about this matter."

Bishop Davis and my mom jumped up almost simultaneously and said, "Thank you, Governor Schricker. Thank you very kindly."

I was fortunate enough to be able to get a copy of the document that Governor Schricker sent to Bishop Davis.

This was an incredible miracle. I have spoken with several attorney friends of mine, and they each have told me that it is inconceivable and highly improbable for a colored man in the '50s, that committed such a crime, to have received a sentence such as this. His extradition under those circumstances should have been irrevocably demanded. Not only was my dad not extradited back to Arkansas, but the governor even reduced his charge from a felony to petit larceny. My mom told us that she later placed a call in to the governor's office to express her sincere appreciation. Governor Schricker accepted her call and spoke to her very professionally but hurriedly and wished her and her family the best of luck.

I want to thank the Office of the Indiana Attorney General for being so gracious to me when I placed a call to them, requesting any information that they might have concerning my dad. Being that it occurred so long ago, I did not know whether they would be able to retrieve his record or not. The Indiana Commission on Public Records expeditiously responded and sent me this true and accurate copy of a document that was on file with the Indiana state archives. You, my reading audience, are quite special because you are the first (besides my family) to have the awesome privilege to read this.

**THIS IS A 'TRUE AND ACCURATE COPY OF A DOCUMENT
ON FILE WITH THE INDIANA STATE ARCHIVES
INDIANA COMMISSION ON PUBLIC RECORDS
6440 E. 30TH STREET
INDIANAPOLIS, IN 46219**

STATE OF INDIANA
EXECUTIVE DEPARTMENT
INDIANAPOLIS

LEROY THOMAS
B-277168

EXECUTIVE ORDER NO. 20589
FOR: **TEMPORARY PAROLE**

TO ALL TO WHOM **THESE PRESENTS MAY COME, GREETING:**

WHEREAS,	One L eroy Thomas **was convicted in the Municipal Court** of Marion County* Indiana on *July* 5, 1955 charged with Petit Larceny and sentenced and committed to the Indiana State Farm to **a term** of 30 days, $25.00 **fine,** $5.00 costs; and

WHEREAS, the Superintendent of the Indiana State Farm recommends that he be granted a ONE DAY temporary parole for the purpose of attending his step-.father's funeral in Indianapolis;

NOW THEREFORE	I, Henry F. **Sohricker**, Governor of the. State of Indiana, by virftue Of the power and authority vested in me by **the Constitution and laws** of said State'. hereby grant the said Leroy Thomas one DAY temporary parole for the purpose of attending his stepfatherts funeral **in** Indianapolis At the expiration of this temporary pa **role the said** Thomas is to return to the Indiana State Farm to serve the remainder of his sentence; otherwise, he Will be Considered a fugitive from justice in the state and treated as such.

IN TESTIMONY WHEREOF, I HAVE HEREUNTO SET MY HAND AND CAUSED TO BE AFFIXED THE GREAT SEAL OF THE STATE OF INDIANA, AT THE CAPITOL. IN THE CITY OF INDIANAPOLIS, THIS 19ᵗʰ Day of **September,** 1955

BY THE GOVERNOR

SECRETARY OF STATE

Henry F. Schricker
GOVERNOR OF INDIANA

Please note that my dad requested that he be granted a one-day temporary parole for the purpose of attending his stepfather's funeral, but I must confess to you that my dad concocted that story. There was no such funeral. My dad just wanted to spend a day with his beautiful wife. Can you blame him? I guess a man has to do what a man has to do. Somehow the governor allowed Bishop Davis to take full responsibility of my dad's one-day release and said that if he did not return at the appointed time to the Indiana state farm to serve the remainder of his thirty-day sentence, my dad would be considered a fugitive from the state and treated as such. That was exceptionally kind and incredibly lenient and unequivocally unheard of. But that's the kind of wonderful God that I serve, and that was the kind of great man that the Honorable Governor Henry Fredrick Schricker was. I don't know if it was just the cow or because of the favor of God. It no doubt was both.

The governor must have taken an exceptional liking to my mom because, when my dad returned to the state farm, he was summoned into the office of parole and he received total exoneration. He only served one day and paid a $25 fine and a $5 court cost. That was an astronomical amount of money back in the day, but when you compare it with the potential of being killed, it was minuscule. My dad was not extradited but, instead, was pardoned and received clemency. The governor had stated when Bishop Davis first met with him that he had the power to pardon or commute the sentence of any criminal offenders except for treason or impeachment, and that's exactly what he did. My dad was pardoned and was now a free man. Excuse me while I shout!

I would be remiss not to tell you a little about this wonderful governor. On October 21, 1914, he and lovely Maude Brown were united in marriage and honeymooned for three days in Indianapolis, Indiana. He was the only Indiana governor elected to two nonconsecutive terms. Due to his popularity and his renowned speaking ability, he was in great demand.

He was chosen to deliver the nomination speech for Adlai Stevenson. Early in 1944, a personal emissary from President Roosevelt delivered to Governor Schricker an oral message from the nation's chief executive, and the message was "The President Roosevelt would like for you to consider running for vice president. Would you consider being his running mate?" Governor Schricker declined the offer saying that "a man ought to know his limitations." I was impressed because some people aspire to be the jack of all trades, but master of none. He was finishing the last year of his term as governor, and he believed his debt of public obligations to his people demanded his service for the full four years. And he wanted to do it without the distractions of a national campaign. As you know, President Roosevelt died while in office and, had Governor Schricker accepted his offer to run as his mate, he would have become the thirty-third president of the United States. What a nice governor! He was more committed and concerned for the people that he was serving than further notoriety. His trademark was his signature white Stetson hat, and he was never too far away from it or his lovely wife, Maude. They were married for fifty years. Governor Henry Fredrick Schricker died December 28, 1966, at the age of eighty-three. I will be forever indebted to this awesome man that did not allow the entrenched ugliness of racism that was pervasive in the '50s to sway his internal conviction that a colored man was well deserving of a second chance. Even now, I would love to meet perhaps some of his descendants so that I could show them some acts of kindness. If there are any relatives of Governor Henry Fredrick Schricker in this reading audience, please contact me. This is a small world, and anything is possible.

What is that smell? It smells like coffee. That is coffee. I know that's coffee! It's my daddy. It's my daddy. I was ecstatic! Before I could get out of bed, my daddy came and picked me up into his big strong arms and swung me around and threw me up high in the air.

"Do me again, Daddy. Do me again. Oh, Daddy, I missed you so much. Where have you been? Daddy, please don't ever leave me again."

"I won't, sweetheart."

"You promise, Daddy?"

"You've got my word, baby. I cross my heart and hope to die."

"I love you, Daddy."

"I love you too, baby girl."

My dad gave me the tightest squeeze ever and it hurt, but it hurt so good. It was a long wait and a lot transpired between the time that I left Blytheville in that crowded car until I saw my daddy again. My mom promised me that I would see him in the morning, and technically I did. I just had to endure a looooooooong night. The scripture that says weeping may endure for a night, but joy comes in the morning is right. But since then, I have been in a multiplicity of situations that have literally rocked my world and tore into the very fabric of my faith. In essence, life has challenged me. Life has rained on my parade. Have you ever been in the midst of disconcerted and adverse conditions? Times like these you feel as though you are holding onto a rope that is threatening to break. David said, in Psalms 30:5, "Weeping may endure for a night but joy comes in the morning."

This scripture is power packed and would bring solace to any believer that is in the blazing furnace of life that is seven times hotter than it ought to be. The furnace could be receiving divorce papers in the mail when everybody thought that you were the ideal, perfect, cute little couple, or a sudden unexpected death, or maybe receiving a phone call from the doctor's office saying that your test results are in and they do not look favorable . . . "Weeping may endure for a night but joy comes in the morning" would bring some degree of comfort and relief, but there is one word in that verse that can leave you shaking like a leaf on a tree. I'm talking about a leaf on one of those trees that is in the midst of a tumultuous windstorm in Florida. The word is *endure*. That verse would be more palatable if it had said "weeping may occur for a night" or "weeping may happen for a night." But it said—and I reiterate—*endure*. Endure, in Greek, literally means to lodge or camp out. In other words, David is saying weeping may check in at the desk of your life with a set of luggage and settle in for a long winter's nap. In other words, your weeping may not be over at the snap of the finger . . . But joy will come. All of the above is really what my mother meant when she most assuredly told me that I was going to see my daddy in the morning. I had to go through the night to get to the morning. You may be able to skip steps, but you can't skip the night. You may skip meals, and sometimes the mirror might reflect that we need to, but you can't skip the night. You may be intellectual and skip a grade in school, but you can't skip the night. While reading this book, you might skip a chapter or two (I trust that you won't), but I promise that you will not be able to skip the night. The delightful part about the night is that morning is coming, and that can't be skipped either. Just as you cannot stop the sun from rising in the east and going down in the west, you cannot stop the morning. Trouble doesn't last always. The joy will come in the morning. Joy is inevitable! I was back on my daddy's lap again and we were having our coffee. That was the best part of waking up. Sharing a delicious cup of Hills Brothers coffee with my daddy meant the world to me. Lots of cream and a little sugar. He always remembered to save some for me in his cup. Grounds and all. My daddy!

My grandfather's house was filled with noise, joy, warm laughter, and a lot of love. It was a bright, sunny Saturday morning and my mom and dad were extremely happy and busy getting settled. They were relieved and in a celebratory mood because they were united again. The immediate crisis from my dad's arrest had interrupted her from sorting out and organizing the boxes of clothes, so my mom had a lot of work to do. We did not have chest of drawers, so my mom just labeled all of the boxes so that our clothes could be easily found. Her father invited us to stay with him until they could make enough money to get on their feet. Since there were so many of us and my mom and dad wanted us together, we all crowded up and lived in my granddad's basement. A humble beginning would be an understatement. There was no carpet on the floor and no linoleum. The floor was made out of what Mother Nature would call *dirt*. Her dad had given her some throw rugs to put down to make it more sanitary, suitable, and comfortable for us to walk around on. My granddad had just gotten running water and an inside bathroom, which we all took turns sharing upstairs. We were amazed at its function and my granddad had to familiarize us with the flushing technique, which was simply mesmerizing to all of us. He still had the pump in the front yard. We were well acquainted with that because that is what we had in Clear Lake County in the front yard at Aunt Mae's house. My brothers and I spent most of our time outside playing and we often forgot that we had running water, so we would go to the pump for a drink. But the pump had to be primed first. Those of you that are not familiar with the pump, let me school you. There was a long handle that was attached to the pump and you had to push up and down on it repeatedly until the suction was established. It was hard work, but once the water started flowing, it was the best cold refreshing water that you could ever drink. The water came from the ground, and I really can't fathom how it came up filtered, sanitized, clear, and ready to drink, but I promise you that it did. I was too young and too little to pump, but when I got thirsty one of my brothers would lift me up to the spout while the other one pumped and I would drink until I got enough, and the best part was there was no water bill for my granddad to pay. Hallelujah! We were having the epitome of fun in and out of that big house. I mentioned that I was three years old and that traumatic and meaningful events that occur in your formative years have the propensity to be indelibly stamped in your mind, and you can recall them as circumstances demand them. My mom pierced my ears (traumatic) later that evening, outside, under a tree. Long ago, before modern inventions, when you got your ears pierced they used a sterilized large sewing needle and thread. The thread remained in your ears for four weeks, and then they removed the thread and immediately placed two straws from a broom that were long enough to go through your ears. The straws remained another two weeks until the healing process was completed. Although the pain was excruciating, the joy was when my ears completed the healing process, and my mom bought me my first pair of fourteen-karat little gold hoop earrings. Joy always comes in the morning.

That Sunday morning, we all got dressed and went to church together. The church has always been deeply embedded into the fabric of the black culture. We may be divided on a multiplicity of issues, but it is the unanimous persuasion of most of us, barring a few exceptions, that God exists and must be acknowledged. The origin of this truth stems from the cotton fields and no doubt even before. The white slave owners could fool us about a plethora of things, but the one thing that we could not be deceived about was the unequivocal existence of God. Colored people were cognizant of the fact that they had been denied from many of life's fringe benefits, but the worship experience was one thing that they refused to be deprived of. Although the black slaves were not permitted to have an organized church as we know of it today, but they devised a way to meet after it was dark, way back in the fields. They were discreet and careful not to be caught because that would have been considered a criminal act. The preacher, who had to keep his identity anonymous, would discreetly select a designated person to walk through the cotton fields and sing,

Steal away, steal away, steal away to Jesus
Steal away, steal away home
I ain't got long to stay here.

All of the slaves anxiously listened for that song because they knew that that was their signal to steal away back into the woods for worship later that night. There was a designated slave that would be discretely stationed by the slave owner's house during their worship time to discover with certainty whether or not their climatic sounds could be heard. The next morning, he would walk through the cotton fields happily singing,

> Couldn't hear nobody pray
> Couldn't hear nobody pray
> Way down yonder by myself
> Couldn't hear nobody pray

When they heard this song, they knew that they had once more successfully avoided getting caught, and then they would celebrate together by singing another song:

> Ride on King Jesus
> No man cannot hinder thee
> Ride on King Jesus
> No man cannot hinder thee
> I said no man cannot hinder thee

There was a song for every occasion. When the slaves saw the satin and the expensive lace and the beautiful bonnets that the slave owner's wives wore, instead of feeling blue and melancholy, they would sing another song:

> I gotta robe, you gotta robe
> All of God's chill'n gotta robe
> When we get to heaven we gonna put on our robe

We gonna shout all over God's heaven

Slaves sang these spirited songs to affirm their validity and to give them consolation, faith, courage, and hope to go on living when life was nothing but incessant physical toil, brutality, and injustice. And although legalized slavery has been abolished, we have continued that legacy of finding a place that we can corporately worship the Lord. There is nothing like the black church experience. It has always been a beacon of light at the end of the tunnel. Creativity and spontaneity is the order of the day on a Sunday morning in the black church. It is unrehearsed and has that aurora of freedom that cannot be denied. What amazes me is no matter what the tough times of life have brought us through the week, when Sunday comes we tend to check them outside at the door of the church. Once inside, you tend to get selective amnesia. It is a mesmerizing act of celebration and thanksgiving, and you are on your own with your expressions. There is usually not a clock in the sanctuary of a black Pentecostal church. Many have asked the notorious questions: What is it that keeps them in church so long? What is it that makes them so incredibly happy after they have suffered such atrocities? Why do they make so much noise? Well, I can answer all of those questions that inquiring minds ask with another song:

> There is something within
> That I cannot explain
> There is something within
> That vanishes all pain
> There is something within
> That I just can't explain
> All I can say is glory hallelujah
> There is something within

There are many doors that have been closed in the face of black people—such as the educational door, the political door, the economical door, and the social door—but the doors of the black church, in one way or the other, have never been closed. We always found a place to worship our God whether it was in a makeshift sanctuary way back in the dark woods, a brush arbor, or in a stained-glass cathedral in the city. And now, the doors of the church were open at the Saints Memorial Church of God in Christ.

On Sunday morning, there was a traffic jam leading to the Saints Memorial Church Of God in Christ. You could hear the sound of exuberant singing, tambourines, piano, organ, drums, and spontaneous handclapping as we entered the door. The atmosphere was electrically charged. When it was time to acknowledge the visitors, the pastor, Bishop J. B. Davis, came to the podium and said, "Church, we are so blessed to have with us this morning an amazing, fine family that has just moved here from Blytheville, Arkansas. They are a tremendously talented family. I understand that the father plays a mean guitar, the mother sings like a mockingbird, and the brothers sing as a group, and they call themselves the Thomas Harmonizers. Oh, incidentally, I also understand that the baby girl that is only three years old has an incredible voice that you would not believe. Sisters and brothers, before I bring the sermon, we want to hear this little girl sing." The black preacher's sermon is the icing on the cake, and he normally announces his lesson text and subject prior to the last song that the choir or soloist sings. Bishop J. B. Davis was extremely joyous about the tremendous outcome of my dad's situation, and I think that his sermon title reflected that victory. The old black preachers may not have had much money, and sometimes they had no formal or academic training, but once they put that black robe on and mounted that pulpit, their economic and their academic fortitude was the furthest thing from the listener's mind. As long as he had integrity and could say his lesson with the anointing and give their congregation an element of hope, every pew would be full on Sunday. Bishop Davis prolifically announced his subject, which was "the dry bones of life can connect and live." He had to wait for a few seconds to allow the church to settle down from expressing their approval of his subject with their "Amens" and their "All right, Pastor's" and their "I know that's the truth's." Once they settled down, he signaled for my mom to bring me up.

The applause was thunderous. My mom took my hand and escorted me to the front of the church. I was so little that they had to stand me up on the offering table so that I could be seen as well as heard. She stood beside me for encouragement. I sang the first song that my mom taught me, which was the following:

> If I ever ever needed the Lord before, I sure do need him now
>
> I sure do need him now
>
> I sure do need him now
>
> If I ever ever needed the Lord before, I sure do need him now
>
> I'm going to need him every day and ever hour

I had not quite learned the technique of how to end a song, so after I sang the verse a few times, my mom just started applauding for me and somehow I assumed that my debut was over. I vividly remember the audience standing and clapping as I smiled unassumingly all the way back to my seat. The stage was now set, and all attention and eyes were now focused on the pulpit. Bishop Davis cleared his throat, and within a few minutes, he had painted a vivid picturesque description and an overall view of Ezekiel and those dry bones. He gave scenarios of how disappointments, poverty, rebellion, greed, and incessant injustice could choke the life out of you and leave you as dislocated, detached, dry bones. He told them that times can get critical, but never be hopeless. By now

the audience is swaying and rocking and saying, "Preach it, Preacher."
He began to exegete in a low monotone; and as the message became
personal to him, he raised his voice in a crescendo, which is a gradual
increase in intensity and loudness. By now the audience, including my
dad and Bishop Davis, had spiritually and emotionally gone to a place
where "ain't nobody was worried." Pardon my Ebonics! Tears of joy
were streaming down my dad's face. This time the tears came easily! He
climaxed his sermon by connecting the head bone to the neck bone, and
the neck bone to the shoulder bone, and shoulder bone to the back bone,
and the back bone to the hipbone, and the hipbone to the thigh bone, and
the thigh bone to the knee bone, and by the time that he connected the
foot bone to the toe bone, the audience was standing on their feet and
moving out into the aisle and shouting and dancing. They were irrevocably
convinced that although they may have entered the church discouraged,
having no expectations or anticipation of good success, and incapable
of redemption or improvement, now they had been persuaded that they
could stand up once again like those once detached, isolated, lifeless dry
bones in the valley and live and face the plethora of challenges in life on
Monday morning.

It was a wonderful worship experience, and after the service was
over, everyone crowded around the Thomas family, and we were
inundated with hugs as they welcomed us into Saints Memorial Church
of God in Christ. There were a lot of people there, but on our way out
of the church, I recognized two faces. It was those two strange men
that had picked us up in Blytheville, Arkansas. They were deacons of
that church. Their names were Deacon Henry Bush and Deacon Toby
James. They both reached down and shook my hand, and one of them
gave me some candy for doing such a fine job with my song. This was
just the beginning of the many inexorable experiences that we had with
our new church family.

I trust that you have not unfastened your seat belts because this plane is getting ready to rise in altitude. I mentioned in the first chapter that my dad affectionately called my mom Kid, and that I would later explain why . . . Well, here I go! Enjoy!

Chapter 3

The Girl at the Well

It was a smoldering hot day in Hickman, Kentucky, and Leroy could faintly see the image of a lovely young girl struggling with a heavy bucket of water. She had just filled her bucket up to the brim and had started her way back down the hill. Most colored people did not have the luxury of running water, and they had to go across the levee to the well to get their daily supply.

"Hey, Kid!" he yelled out so that she could hear him. "Looks like you could stand a little help with that heavy bucket."

"I sure could. This thing is heavy."

Leroy ran and caught up with her and took the bucket out her hand, and they walked across the levee together. "My name is Leroy Thomas, and what might yours be?"

"My name is Beatrice Giden," she responded rather shyly. "I live another mile or so from here, and I sure hope that you plan on carrying that heavy bucket of water all the way to my house."

"Baby, I would carry this bucket and you to the end of the world if you would be mine. Sweet thing, my life would be a dream just like paradise up above if I could just hear you say that I'm the one you could love. Little girl, you would make all of my dreams come true if only you would let me spend my life loving you."

That sure was tantalizing and sounded good to Beatrice's ears. No one had ever said anything like that to her before. Beatrice giggled while trying to steal glances of him when he wasn't looking. He was carrying a guitar over his back and had a red bandana tied around his head. "Why do you have your head tied up?" she asked.

"Oh, I've been up all night playing in the juke joint, and I have a splitting headache."

"What is a juke joint?" Beatrice asked.

"It's a little decrepit shotgun place that colored people meet up at to listen to blues and they boogie-woogie, drink, and dance."

The juke joint was an excellent source of release for colored people after they had worked long hot hours picking cotton or other odds-and-ends jobs for the white man to provide for themselves and their families. Blues is that down-home sound that evolved in the early nineteenth century with colored performers and common people in general. It was the colored people's anthem. Blues was the sound of the holler and cry that they made in the fields. It gave voice to the depression, alienation, and profound despair that colored people endured from being forcibly conscripted to long hard hours of work (sunup to sundown), and then when they grew too sick or too old to function, they were either tossed vicariously aside or put to death. Bad luck and misfortunes are always between every note and beat of the blues. There was no sheet music. The words and the melody were impromptu and called up from deep down in the recesses of their painful frustrations. Some religious people are offended by the music called blues and think of it as low-down and raunchy, but I believe that it is because they are ignorant and do not have a clear perception of it. Please do not take offense from the word *ignorant* because that word simply implies that one lacks the particular knowledge either generally or in a specific subject or matter.

If you take mental notes or comparisons of the blues and the old spirituals, you will find that they both are quite similar in their interpretation. They both, either by notes or by lyrics, paint a vivid picturesque description of the gut pain and agony of the black experience. They both can express the pessimistic, deplorable woes of everyday existence and experiences in hopes of a better tomorrow. And often times, the spirituals end on a sour sad note and leave us with not much to look forward to, but a promise of a recompense, which we will receive by and by beyond that celestial shore. They both are the epitome of the black history and the kind of sufferings, rejections, and the day-to-day frustrations that we encounter. The blues gave an accurate overview of the social situation in which they lived. White people write the blues and sing and play them, but black people live the blues and sing and play them. Leroy's guitar was the instrument that he used to strum out his intense determination to survive in the midst of utter hopelessness. When he played it, the pain hurt so good. It was how he spelled relief. The commercials spell relief as R-O-L-A-I-D-S and A-L-K-A-S-E-L-T-Z-E-R, but Leroy spelled it plain and simple, T-H-E-B-L-U-E-S. It was cathartic and helped him hold on to his sanity until his change came. Spirituals are the same. One articulates that "Oh, my baby, don leave me now what am I gon' to do" or "I've been down so long that gettin' up ain't crossed my mind" while spirituals articulate that "I don't feel at home in dis worl' any mo'" or "Soon I will be don wid the troubles of da world." One is in pain because of a love affair that has gone bad; and the other is in pain because of the maltreatment, disparity, and injustice that has precipitated an alienation and a yearning to be free from life's trouble and a desire to depart and go to heaven. They both are, in a sense, a "somebody has done me wrong" song; and that is what constitutes the blues. But the good news is that the spirituals give you a fervent hope of the hereafter, but the blues well . . . You're kinda on your own.

"Kid, you know colored people are barred from the white people's establishments by the Jim Crow law, so we have our own place across the levee. They have a fish fry every Friday night, and you can gamble and dance until your little heart's content."

That was news to Beatrice because her dad was a Baptist pastor, and they were devoutly religious. The only places that she had been were school, when the weather permitted her to go, and church. *He sure is handsome even after being up all night with a splitting headache*, she thought to herself. "Do you live around here?" she asked.

"No, I'm just here for a few nights, playing at the juke joint across the levee, but as pretty as you are, you could make me like this place well enough to make it my home."

That sounded good to Beatrice because she had said that the next time a real nice man came along and asked her to marry him, she was going to say yes. Her mother had died from tuberculosis when she was eight years old, and she and her other brothers and sisters were just about left to raise themselves. Her father was a Baptist pastor, and when he was not at church, he was busy visiting the sick or taking care of other pastoral obligations that kept him away from home most of the time. In addition to that, he was a widower, and I am sure that he was spending a lot of his time socializing as well. It was quite common to marry at a young age in the '20s, and Beatrice's living conditions at home had a lot to do with her determination to marry and leave home at the young age of thirteen. The nurturing and the advice and discipline that mothers give their daughters was certainly missing in her life and that also played a significant part in her decision. Beatrice certainly did not know enough about life to leave home, but she knew too much to stay. So after a very brief courtship, Leroy popped the question, and he took her to the Justice of the Peace, and they became husband and wife. She was thirteen years young, and he was twenty-nine years old, and that is why Leroy called her Kid. Today that would be considered statutory rape. Beatrice quit school and worked in the cotton fields, and Leroy played his guitar to earn their living. She became pregnant immediately, and after the first baby, Leroy knew that he would not be able to support his family on what he was making at the juke joints. So he began picking cotton during the day, and he played his guitar only on weekends to supplement their income. Because of the zeal that Beatrice had to get married and also her immaturity, she did not inquire about Leroy's background. Although he was a good man, he did have several flaws in his character. She knew that he played a guitar for a living, but what she did not know was that he was a compulsive gambler, loved to drink and party, and was an irresistible ladies' man. Beatrice became pregnant every fifteen months and, in between pregnancies, took care of the babies, maintained the household—which she did impeccably—and worked in the fields when she could. She really had little time and was yet considerably too young and naïve to seriously take notice of his improprieties. Leroy always brought the money home on Fridays for her to manage, which was commendable, but he was always in a rush to take a bath and change clothes, and she would not see him anymore until late Sunday evening. This was his weekend routine without fail. She was aware that the juke joints stayed open until past midnight on weekends, but she could not understand why he was not coming home after it closed.

One Friday night after he left, Beatrice got a babysitter named Ms. Mae, and she walked about a mile or so and crossed the levee to the juke joint. She could hear the sound of the honky-tonk blues as it filled the air before she got to the joint. Beatrice looked through the window; and the place was crowded, dimly lit, and smoke-filled. She saw couples slow drag with their bodies much closer together than she thought was necessary, and she saw other men sitting at the tables, throwing dice and shouting out "seven come eleven." There were other people sitting on the bar stools drinking and behaving quite rowdily. They appeared to be having the time of their lives. She was straining on her tiptoes, looking for her husband, but she could not see him. Just as she was about to turn away from the window, she saw a large crowd of people—mostly women—that had surrounded her husband. The women were spellbound and squirming and wiggling as they listened to him play the blues on his guitar. She stood there for a while, watching him. That was the first time that she had really heard him play his guitar except when he did a little practicing around the house. He was phenomenally, amazingly, and masterfully playing a sweet guitar. She was so proud of her handsome man as she watched the people throwing money at him while clapping and dancing and going crazy. Sweat was rolling off his forehead into his eyes, and a provocative woman that was built like a sculptor's dream dressed in a skintight short black dress sashayed up to him with a cigarette hanging from her red lips and slowly and flirtatiously wiped the sweat off his face. Leroy smiled at her, and she removed her cigarette and kissed him on his lips. His eyes focused approvingly on her voluptuous body as she walked away. Beatrice felt her heart palpitating, and she was weak in her legs. She had never been to a juke joint in her young life, and her husband was an experienced man that was sixteen years her senior, so the only thing that she knew to do was to run back home, crying all the way. She could hardly wait until Sunday evening when he came home so that she could tell him what she had witnessed. She could not hold back the tears as she spoke to him. He did not panic, but he took her into his big strong arms and held her and assured her that what she had seen meant absolutely nothing. He also warned her to never check up on him again because that meant that she did not love or trust him. Beatrice believed him and obeyed him because she was only a kid, naïve and young, and she was madly in love. Leroy continued to work hard and provide for his family, but he also continued his weekend job at the juke joints and his escapades.

By now, they had four babies, all of which were boys. Her dad had grown tired of the South and the antagonistic racial and social climate and had decided to move north. Some of his colleagues in the ministry had moved to a place called South Bend, Indiana, and the word came back to him that life was much better for coloreds in the North. All of Beatrice's siblings had moved with him as well except her younger brother, Henry, who had decided to join the United States Army. Beatrice was ready for a change and so was her husband, but not quite as drastic as moving north. Instead Leroy decided to move his family to Blytheville, Arkansas. He had lived there for a short time before and had established relationships and was not a stranger to the environment. He found a job right away at a place called the Saw Mill, and Beatrice picked cotton to help out financially until she became pregnant with the fifth baby, which was another boy.

All of her babies were born at home under the supervision of the midwives. She was a strong woman that had a remarkable tolerance for pain. None of her babies weighed less than nine pounds and, of course, she had them all by natural childbirth, and naturally they were all breastfed. Her fifth baby, who was named Minor, was a beautiful baby boy with curly jet-black hair. Minor was five weeks old when Beatrice went to check on him one night, only to discover that he had stopped breathing. Beatrice frantically picked the baby up and put her ear to his chest, and she also checked his pulse. There was no sign of life. Her loud shrilling scream woke up everybody in the house. That was a major calamity, and only God got them through the agonizing pain. They were devastated. This was an unthinkable, traumatizing tragedy. Leroy was hurt; and he expressed his helplessness, despair, gloom, downheartedness, and pain through clinched teeth. Beatrice expressed hers through denial, anger, guilt, depression, and insomnia. For days, she could still feel, hear, smell, and even see her little baby. Looking at his little undershirts and his empty crib was unbearable. She was awakened many times in the middle of the night because she heard him crying, only to realize that he was really gone and silenced forever. Most colored people had not even heard of autopsies, so

Leroy and Beatrice laid Minor to rest in his little grave without knowing the cause of his untimely death. Before they buried him, Beatrice cut a lock of Minor's beautiful hair as keepsake and covered him up with his cute, soft little blue blanket, in essence, tucking him in for the last time. The death seemed so unnatural because no parent desires to ever bury a child. It is supposed to be just the opposite.

They did not know it then, but they later heard about SIDS and assumed that Minor must have died from sudden infant death syndrome. Death is so cruel, cold, and final. And the guilty feelings oftentimes are the hardest thing to cope with. She felt guilty for Minor dying alone in his crib, but if he had died in the bed with them, she probably would have felt guilty that she slept through his final moments of struggle to survive. She tried to piece together clues, signs, and reasons as to why a seemingly perfectly healthy baby could just stop breathing. She went over every intricate detail that she could recall of his brief life. She was haunted by the feeling of guilt for every whimper that he had made that might have been a sign that something was wrong. She was desperately looking for something or someone to blame; but the fact is, in SIDS, there is nothing or no one that you can blame the death on. It's a harsh reality, and the guilt and the propensity to blame are the hardest to recover from. Leroy and Beatrice managed to get through it but never got over it. And let's not forget their four little boys. They all experienced this horrible event, and I am sure that they all grieved in their own way as well. Sometimes young siblings' feelings are ignored and not taken into consideration—possibly because of a lack of understanding—but death affects everyone in the house regardless of their age. They may not be able to communicate it, but they are affected nevertheless. One of their little boys had nightmares because he was fearful that the same thing was going to happen to him. I am sure that counseling or therapy would have been highly recommended and therapeutic, but back in those days, that was out of the question. I have never lost a child through SIDS, but I would like to encourage those of you that may have. SIDS can happen at any time to any family to any baby, and there is absolutely nothing that a parent can do about it. Nothing at all. You can do everything right, and it can still happen. Just make certain that the infant's surroundings are safe and healthy and make sure that he or she is seen by the pediatrician for postnatal care. Staying up all night, making sure that the baby is breathing, is nonsensical. Let's face it. We as parents have all done it. I have gone in and out of Erike's room when he was a baby just to check to see if his little chest was still going up and down. But it really makes no sense. Having taken all of the necessary precautions, you should just enjoy your new baby and *go to sleep*. You are going to need your rest for the busy days ahead.

Within three months, Beatrice was pregnant again. She was yet grieving almost to the point of depression, but she needed this pregnancy to help her through the severe pain and shock of the loss of her little baby. Many days she selfishly felt like joining Minor, but she thought about her other children that needed her and her husband that needed her as well. Having another baby just seemed to have been the right thing to do. Some of the neighbors thought that it was much too soon, and some of them gave her the raised-eyebrow treatment. And then, there were those that thought she was not sad enough because she had the nerve to smile sometimes, and then when she cried, others thought that she was grieving too hard and too long. But while grieving from a loss, if you're having a good day, you should not have to pretend to be sad just to satisfy the expectations of others. And likewise, if you are having a bad day, you should not have to pretend to be happy just to appease someone that presumes to know the proper behavior and length of time that a mom and dad should grieve. I told you, in the first chapter of this book, to just "do you." You cannot please everyone; so if you are dealing with a loss, while you are going through the grieving process, be honest when someone asks you how you are doing. I have learned to make it easy on myself and ignore those people that love to wear critical, opinionated hats, and you should too.

Although they needed the extra money, her husband recommended that she not work until after the new baby was born. He was always home with her in the evenings to help her with the boys, but on the weekends, he continued playing at the juke joint. He also resorted back to his other proclivities that Beatrice had known nothing about, and that was making and selling moonshine and running a place where people could shoot craps. Leroy had become a professional crapshooter when he was a young boy. He had become a connoisseur. He knew how to maneuver and arrange the dice in his hand before shooting them. He knew how to grip them and how to minimize the bounce so that the dice would land in the place called the sweet spot. He knew the rhythm that you must have to minimize the chance of throwing the losing seven. He had learned the technique. He had mastered the systematic procedure of how to set your dice, grip your dice, focus your attention, and then throw the dice and land softly. Leroy had learned how to do everything but how to be a good loser. No one likes to lose, but losing is part of the game when you shoot craps. That is why it is called gambling. Every transaction that is based on one party's gain and another's loss, or—if the transaction is obscure—it is called gambling. One party always gains, and the other always loses. Leroy detested losing. Thus, Leroy decided to do what they call hit the wall. That means that he had become so emotionally wrapped up in the game that he could not effectively play it for the fear of losing his bankroll. Hitting the wall means that you quit cold turkey. Only a gambler with self-control and discipline can hit the wall. Leroy knew when to walk away and when to run. This took discipline. He did it without any aids or a step-down program. He experienced many emotional withdrawal symptoms because shooting craps was an exciting, exhilarating, pulse-raising habit that he loved; but the symptoms only lasted a short time. Leroy was smart, knowing that the most important thing you should do when deciding to kick a habit cold turkey is to find something to replace the craving with. Instead of sitting around thinking about how bad the urge was and how much he would love to pick up the dice again, he did something to take his mind off it.

He knew that there was good money in gambling, so because of his financial situation, he thought about the advantages of running the table instead of playing the table. That was a sure way of never losing money because when you do what they call run the table, the players have to pay you. It was a lucrative racket. He built an eight-foot-long craps table, and in addition to this, Leroy built a moonshine table and started making his own moonshine and sold it. This name was derived from the fact that moonshine makers would mix it and sell it at night under the moonlight to avoid arrest for selling it without a license. This was called bootlegging. It was also illegal liquor because it was usually brewed improperly, and it was extremely strong. Aside from reasons relating to politics and money, there were safety concerns to making your own moonshine. There was the potential danger of explosion from the buildup of internal pressure, and it also could be poisonous when the proper temperature while brewing is not maintained. The ingredients were corn, potatoes, and sugar that were slowly cooked. It was a drink with such a potent punch that it could grow hair on your chest and then burn it off. It has been compared to cooked sunshine. The sensation starts with a slight burn at the back of your tongue. It's an innocent tingle that quickly builds into a slow-burning skin-removing inferno. Making it, selling it, and not paying taxes on the proceeds was an enormous revenue loss, which was another reason why it was illegal. No one knew exactly how much money exchanged hands in the moonshine trade, but it was certainly enough for the missing taxes to make a difference. Moonshine was worth more to the government than beer and wine. He became a moonshine connoisseur. All of these activities were conducted outdoors about a mile from their home. Leroy built a craps table and set up a stand for his moonshine, and he was open for business. There was booze, gambling, honky-tonk blues, and good-looking provocative women. In spite of Leroy's improprieties and idiosyncrasies, he loved his wife in his own way and was adamant about supporting his family.

About the fifth month of Beatrice's pregnancy, she took a walk to John Chu's country store. John Chu was a godsend. He was a Japanese immigrant from the prison camp, and when released, he and his family settled in Blytheville, Arkansas. He opened up a store right in the rural area, and he was kind to the colored people by letting them have food and other household items on credit. We would not have made it without his generosity. I am certain that he is sleeping somewhere in Mother Earth now, but I'd like to say *domo arigato* anyway to Mr. John Chu and also to his descendants. There was an older lady in the store that was picking up a few odds and ends, and she introduced herself to Beatrice. She was a nice, friendly lady that had a significant glow about her. After they exchanged pleasantries, she invited Beatrice to a revival that was being conducted at her church. It just happened to have been within a mile or so, which was walking distance back in the day. Leroy agreed to stay home and watch the boys. The older lady and another group from the church met Beatrice down the road, and they walked together to the revival. Long ago, in the rural sparsely-populated areas in the South, some colored people could not afford church buildings. So the men would get together, and they would build a roughed-in shelter that was held up by poles, and the roof was made up of hay and bushes. The hay and bushes served to protect the worshippers from the elements. Benches were made by splitting logs and shaping the seats with an axe, and then the surface was smoothed out with a sandstone rock. The floor was sawdust. This makeshift church was called a brush arbor. There was no form or fashion, and there was an innocence and a sincerity about the congregation. You could hear the singing and the shouting as they were getting close. The walk was long and the road was rough and dusty, and Beatrice was more than glad when they finally arrived. Being that Beatrice's father was a pastor, she was accustomed to singing and shouting, but she had never witnessed this style of worship. They sang with more enthusiasm, fervor, spontaneity, and intensity. She sat in amazement at the level of their freedom of expression and the openness and permissiveness. Today we would say that they really knew how to get their praise on. There was an old gray-haired lady that started singing a song impromptu, right out of the blue. Beatrice was in awe because in her dad's church, you had to be on the program to sing, but this woman just lifted her head and hands up in the air like she really didn't care and began to bellow out,

I love the Lord he heard my cry and pitied every groan
Long as I live and trouble rise, I'll hasten to his throne

Be not dismayed whatever betide
God will take care of you
Beneath his wings of love abide
God will take care of you.

Tears began to fall down Beatrice's face as she thought about the pain that she was experiencing from the loss of her baby. She was overwhelmed with emotion, and the people that were sitting around her hugged her and reassured her that everything was going to be all right. The deacons passed the offering plate and the pastor stood up at the podium, which was made out of the same material that the pews were made out of.

"Has anybody ever made you a promise?" was the first thing that the preacher asked the waiting congregation. "Has anybody ever made you a promise and broken it? I know that they have, but tonight, my sisters and brothers, I want you to know that God has made you a promise, and it cannot be broken no matter how hard you lean on it. God is a promise keeper."

"Praise the Lord, Pastor!" everybody shouted.

"God cares about your burdens and he is inviting you to come unto me all ye that labor and are heavy laden, and I will give you rest. He has promised that if you come to him, he will give you rest." The pastor elevated his voice and began to pound his fist on the podium. "He will give you rest from your worries, rest from your cares, rest from your heartaches. That's a promise that you can lean on and it will not break."

Beatrice stood up and ran to the front of the church and shouted, "I need rest! I need rest!"

The spiritual encounter that Beatrice had that night revolutionized her life forever. She had a change of heart, a change of mind, and a change of direction. She had never experienced so much joy and peace. She embraced the Pentecostal persuasion that night and was fellowshipped into the Church of God in Christ. Her new pastor's name was Bishop Minor Jones. It's ironic that the baby she had just lost had the same name as her new pastor. Beatrice's walk back home was undeniably different from her walk to church. She left for church feeling like the weight of the world was sitting on top of her, but she returned home feeling like she was sitting on top of the world. Her problems were yet there, but she now had someone to help her deal with them.

Her new outlook would be compared to that of going to the dentist to have a tooth filled. The dentist gives you Novocain, which is a local anesthetic, to numb the pain so that he can perform his work. The pain is still there, but your nerve endings have become numbed and desensitized, and you don't feel it as much. That is what God had done that night for Beatrice. He had given her a spiritual injection of Novocain to numb her so that she could continue her assignment in life without feeling as much pain. Beatrice left the church that night knowing, as Yolanda Adams sings so well, that "this too shall pass." You may currently be going through a devastating loss as Beatrice was. We all go through some turbulent, tumultuous times. As a matter of fact, in this life, you are either in a test, going into a test, or coming out of a test. The words to this song by Yolanda have gotten me and, I am sure, a countless number of others through some painful circumstances; and I want to share them with you. Be encouraged because

> This too shall pass
> Like every night that's come before it
> He'll never give you more than you can bear
> This too shall pass
> So in this thought be comforted
> It's in his hands
> This too shall pass

> In the middle of the turbulence surrounding you
> These trying times that are so hard to endure
> In the middle of what seems to be your darkest hour
> Hold fast your heart and be assured

> The Father knows the tears you cry before they fall
> He feels your pain
> His heart and yours are one
> The Father knows that sorrow's heavy chains are strong
> But with his strength, you'll overcome

So set your eyes upon the mountain
And lift your hands up to the sky
And let his arms of love surround you
And take you to the other side

Beatrice and I approve this message: this too shall pass!

They had lanterns to light their path for their journey on that long dark road back home. A group of people eventually came along, riding in an old Ford with the pastor. He had room for just one more, and because Beatrice was in the family way, they offered her a ride. She gladly accepted because she was anxious to get home to tell her husband about the wonderful experience that had taken place.

We don't see brush arbors anymore. Today we have ornate cathedrals with stained-glass windows and with every comfort from air conditioning and padded pews to sophisticated sound systems, orchestras, and entertaining flag-waving liturgical dancers. Perhaps it would do us good to revisit, at least within our hearts, a brush-arbor experience and kneel before our God without form or fashion with unconditional praise.

The house was quiet and dark except for one light that Leroy was using while he played cards. It was late, and the children were all asleep. Beatrice was glad because she needed his undivided attention so that she could tell him all about being born again and that she had joined the church. Leroy was happy for the decision that she had made, but when she invited him to go with her that next Sunday, he let her know in no uncertain terms that church was not for him. Beatrice did not force the issue but was steadfast and faithful in her conviction and church attendance. Periodically she would ask him to go, but when he refused, she was always loving and kind. Leroy continued his riotous shenanigan lifestyle.

In the eighth month of Beatrice's pregnancy, she began to daydream and imagine how wonderful it would be if she could have a little girl. Don't ask me why she waited until the eighth month. My guess is that she was just happy to be pregnant again and just wanted the baby to be healthy, regardless of its gender. She had had five boys consecutively, and the desire to have a girl just began to obsess her. Beatrice was devout in her faith, and she believed that if she prayed for a girl that her prayer request would be answered. One day she got a piece of paper out and wrote down specifically how she wanted her little girl to look. She described in detail that she wanted her to have her husband's pecan complexion, his beautiful big eyes, sandy-colored hair like his sister, and she wanted the baby to have her shape and legs. When she finished jotting down her request, she got down on her knees; and her prayer was

> Lord, I am eight months pregnant. I have had five boys, and one of those boys is now in heaven with you. Jesus, could you please replace him with a girl? Lord, only you know the sex of this baby that I am carrying, but if it is a boy, please change him to a girl, and nobody will ever know it but you.

After the short specific but fervent prayer was over, Beatrice said that the baby starting moving around vigorously and kicking more than usual. There was so much activity in her womb that she thought that she was going to go into labor, but eventually the baby settled down. She went into her bedroom and placed her detailed description in her Bible. And from that point on, when people would ask her what she wanted to have—which is a question that is frequently fired at expectant parents—she answered them emphatically that she wanted a girl and that that is exactly what she was going to have. Beatrice was so confident that she was going to have a girl that she chose the name Jennifer before the baby was born. She admired her bishop's wife, and she wanted to name her baby after her.

It has been scientifically proven that it is the man that determines the sex of your baby as his sperm contains either an X or a Y chromosome. If the mother-to-be's egg is fertilized by an X-chromosome sperm, her baby will be a girl (XX). If the sperm has a Y chromosome, her baby will be a boy (XY). Studies have also shown that the mother's diet may also be a determining factor as well. The idea being that X and Y sperms respond differently to the amounts of sodium, potassium, and calcium in the mother's body. It has been speculated that Y chromosomes have a craving for salt, so if the mother-to-be desires a boy, she should add plenty of orange juice, ham, and pickles to her diet. On the other hand, X chromosomes do not have an appetite for salt, so if the mother-to-be desires a girl, she should cut back on her sodium intake, lessen her potassium, and increase her calcium and leafy greens. This certainly is not an exact science and is mere speculation, so results can't be guaranteed. There are many theories on the market and old folktales about how to determine the sex of your baby during your pregnancy. Some of them have more credibility than others, but bear in mind that none have more than a sliver of validity. Beatrice's sixth pregnancy was before the invention of the ultrasound, which deprives you of the wonderful surprise of finding out your baby's sex at birth. The ultrasound is a useful diagnostic tool in obstetrics that provides real live continuous pictures of the growing fetus. This process allows you to see images that are created from high-frequency sound waves that are emitted from a transducer that is placed in contact with the abdomen and moved like a flashlight all around the uterus. This is a noninvasive accurate way to investigate the sex and progress of the embryo. This would have been wonderful, but it was not discovered until a few years later. Since Beatrice was not aware of the diet recommendations and the ultrasound had not been scientifically discovered, she had to have patience, faith in her fervent prayer, and wait. It has been proven that all organs of the embryo are present and can be determined within seven to eight weeks. Being that Beatrice was in her third trimester, the sex of her baby was clearly already defined and established. The anticipation of counting down the weeks was filled with excitement and anxiety.

That hot muggy Saturday afternoon, Beatrice felt a pain ripping through the lower part of her back that let her know that she was getting closer to the time of deliver. She had had enough experience to know the difference between prelabor and active labor, and she had been monitoring her contractions. Leroy had stayed home that weekend so that he could give his wife all of the emotional and physical support that she needed. He had already notified the midwife, and she jokingly reminded him that Beatrice likes to sit on the fence when it is time to have her baby. That meant that she procrastinated as long as she possibly could before she fully accepted, faced, and embraced her labor. In other words, she was no doubt experiencing some discomfort, but she was probably still more concerned about her hair being in place and her nose being powdered. When you are in serious labor, the tidiness of your hair and whether your nose is shining or not do not take precedence over the severe pain and are the furthest things from your mind.

"How are her contractions coming?" she asked more seriously.

"Well, her contractions are strong, but they do not last very long," Leroy answered nervously.

"I'll tell you what, call me back when Beatrice's contractions are about four to five minutes apart, and they are lasting about one minute in duration and occurring every hour. And if she changes positions and they do not go away, we are in business. I am right up the road with another patient that has just given birth, so I will be able to get there in plenty of time."

Within a few hours, Leroy called the midwife back and told her that it was definitely time. He sent the boys outside and told them to play until the baby was born. During all of Beatrice's deliveries, Leroy always stood by her head to wipe the perspiration from her forehead and to hold her hand. He also always looked forward to cutting the umbilical cord. This time was going to be no different.

"Push, Beatrice, come on, push, you're doing good. We're almost there."

Beatrice had begun to make involuntary deep grunting moans with each contraction. The pain was excruciating. "Please let me get up. Please."

"No, Beatrice, the baby is coming."

"Please, may I have some juice or maybe some ice chips?"

"No, Beatrice, you've had enough to drink. It's time to push. Come on give me another good push."

"It hurts . . . Ouch . . . Lord, have mercy, I want to go to church. It hurts!" It felt like the worst menstrual cramps that she had ever had in her entire life—ever. Every time a contraction would come, the lower part of her uterus felt as if it was coming apart. The muscles in her lower back were slowly twisting harder and harder until the pain became unbearable. Beatrice screamed out, "I've changed my mind, I don't want a baby!" She hated her husband for doing this to her. He was no longer handsome or sexy, and she never wanted to become intimate with him again as long as she lived. Ever!

"Push, Beatrice! Bear down once more. That's good. Give me another hard puuuuuuuuush!" Beatrice was in labor for several exhausting hours, and then finally she heard the midwife say, "Okay, you can stop pushing now. The head is coming. Just pant, Beatrice. Pant like a deer on a real scorching hot July day. Good job, good job. Here come the shoulders." The rest of the baby easily slipped out. "There we go. There we go. Congratulations, Beatrice and Leroy! You've got yourself a beautiful little girl." Neither my mom nor my dad could believe their ears or their eyes. My dad looked at me, his new bundle of joy, with so much love and tenderness. He was madly in love with all of his babies, but there was a special feeling that immediately strummed on the strings of his heart—just like his fingers strummed his guitar—when he first looked at his little girl. His eyes seemed to have been saying,

Isn't she lovely
Isn't she wonderful
Isn't she precious
Less than one minute old
I never thought through love we'd be
Making one as lovely as she
Isn't she lovely made from love

Isn't she pretty
Truly the angel's best
Boy I'm so happy
We have been heaven blessed
I can't believe what God has done
Through us he's given life to one
But isn't she lovely made from love

Isn't she lovely
Life and love are the same
Fair and beautiful is Jennifer
The meaning of her name
Beatrice, it could have not been done
Without you who conceived this one
That's so very lovely made from love.

After having five boys consecutively, they finally had a girl. Daddy's girl. The midwife had to repeat it over and over and over. "It's a girl, it's a girl! Come on, Leroy, it's time to cut the cord."

Leroy had cut the cord for all five babies, but he could not bring himself to do it this time because he did not totally understand its function. Knowledge is power. He faintly said, "I just can't 'cause I might hurt her. She's a girl. My little baby girl."

"Leroy, you cannot possibly hurt the baby by cutting the umbilical cord." The midwife chuckled as she responded. "Technically, it is no longer connected to Beatrice or the baby. The umbilical cord was joined to Beatrice's placenta so that your little baby's nutrients could go in, and her waste could come out through her belly button, via the umbilical cord. Beatrice has passed the cord, and I have tied it and now it just needs to be cut. The stump of it is going to wither within a few days and fall off, thus leaving your baby with her first scar that we call the belly button. I understand your jitters though, especially since it's a girl. So relax . . . I'll do it."

The midwife cut the cord, and she had a nice white cloth waiting to place the baby on so that she could clean her up, but Beatrice anxiously said, "*No*, I want to hold her now." The midwife honored her request and gently laid the messy, wrinkled, beautiful little baby girl on her stomach. My mom kissed my tiny lips and could not hold back the tears because she remembered her prayer request. She had prayed for a little girl, and her prayers had been answered. I weighed in a whopping nine pounds five ounces—healthy and beautiful. My brother, Minor, was born on July 2, and I was born exactly one year later on July 2.

"She's a living doll, Beatrice. Have you selected a name for her?" the midwife asked as she sat down to relax from a job well done.

"I am going to name her Jennifer, after my bishop's wife, because one day—yes, one day—my little girl is going to be a bishop's wife too."

The baby that she lost had her pastor's name, and the miracle baby that she gained was named after his wife. My eyes were struggling to adjust to the brightness of my new environment, and I finally made eye contact with my mom and naturally found her breast and began feeding. Beatrice was overcome with joy unspeakable, and the gut-wrenching pain that she had experienced giving birth to me simply vanished into thin air. Her husband looked handsome to her once again.

My mom has told me this story at least a thousand times about how she prayed for a girl and how she wrote down a detailed description of the precise way that she wanted me to look. She told me that she prayed, "Lord, if I am carrying a boy, turn him into a girl, and nobody will ever know it but you." One would think that an unusual prayer request of this nature would be much longer and filled with magnanimous words, but it was quite the contrary. Her prayer was short, specific, and simple. She told me that I started kicking and vigorously moving around more than usual immediately after the prayer. My mom has shared this incredible testimony many times as she traveled the country and has even told it on television on the Lester Sumrall Show in South Bend, Indiana. She was convinced that I was a boy and that God miraculously turned me into a girl. Albert Einstein once said that there are only two ways to live your life. One is as though nothing is a miracle and the other as though everything is a miracle. I choose to embrace the latter. I believe in miracles, and I am persuaded that they are divinely orchestrated. *Webster* gives a definition of the word *miracle* as an event that apparently contradicts known scientific laws and is hence thought to be due to supernatural causes or an act of God. That is an accurate definition, but if you would indulge me, I would like to share with you my own simplified interpretation of a miracle. I believe that a miracle is an impossible, out-of-the-ordinary, incomprehensible, unaccountable, unexplainable, incredible, inconceivable, unprecedented, extraterrestrial, and superhuman manifestation.

A miracle is an occurrence that will leave you with your mouth open, make your hair stand up on your head, and knock you off your feet. This story has always intrigued me because I knew nothing about it and had absolutely nothing to do with it. I was in a tiny sac under water in a relatively dark, warm, and cozy safe place in my mother's womb. My sex was the furthest thing from my brain. It has been scientifically proven that a baby can hear and is able to recognize the mother's voice and respond to it by the second trimester. I have often wondered if I heard my mom when she prayed that prayer. She was eight months pregnant and in her third trimester, so it is in fact quite possible. Do you suppose that is why I instantaneously started kicking and moving around so vigorously? Although I lack a definitive answer, I do know for certain that God heard it. For he can hear the faintest whisper. Did he miraculously turn me into a girl? Only he knows that answer for sure. That's his secret and my mom's testimony. I must admit that I was always very uncomfortable and squeamish listening to my mom talk about this phenomenal occurrence. As a matter of fact, I found it hard to conceive or believe, and I thought that others would find it preposterous as well, but I never told her. But even if I had, it would not have daunted her faith or conviction because it happened to her and it was real. She believed that I was a boy and that God turned me into a girl. If you have a hundred dollar bill in your pocket, it is irrelevant and insignificant who does not believe it. It would be nonproductive and nonsensical to try to convince a doubter. I mentioned early on in this book that what has been concealed is now being revealed, and this is one of the many things that I am finally confident enough to talk about. I was afraid of the looks that I might get and even afraid of being considered weird. But here I am over forty years later telling the entire world. I do believe that this is possible because I now know who I am and who God is. If God can create this universe, paint the sunset, hang the moon and name all of the stars, and number the hairs that are on our heads, he certainly can answer my mom's prayer. My mom always ended her testimony by saying that if God can turn water into wine, he can do anything. The proof is in the pudding because she got just what she ordered . . . I am a girl (woman) and I was born with my dad's pecan complexion, his beautiful big eyes, sandy-colored hair like his sister's, and I have my mom's shape and legs just as she prayed for. Go figure!

That little house in Clear Lake County was never the same. My four little brothers had to get used to having a little baby girl around the house. So much fuss was made over me until they didn't like me very much. I interrupted, or perhaps disrupted, all of their plans because they were expecting another brother that they could play football with and roughhouse. A new baby can bring both joy and challenges to a family. Leroy and Beatrice were excited about their little girl, but they were also nervous because they did not know how the boys were going to react. They went out of their way to let the boys know that they were still very special, but that they had to be very careful when they held me just as they had with the other babies but girls were, in their opinion, more delicate and needed a softer, more tender touch. Although I had disrupted all of my brothers' plans, my mom was happy beyond words, and my dad was ecstatic and beaming with pride. Initially my dad was afraid to hold me, but when he finally did, he handled me as if I was porcelain and could easily break. I was definitely his pride and joy. Every morning, my dad would get up early, take his bath, and get dressed for work. He would put on a fresh pot of percolated Hills Brothers coffee, fix his breakfast, and then come and get me out of my crib. He cuddled me on his lap and talked to me while he ate his breakfast and drank his coffee. Lots of cream and a little sugar. This was the beginning of our bonding time.

My mom breastfed all of us, and my dad was amazed at how all of his babies' cheeks and thighs would fill out on just the vitamins, the omega-3 fatty acids, and other compounds and nutrients that were in the milk that came from my mother's breast. He was impressed at the capacity that she had to aid in his babies' growth and physical and cognitive development and how we could thrive on simply her milk alone. My dad assisted my mom with all of the babies by changing the diapers, burping them after they finished feeding, bathing them, and singing to them. All of these are very important and helpful means of bonding, but there was something different and special about his bonding time with me. I am certain it was because I was his only baby girl. He watched my mom breastfeed me almost with envy as I was kicking and enjoying what was deliciously familiar to my taste buds. Let's face it, he certainly did not have the equipment that my mom had to handle breastfeeding, but he had formulated a plan in the back of his mind. He could hardly wait until he thought I was old enough to give me what he could—and that was coffee from his cup. He began giving me coffee at the age of one. That was a wonderful and significant plan in his mind that has tremendously affected my life until this very day. Just as a mother and her baby look into each other's eyes and communicate as the baby is feeding from her breast, my dad and I looked into each other's eyes as I was drinking coffee with him from his cup. I wonder what thoughts were in his mind. Probably how important those precious moments that he was spending with me were and probably how our years together could provide a bond that would guide me as I grew into womanhood.

"Kid, I'll be back shortly." This was something that my dad was beginning to say to my mom quite often lately. She was accustomed to him running the craps games and selling moonshine on the weekends, but he was normally at home with her in the evenings during the week. In the evenings, when my dad would leave, she just assumed that he was taking a walk down the road to have a cigarette while visiting his friends. My mom was not aware of the detriment of secondhand smoke, but she preferred that he not smoke in the house because of her religious convictions and also because she could not stand the smell.

One evening, my mom was doing some baking, and she discovered that she had run out of eggs. There was a woman that had befriended her that lived a few houses down the road, and my mom had my eldest brother watch us while she quickly went to borrow the eggs. She knocked on the screen door, but no one answered. She called out her name as she entered the unlocked door. Her friend rushed out of the bedroom adjusting her clothes as she greeted my mom, but she was not as friendly as usual. She was extremely jittery and uncomfortable and tried to avoid eye contact with my mom. There was not a plausible reason to account for her demeanor. Her nervous actions gave my mom reasonable cause to suspect something, but she could not put her finger on it. When her friend went into the kitchen to get the eggs, my mom felt the urge to pull back the curtains to her bedroom, which was near the front entrance. My dad was sitting on the bed with just his undershorts on, and he was sweating bullets. He looked as if he had just seen a ghost. My mom felt sick and breathless. The reality of betrayal and shock was like a double punch to the stomach. She felt terrified and simultaneously furious. The first question that came out of her mouth was "what are you doing here?" My dad had the mitigated gall to get angry with my mom, as if he was the victim, and then he told her—very creatively and convincingly and nicely—that the woman was his distant cousin and that he just needed a break from the noisy house so that he could get some sleep. Of course, he was lying, but he could not admit to her that he was being unfaithful. I always say in jest that a lie is a very present help in the time of trouble. My dad was in deep trouble, up to his neck, and a lie was inevitable. The truth about my dad and his proclivities was so grim and ugly that lying had become a survival mechanism. She told him to get dressed and come home faster than right now and quicker than in a hurry. Needless to say, she left the house without the eggs. There were enough eggs on her face. My mom did not believe his benign explanation, but for the sake of love and the children, she forgave him for his infidelity. What a woman won't do for love.

God helped her through her anger, hurt, humiliation, disappointment, and—yes—even her love-and-hate emotions. My mom began to struggle with low self-esteem from that point on because she thought that she had lost her appeal because of my dad's improprieties; but the truth was she was still a beautiful woman that had maintained her small waistline, her energy, and her desire for love after each baby. As a matter of fact, married life, motherhood, and her love for God seemed to have enhanced her beauty. But a man can have a gorgeous, compatible, and dutiful wife and still have an insatiable need to prow and gallivant. This painful incident heightened my mom's sense of awareness. She had certainly become more knowledgeable and conscious of my dad's extracurricular activities, and it increased her cautiousness of his bizarre and deviant taste. But it did not diminish her ardent love, and with time, her heart healed, and she regained respect for her man. After this discovery, my dad altered his behavior during the week by staying home every night, but he continued his increasingly complicated lifestyle on the weekends.

By now, the church that she had joined had erected a nice little edifice, and she was intricately involved in the ministry. My dad still refused to accompany her, but he did not hinder her from going nor from taking all of us. He did not notice it, but my mom was maturing from the girl at the well and was becoming wiser. She was in essence saying, "Look at me, look at me, I am changing. I'm going to be better than I am." She was changing for the good. Everything must change. Days change, weather changes, time changes, and people change. Bernard Ighner wrote a song that depicts my mom's metamorphosis:

Everything must change, nothing stays the same
Everyone must change, no one stays the same
The young become the old and mysteries do unfold
'Cause that's the way of time, nothing and no one goes unchanged

There are not many things in life that you can be sure of
Except rain comes from the clouds, sun lights up the sky
And humming birds do fly, winter turns to spring
A wounded heart will heal but never much too soon

Everything must change, but it takes time and it is not meant to be easy. Just as it takes time for a butterfly to change, it also took time for my mom to change and also for her wounded heart to heal. Some insects just hatch as smaller versions of their adult size and they just grow, but a butterfly goes through stages. As a matter of fact, they go through four stages. Its origin looks nothing like the finished product. It does not just randomly, accidentally come together; but it gradually, intentionally, and slowly but surely changes. The larva forms a cocoon around itself before maturing into its adult stage. This enables it to survive the winter and then emerge a beautiful butterfly. It goes through a complex ugly metamorphosis, but the end result is breathtaking. It struggles in the cocoon, but if you rush the process, you interfere with the transformation. The struggle in the cocoon empowers the butterfly's wings so that it can function as it was designed to, and that is to *fly*. It seems like my dad just grew from a smaller version to a larger one, but my mom was experiencing a metamorphosis. He later shared with us that the bad habits that had attached themselves to him like Velcro were not totally the fault of his own doing, but that he was a product of his environment. I do understand that one can persevere through the worst conditions and not become a product of their environment, but this was not the case with my dad. He just did not have the willpower, nor did he make the choice to do so. Change is a matter of choice that one must embrace. But that's my dad, and my love for him brightens up his obscure dark side and cancels out his insufficiencies, inadequacies, and idiosyncrasies. However, my mom was a different story. She grew up in a religious environment with *good principles* and a *good foundation*, as much as her parents knew. Clearly, in spite of her environment that was conducive for positive upbringing, it was by no stretch of the imagination impeccable. It still was incumbent upon her to choose to do what was right or wrong. A change was definitely taking place in my mom. She was no longer the kid at the well, and she was surviving the brutal, cold winter that life had afforded her.

My mom had never visited my dad's second weekend job since he had been running the gambling and moonshine business across the levee. Her work was cut out for her with the four boys and a very demanding new little baby girl. My mom breastfed all of us, as I aforementioned, and I was a good eater, so you can just imagine how tied down she was.

My dad was so proud of the dice table and the moonshine stand that he had built. He made them both large enough to accommodate all of his customers. People were coming from all around to party. There was plenty of liquor to drink and good honky-tonk blues that my dad played on his sweet guitar. The dice were rolling, and the women were dancing and ready for whatever the night would bring. One Friday night, my mom got a babysitter and walked across the levee to my dad's gambling den. Because it was set up outside, you could hear the sound of a good time as she approached it, and you could almost smell love in the air. The dice were rolling, and the players were shouting out numbers and nervously digging their fingers into the sides of that wooden table after they tossed their dice. And then they would jump, scream, and yell when the dice landed in their favor. The losers were using language that made my mom's virgin ears tingle. There was an attractive, seductive-looking woman that my dad had hired to keep the moonshine flowing. My mom stood far enough away to avoid being observed but close enough to make a proper assessment of my dad's weekend passion. Although the business made the much-needed money, the environment turned sour on my mom's stomach. Her sober convictions and futuristic plans for her family did not coincide with what she saw. As a matter of fact, they were diametrically opposed to her dreams and aspirations. She caught a glimpse of my dad who was a good-looking piece of sexy eye candy. Her love for him was intense. She watched the women swarm all over him. She wanted to sound the alarm: "He's married, he's mine, and he has five children." But she held her composure. He had skillfully taught her everything that she knew about love and she enjoyed every moment of ecstasy, but she knew that the security of her marriage and her children was at stake and that something had to give. She thought about the future of her boys that idolized their father and that wanted to do everything that they saw him do; and now she had me, a little baby girl that was becoming so attached to my dad that, at the sound of his voice, I stopped nursing. My mom turned on her heels and walked hurriedly across the levee back home with a lonely and sad, but nevertheless determined, heart.

Sunday morning, she got all of us ready for church; and by then, there was a deacon and his wife that my mom had met at the church who had befriended her and agreed to give us a ride every Sunday in their old jalopy. The ride was rough and bumpy, but at least it beat walking. Church was a relief for my mom. It was a sacred place she had found that brought her solace. She enjoyed the melodious singing and the hand clapping.

You could not help tapping your foot to the sound of the upbeat music as everyone anticipated what was to come. The pastor, Bishop Minor Jones, stepped up to the podium; and he was on fire that morning. He told the eager congregation to get their Bibles and turn to Matthew the eleventh chapter and the twelfth verse. They all read it together in concert: "And from the days of John the Baptist until now the Kingdom of heaven suffers violence and the violent take it by force."

"My subject this morning, sisters and brothers, is going to be *take it back*." He said it with fervor in his voice. "Children of God, life is not going to hand you anything of substance on a silver platter. You cannot just sit back and be passive about what you want, but you've got to be aggressive. God has given you a promise and sometimes, either knowingly or unknowingly, you let the devil slip in the back door and snatch your promise right from up under you."

My mom moved to the edge of her seat and shouted amen to what she was hearing.

"Don't let the devil take your peace of mind, take your job, your children, your money, your wife or husband, or your destiny." That was some good preaching, and my mom knew that Bishop Davis was talking directly to her as if he had had a premonition of what she was going through with my dad. Tears began to flow down her face as she stood up clapping her hands and saying, "Praise the Lord."

"You've got to get violent with the devil and take it back by force. Take back your peace of mind, take back your job, take back your children, take back your money, and take back your marriage. You've got to go into the enemy's camp and take back what he has stolen from you. God wants you to have pie in the sky, but he also wants you to have a slice or two down here. You cannot be a half-stepping faker or a lily-livered jelly-backed coward with a punk disposition, but you've got to be real and aggressive and *take it back*."

He preached an emotion-packed sermon, and it went from the crown of my mom's sincere head to the tip of her believing toes. She knew that she had to do something, but she did not know exactly what. She rode back from church very quiet. All of my brothers were noisy; and of course,

I was a quiet, a perfect impeccable little angel. But my mom somehow managed to muffle out the noise with meditation and contemplation.

One Friday evening after my dad got off from work, he ate his delicious dinner that my mom always had prepared for him, and he took his bath and got dressed. He did not put on his usual casual attire, but that night, he wore dress slacks and a nice white shirt that my mom had bought and put away for him to hopefully wear one Sunday to church with her. She watched him get dressed and splash his aftershave cologne on his neatly shaven face. He smelled so good and looked so tall and handsome. "Kid, I am going to a new juke joint that has just opened across the levee down a ways from my place. The owner asked me to come and play a little blues for his opening tonight and tomorrow night. I will be back tonight before too late." This was very unusual for him, to close down his gambling and moonshine sales for the weekend, but she was happy that he would be home those two nights with her and his family rather than be gone for the entire weekend. His buddy, Simon, picked him up in his truck because he had to bring the heavy amplifier for his guitar.

After he left, my mom reflected on the message that she had heard her pastor preach one Sunday about *taking it back*. She specifically remembered that part about going into the enemy's camp and taking back what rightfully belonged to you. My mom got an old lady named Ms. Mae to come over and watch us so that she could go to the new juke joint. My mom put on one of her nice cotton church dresses and her special-occasion heels. She looked beautiful with her hair in curls and her face powdered. It did not take much for her to pass the test because she physically had everything that it took to make an A plus. She started walking across the levee. She was frightened to death because she had never really gone inside of a juke joint, and she did not know how my dad was going to react when he saw her. She could hear my dad playing the blues in the distance as she approached the joint.

The juke joint was dimly lit and jammed packed, and the place was reeking with the smell of liquor and the scent from hot, sweaty bodies. The smoke from cigarettes was burning her eyes as she made her way to a seat at the bar. Every eye seemed to have been on her because she stood out like a sore thumb. She was just as beautiful as the other women, and even lovelier than some, but she stood out for a different reason. She had a look of class, modesty, and dignity. Going to a place like that was an out-of-character thing for my mom to do; but sometimes when you are hopelessly devoted and in love and don't know what to do, you follow your mind in hopes that whatever you do will somehow work out in your favor. My mom ordered a Pepsi with ice, and she stirred it around with the straw and watched it fizzle as she was listening to my dad play the blues. The place was so crowded that he had not even noticed her sitting there. After she was there for a while, a woman came over and sat next to her at the bar. She had seen the woman several times around Clear Lake County but did not really know her. My mom smiled at her, but the woman did not return her smile. Instead she lit a cigarette and took a long draw off it, and then she pressed the cigarette into my mom's arm until the fire went out. My mom was so shocked that she hardly felt the pain. The woman clearly had been drinking, but she seemed to have known exactly who she wanted to burn—and that was my mom. The woman got up and walked away, and my mom sat there for a moment stunned. Then she felt an emotion that she had not felt in her life. She became so angry that she saw red. Her adrenaline, heart, blood pressure, blood flow, and nerves had all shifted into high gear, generating energy that was needed for action. My mom has always been a quiet, loving, and kind person; but people with that kind of temperament sometimes have an edge that you don't want to see. My mom ran out of the juke joint, which was a good thing, but she plotted revenge all of the way home.

My dad did not see my mom that night in the joint, and she was glad because she knew that she was going to go back the next night, and that she was going to be a force to be reckoned with. That Saturday night, my mom waited until my dad left, and she got a sitter and returned to the juke joint. But this time she had an ice pick in her purse. She literally prayed that that woman would be there. Her plan was to pierce that woman's heart with that ice pick and spend the rest of her life in prison because it definitely would have been premeditated murder. She was distraught about the way that my dad was abusing her with his blatant infidelity, and she was still hurt over the loss of her baby, and then to have a woman for no reason at all press a lit cigarette into her arm and use it as an ashtray had ultimately pushed her over the edge. She felt emotionally ambushed. The first thought that entered her mind was that the woman was one of my dad's lovers.

When my mom arrived at the joint, she walked straight to the bar and sat down and firmly placed her purse on the counter. She was waiting and aggressively looking for the woman. Eventually, that same woman came over and sat next to my mom, but this time she had a gentle demeanor. She smiled at my mom and placed her hand over hers and genuinely apologized for what she had done the night before. It was like a Dr. Jekyll and Mr. Hyde comparison. My mom was ready to end her life, but the kind and loving side of her surfaced, and she reciprocated the woman's smile and told her that it was all right. God was working in her favor because one plunge of that ice pick would have aborted her destiny. My mom eased out of that juke joint without my dad seeing her.

I can honestly say that I have never seen my mom get angry in my life. Hurt, disappointed, and displeased, yes. But never angry. My dad and other people have hurt my mom a multiplicity of times, but she always managed to separate the negative actions from the person that did it. Her motto was always "Do not attack the person, but attack the reason." Many times, when people are offended by someone, they retaliate by attacking the person. The attack should be directed at the cause. That is why I am convinced beyond a shadow of a doubt that my mom had lost it when she was about to resort to something as drastic as using the ice pick. This is a true story that my mom has told over and over.

That very night, that woman was brutally stabbed to death by one of her insanely jealous lovers. My dad shared the horrific news with my mom when he came home late that night. He described her explicitly. It was the same woman that had burned her. My mom was both sad and relieved. Sad because the woman had lost her life and relieved that she had not been the one that had taken it. My mom told my dad that she had gone to the juke joint and what the woman had done to her and that she had apologized to her. She told him about the ice pick and what her intentions were. My dad had a frightened look on his face. It was almost that same look that he had when my mom caught him sitting half naked on the bed of another woman. He was shocked, first of all, that my mom would even step a foot in a juke joint, and secondly, he was acutely stunned by the fact that she had the potential to annihilate someone. This young, gentle, naïve kid that he had met at the well had another side to her that he thought he had better sit up and take note of.

My mom was a determined, persistent person, but in a subtle way. She wanted her husband by her side completely, and she wanted him to embrace the loving God that she had come to love. She knew her husband quite well, and he had a poor tolerance for nagging, so she refrained from constantly annoying and criticizing him about his nonchalant attitude toward her spirituality. My dad thought that churchgoers, especially those from the Pentecostal Church of God in Christ, had a ridiculous antiquated perception about God because of some of their doctrinal quirks. He insinuated in essence that she was trying to facilitate neuroplasticity (change his way of thinking and reasoning) on him, and that her pastor was the manipulating force behind it. He perceived her church as having too many don'ts and not enough dos. The don'ts mainly being don't smoke, don't drink alcohol, don't gamble, and don't commit adultery. And he very often facetiously said that the dos were do go to church every night of the week and do bring your money with you when you go. He was cautious not to be specific about the don'ts because he did not want to remind my mom about his erratic after-five lifestyle that he had no intentions of quitting. But my mom was cognizant of the dangers of the don'ts and quite concerned about the negative effects that it could have on her and her children. She knew that her boys looked up to their dad as a role model, and that they would no doubt want to walk in their dad's shoes someday. And now she had a little girl to think about because girls have a tendency to compare other men with their dad.

I personally feel that her concerns were not only spiritually legitimate, but they were also physically and socially legitimate. Physically, her concerns were legitimate because the chemicals in cigarettes can have dangerous short-term effects to the body—which are the constricting of the airways to the lungs, increasing the smoker's heart rate, elevating the blood pressure, and depriving the tissues in your body of much-needed oxygen. These are only the immediate results. The long-term effects are lung cancer, emphysema, and increasing the risk of stroke. In addition to this, smoking is a very expensive habit. Socially, the smell is offensive and gives you halitosis and can affect others by the secondhand smoke.

Her concerns about drinking alcohol were legitimate because drinking alcohol can be one of the worst and most detrimental things that a person can do to their health. Hold on a minute because I hear you saying alcohol, namely wine, is good for your health if you drink it in moderation. That's the problem with alcohol; it's hard to drink it in moderation because it is addicting. And when done in excess, it can cause heart disease, cirrhosis and scarring of the liver, and a multiplicity of other physical ailments.

Alcohol can also cause problems in society such as drinking and driving. Rarely does a person just have one drink. I hear you thinking again . . . I'll get a designated driver. That's a splendid idea, but not a practical one. Usually when people drive themselves to a location, for the most part, they plan on driving themselves home as well. Alcohol has the tendency to numb your sense of reasoning, and you are not aware of exactly how inebriated you are. Alcohol is also a leading contributor to antisocial behavior such as domestic violence, crime, hit-and-run accidents, sexual abuse, and promiscuity. As for gambling, it can pose a significant risk to families and marriage because it preys on the weak and vulnerable and it spreads false hope. It can also cause one to waste and lose money that is desperately needed to sustain the household.

And the last don't that my dad did not want to refrain from was adultery. This don't was not put in place by the sacred book, the church, and society to keep us from having fun but rather to protect us from harm. First, let me establish that sex was God's idea and, might I add, a good one. If he created anything any better, I promise you he kept it for himself. We ought to give him a standing ovation for this stratospheric experience and loving expression. However, God knew that since sex is so powerful that there must be some restraints on how it is to be used, so he specifically relegated sex to the arena and within the confines of marriage. I guess you may be thinking why God would put something so amazingly wonderful on earth and then place restraints on it. Well, for the same reason that he gave man the wisdom to manufacture some cars that can reach the limit of 120 miles per hour and then allow the powers that be to institute the law that will prosecute you if you are caught driving 120. It's for your safety and also the safety of others. I hear you thinking again . . . Why would the manufacturer place 120 on the speedometer and the law forbid you to drive it? I can't answer that. Inquiring minds would like to know! But I do know that the car is for your convenience and also your enjoyment—but with stipulations. So is sex—my, my, my, my, my—but with stipulations. In my opinion, sex is always meant to be in the context of marriage. It should be a private expression and celebration of love and commitment between husband and wife who accept the responsibility that their actions require. Any sex that deviates from that, no matter how satisfying, is wrong in my opinion and according to the Bible.

An alarming amount of people consider adultery to be exhilarating, exciting, passionate, and romantic. Some have said that stolen wine tastes sweeter. They may have a point, but those are short-term emotional results. But the long-term results are damaging, destructive, cruel, painful, time wasting, demeaning, deceptive, and destroy trust. Not to mention AIDS and other transmitted diseases and unwanted pregnancies. So I beg of you, don't believe the hype. I am convinced that the doctrines in my mom's denomination (COGIC) may have been stringent, but they made a lot of common sense.

All of these negative habits that my dad had were wreaking havoc and disrupting the life of his family, and my mom knew that their marriage would not last should he continue in them. My mom knew that she had to be proactive rather than reactive. When you are reactive, you tend to blame other people and circumstances for your obstacles or problems, but when you are proactive, you take responsibility for every aspect of your life. Initiation and positive actions will follow this mind-set. My mom had to be wise to know that in order to effectuate change in my dad she had to emphatically understand him and why he was doing what he was doing, or her efforts would be nonproductive and the end result would be frustration and rejection. First of all, she had to begin her strategy with the end results in mind. She visualized her husband honoring *all* of their weddings vows, which were more important to her than the cake that they fed each other and the pictures that they had taken after the wedding. She was cognizant that her wedding was only an event, but her marriage was an accomplishment. The promises that they had made before the Justice of the Peace and the witness set the parameters for a happy marriage and my dad had dishonored them. She visualized herself coming up with the most effective strategy to bring this into fruition.

Secondly, she understood clearly that my dad's lifestyle were habits that were deeply embedded in the core of his being. His habits were an acquired pattern of behavior that occurred automatically and repeatedly and had become typical or normal to him. My dad's proclivities had become a customary common practice, just as daily bathing or looking both ways before you cross the street. Habits such as his are not usually easily broken, and incessant patience mixed with love would be a prerequisite to facilitate a change. Also, she knew that he had to have an adequate replacement once he kicked his habits.

Thirdly, she knew that there had to be a degree of synergy between them without condoning or participating in what he was doing. This meant that she had to embrace and encourage him for the positive things that he was doing to provide for his family, and then she had to continue working collaboratively with him as a wife and mother without nagging. It's called team work to make the dream work. Then last, but certainly not least, she had to continue engaging in her recreational activities that had given her personal satisfaction, and that was being faithful to that little happy church and loving her God with everything in her being. My mom could not get the message that her pastor preached about *take it back* out of her mind. He told the congregation that they could not sit passively by and let the devil take what rightfully belonged to them. What he was saying, in essence, was faith without works is dead. My mom earnestly prayed as to what she needed to do that would be most effective and bring positive results without upsetting the apple cart, if you will, and the Lord gave her exactly what she should do in order to make this happen.

After a few months of contemplation and careful planning, my mom came up with an idea that only a woman with courage, grit, and determination could successfully carry out. Early on, I mentioned that my dad had been a habitual gambler, but that he had hit the wall (quit cold turkey) because he had a fear of losing his money. But losing is one of the consequences of gambling that you have to expect. My dad had decided that rather than shoot craps and chance losing his money that he would set up his own business and do what you call run the table. By doing this, he was certain never to lose money but rather make it. My dad built an eight-foot gambling table to accommodate his customers and also a stand where they could buy the moonshine that he made every weekend. One Friday morning after my dad had gone to work, my mom got an axe and wrapped it in newspaper and walked across the levee and literally tore down the gambling table piece by piece and also the stand for the moonshine. She swung that axe until the table and stand were destroyed beyond recognition. After completing this arduous task, she walked back home with a feeling of mission accomplished. Her pastor had preached the sermon *take it back*, and this was her way of doing exactly that.

Please understand that this was a difficult and physically exhausting task for a petite woman to undertake, but my mom was always a strong brave woman of action. She was a little piece of leather but put together well in more ways than one. She always was of the persuasion that action produces results. The action that she had taken might have been a bit drastic and risky, but a woman has to do what a woman has to do to rescue her family. Being brave does not mean that she wasn't afraid, but being brave meant that her fear did not hinder her from doing what she needed to do.

When my dad came home from work, he ate his dinner and quickly changed his clothes. My mom observed him out of the corner of her eyes, and she could see the anticipation and the excitement of an action-filled weekend on his face. "Kid, here is the money to pay the bills and buy groceries." He kissed my mom on the lips and told her that he loved her and that he would see her later. On weekends, his later always meant sometime that Sunday evening. She smiled at him and told him that she wished that he would stay home with her and the children but, nevertheless, have a good time. Within an hour or so, my dad returned home in a rage. He told my mom that someone that was jealous of his thriving business had torn down his craps table and moonshine stand. "I think it was the man that just opened up the new juke joint a little ways from my place," he said in disgust. "And I was nice enough to close down my business and play for his opening those two nights." My mom felt sorry for my dad because of all of the hard work that he had put into building the craps table and moonshine stand, and in addition to that, he was accusing the wrong person as the culprit for the damage. She managed to conceal her guilt, and she remained focused on her pastor's message, *take it back.*

To say that she felt joyfully fulfilled that he was home with her for the weekend would be an understatement. He got up that morning and put on a pot of coffee and fixed breakfast for the boys. This was also a perfect time for him to cuddle me on his lap and secretly give me little sips of coffee out of his cup. The next week, my dad purchased some more lumber; and he and his friend, Simon, worked hard every evening after work, building another craps table and moonshine stand. By Thursday, they had it all ready for business on Friday night. That next morning, after my dad left for work, my mom got that same axe and wrapped it in newspaper and walked across the levee and tore down the gambling table and stand piece by piece again. While she was swinging the axe, she was soliloquizing to herself, saying, "Leroy, you are going to be the good husband and father a real man is suppose to be. And until then, I'm going to tear it down as fast as you build it."

Walking back home across the levee, she felt as if her senses had taken a leave of absence. The questions that were lurking in the back of her mind were would my dad ever discover that she was the one that was tearing his gambling den down, and what would be the consequences for doing it? When my dad came home from work, he was relieved because he had checked on the craps table and stand before going to work that morning, and everything was just the way that he had left it the day before. My dad was a bit anxious to leave, so he just changed clothes and gave my mom money for the bills and food and a quick kiss and left. She followed him to the door and told him that she loved him and to have a good time. She was nervously and anxiously watching the clock because she knew approximately how long it should take him to go across the levee. Within an hour or so, she saw my dad coming down the road with both hands in his pockets and his head down. *Oh god, have mercy*, she said within herself. *This man is going to kill me if he ever finds out that I am the one that is destroying his craps table.* All of the children were asleep except me when my dad stormed into the house. He was using some of the foulest and shocking words imaginable, and that was something that my mom had never heard him do. In spite of his bad habits, he always was a gentleman and respected my mom and his children.

"Kid, I'm sorry for cussing, but somebody did it again. If I ever get my hands on the d---person that is doing this, they are going to be sorry"

"Did what?" my mom asked innocently convincingly.

"Somebody tore down my d---- gambling table and moonshine stand. I'm sorry, Kid, but when you are as angry as I am, cussing seems to help relieve the frustration. I've got an enemy somewhere, and I don't know who in the h--- it is. I have an idea, but when you are not certain, you're just shooting in the dark. I just can't seem to be able to wrap my head around why someone would continuously do this to me."

My mom allowed him to rant and rave and use profanity, but she reminded him that all of the children were asleep except me, and that he should keep his voice down while doing it. My mom had such wisdom. She allowed her husband to blow off steam for something that she was responsible for. Blowing off steam and relieving the pressure no doubt prevented an explosion. My dad picked me up, and just the big smile that I gave him seemed to have been the antidote that he needed to calm him down. Babies are so innocent and carefree. Although they are intelligent beings and can sense the slightest inkling that something is going on that is not pleasant or desirable, it is short-lived and easily forgotten the moment that they feel secure by your warm cuddle. I gave my dad the biggest toothless smile ever. He began to play with me and I was a cooing and gurgling machine. My daddy!

My dad had no other alternative but to build another craps table. The job at the Saw Mill was not sufficient enough to take care of five young children, a wife, and all of the other responsibilities that went along with that. After he and his friend, Simon, completed the table, he told one of the neighbors across the levee what had been occurring; and he asked him to look out for any suspicious person that might vandalize his business. My mom got her axe and wrapped it in newspaper and walked across the levee. She saw two men standing around, laughing and talking, and she waited out of sight for a while for them to leave. But they didn't appear to have any place to go anytime soon, so my mom went back home disappointed.

The next few weeks were a happy time for my dad. Every attempt that my mom had made to tear up his craps table was unsuccessful because of my dad's lookout man. Several weeks passed, and my dad must have felt confident that whoever was destroying his property probably had had a change of mind because, when my mom went across the levee that day, there was no one in sight. She quickly started swinging her axe and tore down the table and stand to pieces. As she turned to leave, a man came from out of nowhere; and when he looked in my mom's face, he recognized her.

"Aren't you Leroy's wife?"

"Yes, I am, but please don't tell my husband what I have done."

"So you're the one that has been tearing down his craps table all of this time?"

"Yes, I am the one, but please, I beg you, please don't tell my husband." She went on to explain to him the reason why she was continuously tearing it down. She promised him that if he didn't tell her husband, she would tell him when he got home from work.

"I am not going to get into married people's business. I got six months to mind my own business and six months to leave other folks' business alone. I am going to leave that up to you," he said rather convincingly.

She was both relieved and afraid because she did not know whether to trust a stranger's word or not. When my dad got home from work, she attempted to tell him several times, but she could not bring herself to do it.

"Kid, here is the money for the bills and groceries." He kissed my mom as he usually did and told her that he loved her and that he would see her later. She watched him as he walked down the road. She loved that man, and she wanted to call out to him to come back so that she could tell him what she had done, but fear gripped her and she didn't. Hours had passed, but my dad had not come back home.

Where in the world could he be? I know that he must have gone ballistic when he saw that his craps table was demolished again. Oh god, please don't let him have done anything to that innocent man that owns the juke joint down from his place.

My mom tossed and turned in bed until almost one in the morning. She was awakened by the sound of a truck. She got up and ran to the door to look out, and she saw my dad's friend, Simon, helping him out of the truck and up the walkway. He was so drunk that he could hardly stand up by himself. This was the first time that my mom had ever seen my dad in this condition.

"This must be affecting him much worse than I thought," my mom said out loud. "I can't keep doing this to my husband. I've got to tell him that it is me and that I'm only doing it because I love him so deeply."

She opened the door and helped him into the house and thanked Simon for bringing him home safely. He was as gentle as a lamb. He just kept saying over and over that they did it again . . . They did it again. My mom undressed him and got him into bed. Maybe it was a blessing in disguise that he was drunk because that gave her time to strategize about how she was going to tell him that she was the guilty one when he awakened from his drunken stupor. My mom quietly slid into bed and eventually drifted off to sleep. She was awakened by the smell of bacon and eggs and coffee. She got up and went into the kitchen, and my dad had gotten up already and was holding me on his lap while eating breakfast and sipping on his coffee. The boys had already eaten their breakfast and were terrorizing each other around the house.

"Good morning, honey," my mom said while yawning, wanting to avoid the inevitable.

"What is so good about it?" my dad disgustingly responded. "Somebody tore up my craps table again, and I am sick and tired of rebuilding and rebuilding. Kid, I just don't know what to do. It's bad enough that somebody is destroying my property, but to make bad matters worse and add insult to injury, I don't know who's doing it."

"Honey, when the boys go out to play and Jennifer takes a nap, I would like to talk with you." My mom quickly had a second thought that it probably would be better and safer to tell him while the children were around so that my dad would be forced to control his anger. She also knew that he wouldn't possibly lose control of his emotions while he was holding me on his lap. "Honey, I . . . ah . . . I . . . well . . . ah—what

I am trying to tell you is that I have been the one that has been tearing your craps table and your moonshine stand to pieces."

My dad was jumping me up and down on his lap and heard what my mom said, but then again, maybe he hadn't because he did not respond. There is a saying that goes I can't believe my ears, and this was a perfect example of that. He just continued bouncing me up and down on his lap.

"Honey, did you hear what I said? I am the one that has been tearing down your craps tables." The room struck silent and cold, and my dad just stared at my mom. If looks could kill, my mom's life would have ended then. "Honey, please don't be angry with me. I wanted to tell you long before now, but I just couldn't find the words or courage to do it," she said, waiting for his response. But he just continued to stare.

When my dad finally spoke, he said, "Kid, I am angry, shocked, hurt, and confused. I have never hit a woman before in my life, and you better be glad that I'm holding this baby because you would be the first. Is this your way of getting back at me for the things that you think that I have been doing?" my dad said, sounding angry and serious.

"No, honey, not at all. Yes, you have hurt me, but that is not the reason that I did it. I did it because God told me to do it."

"God told you," he echoed back. "Now I'm really angry. You are taking this God thing a little too far," my dad disgustingly responded. "Are you fixing your mouth to tell me that God told you to tear down something that I built that was helping pay bills, keep a roof over your head, and put food on the table for you and these five kids? Are you sure that you were not being vindictive and just retaliating by giving me what you thought that I deserved?"

My mom could see the sincerity and the bewilderment in his eyes. "Honey, I know that you have always been a good provider for me and the children, but God does not want you to provide for us by gambling, selling moonshine, and playing at the juke joint. Yes, it makes good money, but gambling and selling moonshine is illegal, and it keeps you away from your family every weekend. And I don't really like you playing at the juke joints because . . . well . . . Because it's just not a good environment. Those places are just rowdy, and all of the swearing and drinking, and remember the lady that burned me with her cigarette?" My mom pointed to the scar that was on her arm. "Honey, it is so dangerous. Remember, that lady was murdered the very next night just a little ways from that place. And the women that hang out there . . . Well, they are so loose and provocative, and it just seems like they don't care whether you are married or not. Fornication seems to be very popular, and sexual promiscuity seems to be acceptable in that crowd. Those women obviously just want to satisfy themselves at the expense of others and they don't even blush when they do it. Honey, that's like playing in the traffic. Eventually somebody is going to get hurt or killed."

My dad just sat quietly and listened. That was a lot for him to ingest and rationalize because he was accustomed to doing all of those things since he was old enough to remember. Most of the time, you are a product of your environment, and those were habits that had attached themselves to him, which he had picked up from his dad who picked them up from his dad's dad and so on. My dad continued to listen as he was wearing a distant half-hearted look of conviction on his face.

"Honey, it is time that you make a change. You are the head of this house, and change has to begin with the head. This home can only be as good as the head of it. Just as your head is the command center for your body, you are the command center for this house. You are a good man, and you have some exceptional, phenomenal qualities, but your lifestyle has been weighed in the balance and found lacking. Leroy, a doctor can successfully prescribe medication for the body, but if the head does not choose to follow the proper recommendations for good health, the doctor's request to prescribe medication is a waste. It's a matter of choice. It's not going to be easy because change forces you out of your comfort zone into unfamiliar territory, and that can be frightening and overwhelming. No one likes a change but a baby in a soiled diaper, and most of the time, they even cry the entire time that they are being changed. They are shortsighted and do not consider the wonderful end results. Change is difficult, but change is a choice. I wish that I could tell you that it's going to be a cakewalk or a zip-a-de-do-da, but it's not." My mom had made it crystal clear to my dad—in a wise, feminine, discreet, but candid way—that a change was imperative.

"Kid, I'm scared," my dad said helplessly in a tone that reminded her of a little frightened boy. "I don't know what to do."

"Well, that's one of the reasons that you met this kid at the well that hot summer day," my mom said as she seductively gave him a love bite on his neck. "I'm here to help you and not judge you, and not only am I here, but God is here for you as well. He just needs your permission and your cooperation."

Readers, may I pause for this sidebar? One of the reasons that people go in and out of the Betty Ford Clinic is because they leave out the one most important element—and that is God. Now may I resume? It was not difficult for my dad to be receptive to my mom because she had always dealt with my dad's proclivities in a loving way. She never raised her voice, gave him an ultimatum, did any finger-pointing, or threatened to kill him although she told me a few times she contemplated it. After all, she was a pro at swinging the axe, and I am sure that she could also have used the ice pick. But love would not let her do it, and most importantly, mercy said *no!* In spite of all of the curve balls that her life with him had thrown at her, she never stopped loving on him, and *never* did she *ever* degrade his position as a father to his children and the set man of the house. I would hope that I would be able to mimic her docile and patient demeanor under those adverse circumstances. Discovering that her husband had desecrated his marriage vows by having an affair, or perhaps affairs, must have been emotionally devastating. She felt betrayed, abused, and violated. It is no doubt very natural for my mom to have had the desire to be confrontational with the woman that she caught him red-handed with, but what would that really have accomplished? Killing her probably would have been an option, but my dad was the one that should have been held responsible and liable. The other woman could not have entered their marriage if he had not opened the door and allowed it to happen. However, while taking extreme measures would have brought some sense of relief to my mom, it would not have fixed the problem. An irrational move is not always wise and could cause other heartaches and disruptions. I celebrate her!

I had fallen sound asleep in my daddy's arms, and the boys were making incredible noise while playing, but there was a tranquility that had covered that house like a delicate, soft warm blanket.

My mom and my dad were both quiet for a long time, and then she stood up and made an announcement. "I am ready for the curtains to rise on the set of our new beginning . . . Places, everyone . . . Lights, cameras, action."

The next morning was Sunday, and the sun was seemingly shining brighter than ever. My mom got up to get all of us bathed and dressed for church. My dad had already fixed breakfast and his delicious pot of coffee and fed the boys. Then my mom heard my dad ask her something that made her freeze in her tracks.

"Kid, do you think that you could put me something out that I could wear to church?"

She was speechless! "Honey, are you . . . I mean, did I hear you say . . . What I mean is are you really going to church with us today?"

"Kid, I think I am, but I am so scared. Honestly, I am so scared that I don't know what to do."

"No, honey, you are so scared that you *know* what to do, and that is to go to church today with your family."

My mom hurried and found him something to wear before he changed his mind. When the deacon and his wife from the church arrived to pick us up, they were pleasantly surprised to see their new passenger. We all packed in that old car, and my mom's countenance beamed all of the way to church. You could tell when we were getting close because you could hear the familiar sounds of singing, tambourines, drums, and shouting. That was welcoming noise to my mom's ears, but my dad was scared to death. My dad had never stepped a foot inside a church in his life. This was indeed an experience for him, and my mom constantly looked at him, giving him that heart-melting smile that made him feel at ease. My mom was hoping that that old gray-haired woman would sing one of her impromptu songs and . . . She did. My dad was startled and amazed as she stood up and stretched her hands toward heaven and bellowed out one of her favorite songs:

> Amazing grace how sweet the sound
> That saved a wretch like me
> I once was lost, but now I'm found
> Was blind but now I see

That was just the song that was tailor-made for my dad, and my mom was sitting there, hoping that he was listening to every significant word. The deacons passed the offering plate; and then the pastor, Bishop Minor Jones, stepped up to the pulpit. He was on fire as usual and seemingly even more so when he looked out in the audience and saw who he assumed was my dad. He told the congregation to open their Bibles and turn to a familiar scripture: 2 Corinthians the fifth chapter and the seventeenth verse. They read it in concert: "Therefore, if any man be in

Christ, he is a new creature: old things are past away; behold, all things are become new."

He told them to look at their neighbor and say, "Brand new, Hallelu." My mom looked at my dad, and his eyes met hers. She read his lips as he softly and slowly repeated the pastor's subject: "Brand new, Hallelu!" The pastor's voice echoed out, "If any man be in Christ, he is a new creature. Colored man, white man, rich man, poor, man, tall man, short man, fat man, skinny man. Any man. If any man be in Christ, he is a new creature. Not around Christ or near Christ but in Christ. It does not matter to God what you have done or how long you have been doing it." The congregation was in agreement with their "Amen's" and their "Thank you, Jesus's."

"Though your sins be as scarlet, he will wash them whiter than snow!" the pastor shouted as he was climaxing and bringing his sermon to an end.

My dad was thinking to himself, *Wow, the man upstairs must have some awfully strong detergent to wash all the sins that I have done whiter than snow.* While the preacher was preaching, my dad's mind reminisced about all of the moonshine that he had drunk and all of the times that he had gambled and sometimes cheated people out of their money. He had also been with more women than you could shake a stick at—single, married, old, and young, just as long as they were pretty things. Promising them everything until they gave him everything; and when they mentioned future plans, he would remind them that he thought it was understood that they were just having fun—and perhaps even a one-night stand—because, after all, he was a married man. Many times, even before he was married, he told women that he was married just so after he had his fun with them he could move on to the next one.

His charisma, good looks, and sense of humor made it easier for them to believe his lies and his deception. It took my dad a while to grasp the concept that being in Christ makes you a new creature. *How could that be?* he thought to himself. *That's just like you telling me that if I am in a garage, I am a car.* His attention was going in and out as the sermon was being preached. He focused back just in time to hear Bishop Jones say, "I know that some of you may be sitting there thinking about all of the wrong that you have done, but once you accept Christ as your personal Savior, he forgives your sin, and he will cast them into the sea of forgetfulness, never to be remembered anymore. God has selective amnesia. Now if a God that is all-knowing can forget, then why can't you? But my brothers and my sisters, I want you to know that there are some self-righteous Jesus-junior deep-sea-diving churchgoers that will put on their sanctimonious diving gear and attempt to go and fish up your sin. But glory be to God, when they get there, there will be a big sign that says No Fishing Allowed and Violators Will Be Prosecuted to the Fullest Extent."

My dad laughed out loud and then quickly put his hand over his mouth. The pastor concluded his sermon by saying, "My brothers and sisters, God is standing at the door of your heart knocking, but there is only one knob, and it's on the inside. You have to open the door and let him in. He's knocking . . . Will you open the door?"

I was getting a little fretful, probably ready for another bottle, and my mom was busy trying to quiet me down when she noticed that my dad was moving to the edge of his seat. The pastor gave the invitation again. "Will you come?" My dad slowly stood to his feet and moved out into the aisle, and the church exploded with praise. My mom was so emotional that she never remembered who took me out of her lap. She walked down to the altar with my dad, shedding tears of joy.

That day, my dad received Christ as his personal savior. He never received so many hugs (at least not of that kind anyway) and handshakes in his life. They fellowshipped him into the Church of God in Christ that day. The ride home was jubilant, and a "this is just too good to be true" atmosphere invaded that old car. My mom always cooked a delicious dinner on Sundays before she went to church. Southern fried chicken, rice and gravy, collard greens and okra with hot water cornbread, and a three-layered coconut cake were the usual. Unfortunately, my dad was never there to enjoy it because he was wherever his lust dictated him to be, but this Sunday, we all sat down together to eat. My mom and my brothers all bowed their heads almost simultaneously to say grace, but my dad quickly took a big bite of his Southern fried chicken, only to discover that he was the only one eating.

"Daddy," one of my brothers said rather emphatically, "you've got to bow your head and fold your hands like this, and you must close your eyes and say grace before you eat."

"Okay, son, okay." My dad carefully watched my brother, and he acquiesced by folding his hands, closing his eyes, and bowing his head. A little child shall lead them.

That night, my mom felt a bit awkward and fear gripped her heart. She wondered if my dad's spiritual encounter and commitment was going to be a lasting one. The wonderful change that he had made was phenomenal and amazing, but it was just too soon to tell whether he would be strong enough to withstand all of temptations that were deeply ingrained in his soul. When all of the children were tucked in, my mom slipped into bed beside my dad, and her heart literally began to race.

"Kid, you are trembling," my dad said as he took her into his arms.

"Honey, I'm just so happy," my mom said. "This is like a dream, and I am afraid that I am going to wake up."

"Kid, all I know is that what I felt today in church was real, and all I can do is to take it one day at a time. I'm probably just as afraid as you are, but we are in this together, and I believe that I can make it with you by my side . . . And of course, the man upstairs. Yes we can!" His words echoed in her head over and over as he held her. Her doubts slowly began to fade away as he kissed her. It was a tender time that was filled with pure delight and intense ecstasy. "Your love is better than the best wine, and my desire is toward you only," he whispered in her ear.

Let day never break.

My dad fell asleep with satisfaction while holding my mom tenderly in his arms. She watched him breathe as she basked in the afterglow of the love that they had just shared. But as she lay there, she began to recall some dreadful memories of some of the things that my dad had done to her. She tried to stop the flashbacks that continued to show up on the screen of her emotions. She saw instant replays of him sitting on the side of that woman's bed half naked, and she quickly shut her eyes tight, but the memories kept getting in the way. She began to mentally capture a picture of that beautiful woman at the juke joint who had on that skin-tight dress that showed every curve on her vivacious body and those ruby-red parted lips that kissed him unabashedly. Those were only two women that she was aware of.

Only God knows who else was out there that was competing for his attention. Many thoughts bombarded her mind as she reflected on my dad's lifestyle, and she became the frightened *little girl at the well*! She knew that the rhapsody that they had experienced that night was real, but as she watched him sleep, her emotions vacillated from certainty to uncertainty. And while looking at him through the eyes of tears and the mystery and the unpredictable feeling of tomorrow and the ambiguousness of the days to come, she thought to herself,

> Tonight you're mine completely
> You gave your love so sweetly
> Tonight the light of love was in your eyes
> But will you love me tomorrow?

Is this a lasting treasure

Or just a moment's pleasure

Can I believe the magic in your eyes?

Will you still love me tomorrow?

Tonight with words unspoken

You said that I'm the only one

But will my heart be broken

When the night meets the morning sun?

I'd like to know that your love

Is a love I can be sure of

So tell me now and I won't ask again

Will you still love me tomorrow?

I'd like to know

Will you still love me tomorrow?

"Good morning, Kid," my dad said as he was yawning and reflecting on their blissful night of love. "I had a dream about you, and in the dream, you had doubts as to my stability. You were asking me in the dream if I would still love you tomorrow." He gathered my mom in his big strong arms and answered her question. "Yes, I'll love you tomorrow. I will love you as long as there is breath in my body. I am so glad that I met this beautiful *girl at the well*!

The week was amazing and filled with wonderful laughter, love, and tranquility; and it went by so fast. Time has the tendency to take on wings when you are having fun. But when Friday came, fear gripped my mom's heart again because that was going to be the test. My dad had never spent his weekends at home with his family since they had been married, with the exceptions of when she was in labor. When my dad came home from work that Friday evening, he ate his dinner, and he was restless and quiet.

"Kid, I have been worrying about our finances all week. There is no way that we can make it on what the man is paying me at the Saw Mill. Kid, our outgo exceeds our income. The money that I was making running the craps table and selling moonshine sure was helping out a lot."

"Yes, honey, it sure did help out, but I've been thinking too. Today our babysitter, Ms. Mae, stopped by and asked me if we would like to move in with her since she lives all alone and since we also need her to watch the children periodically anyway. She said that her arthritis is getting so bad that she can hardly take care of her cow anymore, and that she would be willing to deduct half of our rent if you and the boys would assume that responsibility. And, honey, she said that if I would help her churn the butter and make the cheese and also bottle up the milk to sell to her customers, she would give us some of that money too."

"Kid, the man upstairs is looking out for me," my dad responded. "Because I thought that I was going to have to build another craps table only for you to destroy again with that infamous axe of yours." They both laughed hysterically. We moved in with Ms. Mae, and we were a happy little family. My dad continued to go to church, and his faith increased exponentially.

My mom had begun to mention to my dad that she wanted to move north to a place called South Bend, Indiana, where her dad and the rest of her siblings had moved. Quite frankly, she had not just casually mentioned it to him, but she had become rather adamant about it. She wanted something better for her children, her husband, and herself. They had grown weary of being treated as second-class subservient citizens. This was in the '50s, and social injustice and legalized discrimination and racism were prevailing at an all-time high. Colored people being lynched, raped, beaten, emasculated, excluded, and exploited was common in that era. My mom and dad both wanted to go to the land of opportunity. She also wanted them both to find jobs and work together to purchase a home of their own. Her dad was also getting older and having some health issues, and she wanted to move close to him to help take care of him and enjoy whatever time he had left.

I was three years old, but I remember the morning that my dad and I shared our last delicious cup of coffee before he left for South Bend, Indiana. My dad had been secretly giving me coffee every morning since I was around one year old. When my mom first discovered it, she was adamantly against it. She thought that it was negatively affecting my intake of nutrition because I definitely had substituted my desire for milk with coffee, but my dad had convinced her that the small amount that I was consuming would not interfere with my nutrition. Neither would it aggravate my system by causing jitters, irritability, or make me black as the old colored folktales warned. But just between you and me, coffee was my dad's favorite beverage, and it had become mine as well. I was addicted. Perhaps it was the caffeine, but I had acquired a compulsive physiological and psychological need for coffee. I had developed a dependency on the substance and the time that it afforded me with my dad. That was the best part of waking up. That's how we spent our precious nurturing and bonding time together every morning, drinking coffee with lots of cream and a little sugar.

The details surrounding my family's sudden move to Indiana were too complicated for me to comprehend, but it significantly impacted my life forever. I certainly do not condone my dad taking the measures that he did to facilitate that move from Clear Lake County, Blytheville, Arkansas, but sometimes a man has to do what a man has to do. I have adopted a saying that goes, "Your friends do not need an explanation, and your enemies do not want one." That's my daddy, and no apologies or further explanation is necessary.

Chapter 4

Somewhere to Lay My Head

After our move, my mom applied for a job at the Kingsbury plant—about thirty miles outside of South Bend—where they produced shells, cartridges, and mortar rounds for World War II and the Korean Conflict. The plant had closed down because World War II had ended, but when the Korean Conflict broke out, they reopened and hired hundreds more employees, and my mom was one of them. Her job description would be to work on the assembly line and fill ammunitions with powder. Although my mom needed the job desperately, she was reluctant to take it because we had no transportation; but when our new neighbor, Mrs. Johnson, came over to welcome us into the neighborhood, my mom found out that she was employed there, and she offered to give her a ride to work every day. That was such a blessing. She accepted the position and began working there immediately.

My dad already had been hired at the South Bend Iron and Metal Company. His boss was kind enough to hold his job for him until he was released from jail. This company was founded in 1942, way before I was born, and still ranks among the largest and most successful scrap metal companies in America. His responsibility was to recycle enormous amounts of scrap metals and other recyclable materials. Even automobiles and buses had to be chopped, crushed, or shredded and converted into reusable resources for use in manufacturing, business, and industry. He worked hard for his money, so they better treat him right. My daddy!

Things were really coming together just as they had desired. My mom and dad saved their monies, and within one year, they had enough to have a house built from the ground up in a new development. I will never forget the address of my first house—129 South Illinois Street—and my first telephone number—288-3709. We had come "a long way, baby" from that dilapidated shotgun house in Clear Lake County with no inside toilet to the basement with a dirt floor in my granddad's. It was an exciting time for us, and you would have thought that we had just moved into a huge mansion in a gated community, but it was a modest, beautiful two-bedroom house that my mom and dad worked hard for, and it was ours. What stood out for me were the lovely hardwood floors in the living room, and thank you, Jesus, for the inside toilet. All four of my brothers happily shared a bedroom with bunk beds, and of course, my mom and dad had their own bedroom. I was waiting for them to show me to my bedroom, but there were only two in that small house. I was wondering where I was going to sleep until my mom brought out something called a hideaway bed.

The place where I was going to lay my head had to be folded up and stored in the utility room during the day and then rolled out in the living room and unfolded when it was bedtime at night. My bedroom was, in fact, the living room. I was never the type to complain much about anything, not even as a four-year-old. There was something innate in my persona that allowed me to be content with such as I had. My mom often complimented me on the ability that I had—even as a child—to persevere through uncomfortable times. She often marveled with amazement at the capacity that I had to endure inconvenience without excessive complaining. The serenity prayer has always been ingrained in my psyche. I have always made a conscientious effort to accept the things that I could not change, and I have always tried to change the things that I didn't have to accept. I was just happy to have *somewhere to lay my head.* I soon discovered that my bed was positioned in the right place because when my dad got up for work, he had to pass by me every morning to get to the kitchen. My bed was strategically in the perfect place. There is a reason or a purpose for everything.

There is a reason for the sun; it warms the earth. It is where we get our light and heat. The sun is ninety-three million miles from the earth, but it is strategically in the right place. If it was one inch closer, we would probably burn up. As far away as it is from us, it is still hot enough for some of us to enjoy a nice suntan or endure a painful sunburn, and we can even fry an egg on the sidewalk. But if it were one inch farther, we would no doubt freeze to death. And just as there is a reason that the sun is positioned where it is, there was a reason that my bed was positioned in the living room. My dad was the first to get up in the morning, so when he made his breakfast and a pot of Hills Brothers coffee, he would quietly get me up every day of the world without disturbing anyone, and we would have breakfast and he always drank one and a half cups of coffee. Of course, the other half he would always save for me. Lots of cream and a little sugar. Occasionally, there were some black things in the bottom of the cup that he called coffee grounds, and he told me not to swallow them. He never told me why, so I promise you that I ingested my share of them. That coffee was so good—grounds and all—especially because I was drinking it from my daddy's cup. It wasn't that instant stuff, but he made fresh percolated (today it would be called brewed) coffee, and that aroma permeated every room in our entire house.

The first Sunday morning in our new house was the happiest ever for everyone. That morning was everything that my mom could ever wish for . . . and then some. It was simply a dream come true and an answer to prayer for my mom to have all of us getting dressed for church together. We did not have a car, and there were too many of us to ride with some of the members of the church, so we always rode to church in a cab. Fortunately, it was only eight or nine blocks away, so it was somewhat affordable. That morning at our new church, Saints Memorial COGIC, was phenomenal. You could hear the electrifying singing and other expressions of thanksgiving as we entered the sanctuary. This was definitely a hand-clapping, foot-stomping, tongue-talking Pentecostal church. The choir rocked!

Bishop Davis looked out over the audience and observed us sitting together as a family, and he gave my dad the thumbs up sign. Tears of joy filled my dad's eyes as he reflected on all that Bishop Davis had gone through to get him exonerated from the felony charge. My mother had told my dad that Bishop Davis pleaded with the governor until sweat literally poured off him. He thought intensely about the governor of Indiana, Governor Schricker, who was a white man that showed kindness to him and his wife in the '50s. The sheriffs from Blytheville had intended to *get that nigger* and extradite him back to Arkansas and probably kill him, but here he was, sitting in church with his family a free changed man. A new creature. He felt sympathy for Aunt Mae and how she must have felt and been impacted by him stealing her cow, but he knew that he had to stop looking back and turn the page to a new chapter in his life. He felt absolutely no guilt or shame. You show me a person that has never made a mistake, and I will show you a person that has never made an attempt to do anything. Old things were passed away and behold, all things had become new. That was the Sunday that I made my singing debut. The audience gave me a thunderous applause, and my dad stuck his chest out as far as he could without popping the buttons on his shirt.

Later on in church, my dad heard a familiar sound. He looked over in the corner near the choir, and he saw a man with his eyes closed and a frown of enjoyment all over his face as he played his guitar. Now that's what I call a dichotomy, frowning from enjoyment! He was simply flabbergasted to hear someone play a guitar in church. The little church in Clear Lake County did not have that instrument, and the thought never occurred to him that a guitar could be played in a church. He had only heard the guitar played at the honky-tonk dances in the juke joints. Immediately after church, my dad made his way to the man and introduced himself to him, and he complimented him on his skillful playing. His name was Deacon Henry Jones.

"Maaaaaaaan, you're good," my dad said with excitement.

"Thanks, brother, and I hear that you can play too."

"Yes, the guitar is my passion. I have played the guitar since I was knee-high to a duck. I used to play in the juke joints for a living Down South until I joined the church. I guess you call them night clubs up North," he said jokingly. "Man, I didn't know that you could play a guitar in church."

"Yea, brother, the Bible says praise God on all of the instruments. Why don't you bring your guitar next Sunday, and you and I can take turns playing?"

My mom had to pinch herself when she heard my dad play his sweet guitar in church for the first time. He looked so handsome and she was so proud. My dad had no formal training on his guitar, but he played by ear. That is what you call real God-given talent because a person that plays by ear can practically hear a song once and play it without sheet music. Deacon Jones could play, but my daddy could mesmerize you into a breathless frenzy. The same guitar that he used to entertain that rowdy crowd in the smoke-filled, hip-swinging, finger-popping, dice-throwing, cussing, and God-only-knows-what-else juke joints was now being used as an instrument unto God to make his praise glorious. My daddy!

We were so proud of him and the tremendous consistent change that he had made and was continuing to make. He had his struggles, I'm sure, but he was becoming the man that God intended for him to be. I love the word *becoming* because when it is used as a verb, or an action word, it indicates process, movement, and change. My mom had gone through a metamorphosis, and now her man was doing the same. A metamorphosis is a change in form, a change in structure, or a change in function as a result of development. An instamatic camera takes a picture of something or someone and shoots it out. Initially there is nothing there, but you don't throw the paper away because it is *becoming* a picture. It has to develop.

When my dad was conceived, he did not start as a man, but he began as an embryo, and then he changed or developed into an infant and eventually became a man. A frog does not begin as a frog, but it starts as a tadpole and it becomes a frog. I mentioned earlier that a butterfly starts as a caterpillar in a cocoon, and it eventually becomes a beautiful butterfly. It's a process that requires some waiting, some shedding, and some coming out. But once an embryo or a frog or a butterfly turns into its final state, it never turns back into its origin. My dad had come a long way from the craps table, moonshine, and womanizing—and even his brief jail sentence—but there was no turning back. Sometimes he probably had the propensity to look back, but that is normal. I am glad that my mom did not throw him away when the instamatic camera of life shot him out, and there was nothing on the paper. He had to develop, and now he was finally getting his wings, and he believed that he could fly. I can hear my dad saying,

> I use to think that I could not go on
> And life was nothing but an awful song
> But now I know the meaning of true love
> I'm leaning on the everlasting arms
> If I can see it, then I can do it
> If I just believe it, there's nothing to it

I believe I can fly

I believe I can touch the sky

I think about it every night and day

Spread my wings and fly away

I believe I can soar

I see me running through that open door

I believe I can fly

See I was on the verge of breaking down

Sometimes silence can seem so loud

There are miracles in life I must achieve

But first I know it starts inside of me

Oh, if I can see it, then I can do it

If I just believe it, there's nothing to it

"Kid, it was worth your wait and all of the pain that I put you through because now I can fly. I can fly above my gloomy past into our bright future. I'm going to make it up to you, baby, if it's the last thing that I do." His faith continued to increase exponentially. My daddy!

In spite of my dad's extracurricular activities on the weekends in the South, he always was a hard worker and an excellent provider for his family. We always had food on the table and somewhere to lay our heads. He continued his same work ethic at the South Bend Iron and Metal Company. My dad took the bus to work faithfully, and I never remember him missing a day from work the entire time that he was employed at that company. Every day after school, at around four thirty, I would see my daddy walking home from the bus stop about a half mile away. The bus stop was on the corner of Western Avenue and our street. He always stopped at the grocery store called the A&P to buy food for his family.

Without fail, I would see him carrying two bags of groceries in his arms at least twice a week. My mom would let me run and meet him when he got within a safe distance of our house and I would help him with one bag if it was not too heavy. My brothers were busy shooting marbles or playing basketball, but I knew what time my dad got off from work and my mind was on him. I can close my eyes right now and see my daddy making his way down the street to the new house that he and my mom had worked so hard together to build. Sometimes he looked so tired, but that look soon vanished when he saw me running to meet him and also when he got home to his comfortable chair and watched my mom move around in the kitchen as she prepared his dinner. He always offered to help her, but he worked much harder than she did, and she wanted her husband to relax after a long day.

In those days, women catered to their husbands by bringing them their slippers and the newspaper. My mom always ran my dad's bathwater, and his dinner was always served first. My dad needed all of the tender love and care that she could give him because it was not easy for colored people and especially men. They had to work twice as hard to please the white man. We had moved up north to the land of opportunity, but little did they know that that land was also polluted with the ideology that the white race was inherently superior. They had moved to the North to get away from the injustice and the degrading acts that were subsequently imposed upon them, but what they were oblivious to was that systematic racial discrimination was prevalent everywhere just under the disguise of a different zip code. In the South, racism was overt, public, and obvious; and in the north, it was covert, subtle, and suppressed. It was masked perpetuated injustice. They had to work hard and persevere under difficult unfair taskmasters. My hat is off to them because I probably never would have made it.

One day, my dad came home from work so excited! "Kid, guess who has moved from Blytheville to South Bend?"

"I have no idea," my mom said as she continued to peel the Idaho potatoes that she was going to twice mash and serve with mushroom gravy and meat loaf.

"Do you remember my old buddy, Simon?"

"As a matter of fact, I do," she responded. For a split second, my mom had a flashback of that night that Simon had brought my daddy home sloppy drunk. She also briefly reflected on the reason, being that she had tore his craps table and moonshine stand to pieces with the axe, and he had drowned himself in liquor to help him get it off his mind. "Oh, that's nice," she said without looking up. And then she added, "What a coincidence."

"No, Kid, it is not a coincidence. He heard that I had moved to South Bend and had gotten a good job and built a nice new home. He wanted to come here so that he could better himself as well. He applied for a job at my company, and they hired him today. You know, Kid, Simon has always been competitive and somewhat jealous of me. I think it is probably because of his old lady that he was shacking up with that left him for me. He was really crazy in love with her, but feelings just weren't mutual. Ah, come on, Kid, don't look at me like that. That's water under the bridge, and God has forgiven me and Simon acts like he has too."

"That's nice! Honey, get washed up because dinner is almost ready."

"You won't have to call me twice because I'm starved," my dad said as he made his way to the bathroom.

My brothers were doing great in school and, of course, being mischievous as boys can be around the neighborhood. I was the one that was daddy's perfect little angel that never did anything wrong and reported everything that I saw them do. I was what you call a tattletale. A snitch, a whistle blower, a blabbermouth. You got me? I assure you that I did my share of mischief, but I was always afraid of my mom's discipline measures and that kept me pretty much in check. My dad would occasionally spank the boys, but my mom was the disciplinarian. My dad spanked me once in my life, and my mom had to force him to do it.

My dad had a sweet tooth for this candy called coconut balls. They came in different colors. White, pink, yellow, and chocolate. Yummy! He kept them in the pocket of his work coat that he always hung up in the utility room. He had already shared some of them with me, but I got greedy. When I went into the utility room to get my hideaway bed, I checked his coat pocket; and yes, there were more and I ate them all. Of course, my dad thought that my brothers were the guilty ones, but my mom told on me, and I admitted that I was the guilty one. It bothered her that I had eaten the rest of his favorite candy that he had saved for himself for dessert after dinner. It was the first time that my mom had ever given my dad an ultimatum since they had been married. She told him that if he did not spank me, she would not let him into her bed that night. I guess you know; he tore my behind up. I deserved it though, and my brothers teased me to the high heavens. That next morning, I was awakened by the smell of coffee. I must have slept through my dad's morning kiss on my forehead. I suppose that spanking was quite a sedative. Why had he not awakened me? *I wonder if he is still upset about his candy*, I thought to myself. I covered my head up and cried from guilt. I always covered my head up in bed when I was sad about anything, and I still do it until this very day. I guess that means no more coffee with my daddy.

Within a few minutes, I heard my dad quietly say, "Hey, baby girl, your coffee is ready." I jumped up out of bed and ran to hug him.

"I'm sorry, Daddy, about eating your candy," I said, relieved while showering him with kisses all over his face. He looked at me with so much love.

"All is forgiven," he said, and he never mentioned it again. Life was a dream. Oh, we had our share of challenges, typical disappointments, and ups and downs as families do; but compared to the shotgun house and the outside toilet at Clear Lake County and the dirt floor at my granddad's, life was but a dream.

Late one night, the phone rang, and it had a strange sound to it. It is just something about those phone calls in the middle of the night that can frighten you out of your wits. They can be quite startling and alarming. My mom had a funny feeling down in the pit of her stomach that it was not going to be a pleasant call, and she was a bit apprehensive about answering it, but after a few rings, she slowly picked up the telephone.

"Hello, Thomas residence."

It was my mother's sister, Aunt Pearl, on the other end in distress. "Beatrice, Daddy has just had a massive stroke. Please hurry and get dressed, and I will pick you up so that we can get to the hospital."

My mother's premonition was right. She had told my dad that she wanted to move north where her father lived so that she could spend some quality time with him before something happened. He had suffered from high blood pressure for years, and I am sure that he was not under the best medical care. He passed away shortly after they arrived at the hospital. That was my first experience with death. I was five years old; but I remember my mom crying and lots of people, flowers, and food. I asked questions like why and how. I remember experiencing emotions of sadness, anxiety, and fear until my dad explained to me that my granddad "went to heaven." I guess I was okay after that because that seemed like a good place to me. The solace that my mom found was in the fact that she had a chance to live in the same house with him for a while, and after she moved into her own home she still had some time of joy and happiness with him. Nothing teaches us more about life than death. It makes us question why we take for granted something that is so precious and . . . transient.

The next few months were tough for my mom. My dad wanted to do something special for her that he thought would make her smile again.

He missed that bright gleam in her eyes. My granddad's death actually affected the entire house, and we all needed an emotional lift. One Saturday morning, he went out and stayed for a few hours, and when he returned, he came to the back door instead of the front. He called out for all of us to come to the back door. All of my brothers, my mom, and I ran to the back of the house and there stood the cutest little puppy ever. He was a Golden Retriever. You would have thought that that dog was a human being. We took turns holding him and playing with him. It was love at first bark. My brothers named him Sisco. Please do not ask me why. Dogs are incredible because they are not prejudiced. You can be colored or white, Catholic or Baptist, republican or democrat. If you treat them with love and care, they will be loyal and show gratitude to you until the end. Selecting the particular type of dog that would best suit our family's needs was an arduous task for my dad, as it would be for anyone for that matter. It kinda reminds me of the instructions that some ministers give when they are performing the marriage ceremony. They remind the anxious, Chantilly-laced, beautiful bride and the handsome groom with his tuxedo and bowtie that the step they are embarking upon is not to be entered into lightly, but soberly and discreetly. Most of the time, because of the euphoria and the excitement, this bit of chilling, thought-provoking advice flies over their heads, only to boomerang and stare them in the face at a later, challenging date after the novelty has worn off. Both scenarios, getting married and selecting a dog, are a "'til death do us part" undertaking. I admire the Obamas for taking their time rather than succumbing or bowing to the pressure of their lovely girls—and America, for that matter—and making a decision hesitantly and flippantly that could negatively impact them and the dog. I can just imagine what President Obama and Michelle were going through trying to decide what kind of dog that would be best for Malia and Sasha. The job is a major one. It was so important and difficult that on his first press conference as president-elect, instead of addressing solely the housing crisis, the war in Iraq, unemployment, and Wall Street, he referenced the dire need to find a hypoallergenic dog for his girls. But my incredible dad hit the jackpot in a few hours. He selected the right kind of dog because a retriever is a family dog and they are friendly, easy to train, and excellent with children.

There is a saying that goes a dog is a man's best friend, but in our house it was reversed because my mom became our dog's best friend. Sisco responded to all of us, but when my mom walked in the room his tail would wag so hard that his entire body would move. He was able to distinguish her voice from ours, and his ears would stand up when he sensed that she was within a half block of our house. As you know, a dog should be walked twice a day. In the morning before he eats and in the evening. If the dog is properly trained, he will focus on his leader and will walk beside him or a few steps behind him. We all had the chore to take turns walking the dog, but only my mom could get him to cooperate obediently and walk along side of her or a few steps behind. You should have seen us taking Sisco for a walk. He really was taking us for a walk and dragging us all of the way. It was a hilarious fiasco. Sisco was not a happy camper, if you will allow me to say, because he preferred my mom to be his designated primary caretaker. He wanted his friend to walk him . . . my mom. That unquestionably was her dog, and she was his best friend. She trained him to fetch her shoes rather them chew them, and when all of us gathered in the living room in the evening after dinner, his spot would be curled up right under my mom. You would not think that a dog would be the antidote that my mom needed to help her through her father's death, but it was.

I shared this very simple and true story with you to show you how much my dad loved his wife and how important it was to him that she be happy. His feelings for her had grown deep. He never thought they he could be committed to one woman, but he was. He had discovered that his infidelity was a symptom and not the cause. When you have a common cold, the symptoms are a scratchy throat, fever, sneezing, nasal stuffiness, general malaise, and achiness. Those are only signs or the manifestations of the disease or disorder. The cause or the reason that precipitated the symptoms is a virus that has been transmitted between people either directly or airborne, and through contaminated surfaces. My dad's insatiable desire to womanize was the symptom or the manifestation, but the cause was his sinful nature. Our purpose in life is to worship our creator. Until we do that, we will aimlessly seek other things to substitute and satisfy that purpose. But it is a mission impossible because the void that each of us has can only be filled by the one that placed it there. Your life must include him. It must begin with him and end with him. Only God can help you connect the dots in your life. He makes everything else in this complex life palatable and more often, wonderful. The kid he married satisfied him completely, and he felt content knowing that her love was reciprocal. She had forgiven him. To error is human, but to forgive is divine. Yes, there was a big hole in her heart from the hurt of betrayal. But that can be compared with a guitar. Some guitars have a big hole in them also, for the purpose of sound projection. You play it for all it's worth and what a sound. The hole in her heart didn't need to be repaired, just strummed with the fingers of passionate love, communication, and forgiveness. Their moments together when they were alone seemed to escape much too quickly. He found that it was significantly easy to love her after he learned to love himself. What a tremendous change. He loved her more than he loved his guitar. He was definitely not the same man that she met at the well, and neither was she the same little thirteen-year-young girl—she was a woman, phenomenally.

Sisco brought joy and excitement to all of us, but within the next month or so my dad had saved up enough money and surprised my mom with something else that was expressly for her, to put a smile on her face and make her job around the house undeniably easier. One Saturday morning, he told my mom that his friend Simon had asked him to do some odd jobs with him on his truck. When he returned later, she had the surprise of her life. He needed Simon's truck because he had purchased her a brand new washing machine. My mom had been accustomed to making her own soap with lye since she was a young girl in the South, and washing all of the laundry by hand. When she became a mother, Pampers were out of the economical question, and Pull-Ups had not been invented, so she had to wash our diapers out by hand also. She was always a perfectionist and frowned upon dingy clothes, so she made certain that our clothes were the brightest and the whitest by using a simple wash board and a pair of strong hands. As she grew older, my mom was embarrassed about the roughness of her hands from the laborious scrubbing that went into sometimes daily laundry, but I never saw roughness. I only saw tender love and care. She was so happy for her surprise gift from my dad. Please know that it was not the kind of washer that we have today with the customized cycles and different water levels and temperatures, but it was a tremendous improvement and welcomed relief. It was a very interesting-looking machine that required a great deal of skill, but it definitely gave my mom's poor hands a break. It had an attached wringer, and the clothes had to be carefully fed through the two rollers in a steady and careful fashion. If you put too many through at once, the wringer would pop its top and make a horrendous noise that was loud enough to frighten everyone in the house. I hear you thinking! What about the dryer? Well, the dryer was located outside. She had two clotheslines and the only other things that she needed were clothespins and a sunshiny day. God's sunshine was her clothes dryer. My dad's lavishing of gifts on her did not stop there. The next thing he did for her was bought her some nice dresses for church. He had excellent taste, and he knew how to pick the appropriate dresses that complimented her and accentuated her slim waistline and her other assets. My mom owned two nice dresses, one on the hanger in her closet and the other one on her back, but she was content knowing that brighter days were up ahead. His acts of kindness did not replace the loss of her father, but they certainly were thoughtful, and they aided in the healing process.

My mom and dad worked extremely hard together to provide and maintain a roof over our heads, food on the table, and nice school clothes for five growing children. It was not easy by any stretch of the imagination because they still were facing head-on the woes of social, political, and economical injustice and disparities. It would be nonsensical for me to suggest that they were financially making enough to make ends meet because they were barely doing that, but considering the sobering fact that colored people worked for free for 300 years, their small salaries were a major, welcomed improvement. They were yet fiercely struggling to maintain their dignity in a society that considered them to be less than human. I admire them and celebrate them for their incessant perseverance while living under the harsh reality of covert discrimination and blatant exploitation. I will not apologize for reiterating the history of injustice in this country, because we need to be reminded that the disparities that my parents suffered are not a thing of the past, but remain a very present issue that we must continue to address. Granted, some progress has been made in that this country has made it possible for a black man to run for the highest office in this nation and win, but we still have a long way to go.

When my brothers and I began school up north, my mom noticed that our school pictures were extremely darker than our own physical hue. She had observed the same in the South as far as my brothers pictures were concerned (I had not, as of yet, began school), but she assumed that it was just that Southern "tar baby" stigma representation. When we moved up north, she noticed that the same photo-technological misrepresentation existed. My mom held her peace until I was in the second grade, and then when our pictures were sent home for her perusal and purchase, she sent them back with a note of refusal, and the reason being that their technology of photography obviously had been developed for white skin tones only. She added that additional skills were mandatory and would be essential in order to capture the true beautiful *variety* of the skin tones of colored people, whether it be an amazing jet black or an amazing high yellow. My mom had an element of pride, and she refused to put her hand over her mouth and keep silent about something that was clearly a superficial determining factor that white was superior and beautiful and colored was inferior and ugly. She did not stop at that, but she solicited as many colored parents as she could to refuse to purchase school pictures until there was a conspicuous improvement. This was a very "touchy" issue and had to be handled discreetly and professionally, but nonetheless handled. There was not an immediate change, but gradually there became more satisfied customers. She definitely believed in voting with her feet, so to speak, as opposed to taking whatever was given, and it worked.

She not only took on the challenge pertaining to her dissatisfaction with the quality of our pictures, but she also expressed her displeasure on other racially pertinent issues. They were yet feeling their way in an unfriendly world with one hand, while trying to hold on to their sanity with the other. Both my mom and dad were adamant about not allowing their oppressor to have the last say about their right to the tree of life, both natural and spiritual. They would thus have become enslaved, which means to be subjected to a dominating influence that takes away his or her right to equality and freedom. Shakespeare once said that a slave bears the power in his own hand to cancel his captivity. She always believed that it took less energy to remain enslaved and that it was more strenuous to pursue liberty and justice, and she did not mind the exertion or the fight. Remember in the movie *The Color Purple* when Sophia, Harpo, and Ms. Ceely were in the field and Sophia was bad-mouthing Harpo? Well, Ms. Ceely told Harpo to beat her and Sophia said, "I got to fight all my life." Well, my mom said ditto, ditto. My mom had found a cause worth fighting for, and that was to strive for a more perfect union with liberty and justice for all. It was no cake walk for my mom and dad, but it was much easier together.

It was neither the multiplicity of things, nor the extravagant things that filled the house on 129 South Illinois Street, but it was the love that filled the house that made us content with such as we had. Love and contentment make a house a home. My hideaway bed that had to be folded up in the morning and rolled into the utility room was just as beautiful to me as a princess bed with a canopy on top, just as long as there was love. I was content just having *somewhere to lay my head*. I can proudly say from experience that where you are currently laying your head is not an indication of where you are going to end up laying it. It does not even indicate who you are.

The awesome examples that come to mind are, first of all, Tyler Perry. Ten years ago, he was homeless, hungry, unsure of where his next dollar was going to come from, and not so sure as to whether life was even worth living. But through the pain and shame, he persistently held on to his dream and faith in God, and today he has single-handedly built a billion-dollar entertainment empire that is the envy of Hollywood. He is a successful playwright, author, film and TV actor, producer, and director whose eleven stage plays (and counting) have earned him more than $200 million; whose five films have made him $240 million overall in North American box office sales, and whose television show *Tyler Perry's House of Payne* became the highest-rated sitcom on cable in history. One decade ago, he had *nowhere to lay his head*, but how do you like him now?

Another example is our new president, Barack Obama. I read that one of the colleges that he attended was in New York, and that when he first arrived in the city, he somehow missed connections with his roommate and he ended up laying his head on his luggage in a rough, risky, dirty, and unsafe alley and sleeping until morning. Where he laid his head that night was no indication of where he was going to end up laying it, because on January 20, 2009, he will be our forty-fourth president of the United States and he is going to lay his head at 1600 Pennsylvania Avenue NW—in the White House. He was not the likeliest candidate to end up in the White House. He is the son of a black man and a white woman, but was raised partially by his white grandparents. He had a very modest beginning in life. He did not have much money or endorsements when he decided to run for the presidency. The conception of his campaign was very humble and launched from the backyards, living rooms, and front porches of some cautiously-optimistic, and I am sure skeptical, supporters, but look at him now.

I must be candid with you and admit that I did feel somewhat embarrassed to share with my classmates at school where my bedroom was, especially after they had invited me to come over and play with them, and they had proudly showed off their pretty, girly bedrooms that had nice beds and pink ruffled bedspreads. When my friends came over to play with me, they wanted me to show them my bedroom and I always managed to make up an excuse as to why I couldn't. Although I felt a bit ashamed, deep down inside, I knew that I was still somebody, and that one day I was going to have a nice bed and bedroom just like everybody else. I knew that God had a timetable or an expiration date stamped on my humble sleeping arrangements and on all of the other discomforts that life had afforded me for that matter. That mind-set comes from knowing who you are.

Unfortunate circumstances never make a man; they only reveal who he already is. I must refer back to Joseph in the Bible when his brothers sold him into slavery and he ended up laying his head in the pit. Joseph knew who he was and considered that pit to be only a pit stop. A pit stop is not your final destination; it's just a hesitation, if you will. It's a time of refueling, refreshing, and re-servicing; Joseph laid his head in the pit as a slave, but he ended up laying it in the palace as a governor. And for your consideration, Jesus is our perfect example. When he was born on that cold night in a town called Bethlehem, he needed somewhere to lay his head also. His adoptive father, Joseph, searched for a convenient place for him to be born but was flatly turned away because there were disheartening signs in every window where he inquired that read *no room, no vacancies, all sold out, all filled up.* There were no rooms available anywhere. That precious baby had to lay down his sweet head in a manger, which was a box or trough in a stable from which the animals would eat. But no crying he made because he knew who he was. He was Jesus, the Son of God that owned the cattle on a thousand hills, the whole earth and the fullness thereof, and all of the silver and gold, but he laid his head in a box that was filled with hay. But the wisdom of this is he knew that where he was wasn't an indication of who he was. The manger was just temporary, and it was orchestrated to teach us a profound message in humility.

Many times, our starting place in life is marginalized and vulnerable. I would not have chosen to live in a shotgun house with no inside toilet. I would not have chosen to live in a basement and walk around and play on dirt floors. And I would not have chosen to sleep on a hideaway bed in the living room while everyone else had a comfortable bed and a bedroom to sleep in. But it was instilled in me that I am somebody wherever I am. In our church organization, when we have state or national conventions, you should see some of the people racing for the front row seats. I always look at those people with sympathy because they are confused in their identification and perception. They perceive that the front seat transitions them into an upper-echelon status. It makes them feel special. I always smile to myself as I observe their disruptive, un-Christlike, cavalier behavior. It just makes me want to holler and raise both of my hands and shout out with a loud voice, "The seat does not make you special, but your character and your integrity do." I was always unequivocally of the persuasion that wherever I sat was the front. It's a mind-set. It was my mom's philosophy and it has become mine as well, that you make the place, the place does not make you. Although all seven of us crowded into the basement of my granddad's house to lay our heads on makeshift beds with dirt for a carpet and had to use cardboard boxes for chest of drawers, my mom always reminded us that we were somebody, and that this is home and we should keep it neat and clean. She beautified it by adding throw rugs, fresh-cut flowers, and little whatnots here and there. When you ride into a neighborhood and you see an occupied house with a broken window that has been negligently overlooked, you automatically assume that it is okay to throw garbage in the yard and park your car on the lawn for repairs. It only takes one bad apple to send that kind of negativity or message.

I have come to know that if you can muster up the will to endure difficulties and learn what you need to learn while you are going through them, you will not have to repeat that test. Here is a news flash: just as the products that we purchase have an expiration date stamped on them, so do the challenges of life. I am so glad that troubles don't last always. I was content and happy just having somewhere to lay my head and drinking a half of a cup of coffee with my daddy every morning before he went to work. Lots of cream and a little sugar. That was the best part of waking up.

Chapter 5

Someone to Watch Over Me

It sure looks cold outside. It is snowing so hard, and I don't want to get up. My dad had already gotten dressed, and I could hear him in the kitchen putting the coffee on and getting ready to fix his bacon and eggs. I am going to stay in this bed where it is warm as long as I can . . . until I smell that coffee. The smell of coffee was really my alarm clock. My dad had an old clock that would literally dance almost off their nightstand when the alarm went off, but that did not arouse me. But when my dad got up and brewed his Hills Brothers coffee, that aroma instantaneously sent a message to my brain telling me it's time to get up. Oh, that's right. I've got to remember to get a dollar bill and a quarter from my dad for a special project in school. Tomorrow is George Washington's birthday, and my fourth-grade class is doing a special presentation about him. Mrs. Carmichael had gotten a large poster with his picture on it and told us all about him being our first president, the father of our country, and she explained to us that because George Washington was such an important person and did so many wonderful things to help our country, we should do something special on his birthday to commemorate him. Three of the kids in my class were selected to share any information that they had learned from the lesson that our teacher had taught, and the remainder of the class was going to do a skit. I was one of the three that was selected to share something that I had learned. Also, the three of us had to look for anything in our house that reminded us of him (within reason of course) and bring it to class. I chose the dollar bill and the quarter. That was a brilliant idea, if I may say so myself, but now I needed to get it from my dad. I was daydreaming about my presentation when the smell of coffee interrupted my train of thought.

My dad came into the living room and kissed me on the forehead. "Baby girl, get up. Our coffee is ready," he said with the biggest smile on his face.

"Oh, Daddy, it is so cold, but I've got to get up and have my coffee."

"Come on. Get up, girl. I'll turn the furnace up a little, and the coffee should help to warm you up some too."

"Okay, Daddy." I talked my dad's head off that morning before he left for work about my project in school. I told to him all about George Washington being the first president of the United States. "Daddy, did you know that he had false teeth that were made out of cow's teeth and elephant ivory and that the base of them had springs that allowed him to open and shut his mouth?"

"No, I didn't know that, but I do know that cows have some very strong teeth. We had a cow when we lived Down South, baby girl."

"I kinda remember that, Daddy. Did you know that he didn't really chop down his dad's cherry tree, but that that story was just concocted?"

"No, I didn't, honey." Although I was engaged in deep conversation, I still had my eyes on my dad's cup. I could hardly wait until he finished his cup and a half, because I knew that it was going to be my turn.

"He was six feet tall when he grew up, just like you, Daddy. And guess what? His father nicknamed him Sweet Face because he was such a nice, honest, and well-mannered little boy. Daddy do you know why Mason Weems invented that story about the cherry tree?"

"No, I don't, baby girl."

"Dad, you really got to hear this. In fact, I have to give a speech on this in class tomorrow for George Washington's birthday. You want to hear it, Daddy?"

"Of course, honey."

"Well, George Washington's father sat him down one day when he was little and told him that truth is the best quality that a child can have. He told him that he would rather ride fifty miles to see a little boy whose heart was honest and his lips pure than to live with a child that would lie. He told him that if a boy lies, nobody can believe a word that he says even when he tells the truth.

"Daddy, George Washington's father told him that he would rather nail him up in a coffin and bury him in the grave rather than see him become a liar. 'Never lie to me,' he told his son. 'I have always told you, and now tell you again, that whenever by accident you do anything wrong, which will be often because you are yet a little boy, rather than spank you, George, I will love you instead.' Daddy, when the president was a little boy, his father gave him a hatchet for his birthday, and he cut his dad's favorite English cherry tree down. The next morning, when his dad noticed that the tree was cut down, he asked him if he knew who killed his tree in yonder garden. This was a hard question for him, Daddy, but he thought about what his father had told him about lying and he cried out, 'I can't tell a lie, Pa, you know I can't tell a lie. I did cut it down with my hatchet. I cut down your cherry tree. Run to my arms, you dearest boy,' said his father. 'Glad am I, son, that you killed my tree for you have paid me for it a thousand-fold. Such an act of integrity in you my son is worth more than a thousand trees blossomed with silver leaves and their apples of pure gold.'"

My daddy listened to me so intensely and told me that I should always pattern my life with integrity the same as George Washington did when he was a little boy. I reminded my dad about that evening that I took his candy out of his pocket, and I told him the truth and still received a spanking. He smiled at me and handed me my half cup of coffee and told me that that was my mom's idea, but regardless of that, he was proud of me for not lying. "But George didn't get a spanking, Daddy, but I did."

"Yea, yea, I know, but now I want to tell you a story. Once upon a time, there was another little boy that lived in the country that cried wolf all of the time and his parents would run out to save him, and there was no wolf anywhere in sight. Baby girl, he did that about three times, and on the fourth time that he cried wolf, no one came to see about him, but that time there really was a wolf, and he was eaten up. Maybe his parents should have told him that cherry tree story and gave him a little spanking for lying. Always tell the truth," my dad said. "Remember that a lie travels fast because it has wings, but the truth travels slow because it only has feet and it has to walk. But when it gets to where it is going, it can *stand*. Now that's integrity."

"Yes, Daddy. Oh, by the way, Daddy, could you give me a dollar and a quarter?"

"Wow, that's a lot of money. What do you need that kinda money for?"

"I'm going to bring it back home, Daddy, I just need it for my presentation in school because President George Washington's picture is on both of them and we are suppose to bring something from home that reminds us of him."

"You are a smart little cookie, baby girl. I will leave it for you on the kitchen table." My dad had to rush because we talked so long that he had almost missed his bus.

My dad and I had so much fun sharing that morning. When he got up from the kitchen table, he held my face with both of his hands and told me that he loved me, and that he was so proud to have a nice pretty little princess as his daughter. Those times that I spent in the mornings with my dad drinking coffee—and him listening to me chatter about not much of anything—meant everything to me. He had his way of looking at me with those handsome big eyes as he listened with so much interest and fascination. I was definitely daddy's little girl and I only had eyes for him. I loved my mom, but there was something special about the relationship that my dad and I had. I was so happy that I didn't have a bedroom so that my hideaway bed was in the living room near the kitchen. He had to pass my bed every morning and he always gave me a kiss on my forehead on the way to the kitchen to fix his breakfast. He actually felt bad because they could not afford a third bedroom when they built our new house, but I could not have been happier. While everyone else in the house was asleep, I could sneak out of my hideaway bed into the kitchen every morning and have coffee with my daddy. Lots of cream and a little sugar. That was the best part of waking up. My daddy!

I practiced my little cherry tree speech over and over at school that day, and I could hardly wait until the next day to recite it and also to show off my dollar and a quarter with George Washington's picture on it.

When I got home from school that evening, I was surprised because my dad was already home from work. I didn't understand why he was home so early. I always looked forward to meeting him half way down our street everyday of the world as he walked from the bus stop. Sunshine or rain, hot or cold, I met him every day. My dad was sitting on the couch in the living room with his head completely bandaged. Blood had seeped through the bandages, and his eyes were red. I ran over to the couch and asked him what had happened. He told me that he had gotten hurt on the job. He said that he had stooped over to pick up a piece of iron and he suddenly felt a crushing pain in his head and everything went black. He was knocked unconscious, and he woke up in medical on his job. He told me that he had an excruciating headache and he just wanted to lay down on the couch and rest. I went in the utility room and rolled out my bed

WILL THERE BE ANY COFFEE IN HEAVEN?   187

into the living room next to the couch and sat down and held his hand until he drifted off to sleep. When my brothers got home from school, I motioned for them to be quiet because dad had gotten hurt on the job and he was asleep.

My mom was always the first one to leave in the morning and the last to get home in the evening because she had to travel about thirty miles. When she got home, my dad had awakened from the excruciating pain and was sitting up on the couch. He explained to her as best as he could remember what had transpired. He told her that his friend, Simon, had witnessed the accident and told him that a huge heavy piece of iron that weighed a considerable amount had fallen from the upper level and had hit him on the head.

She said, "Honey, I've got to take the bandages off so that I can see your wound. I will be gentle I promise." It took her some time to unwrap my dad's head, and when she finally saw his wound, she nearly fainted. I started crying, and my mom signaled for me to go in the kitchen because she clearly saw how upset I was. My mom had to be strong to stomach the sight of an injury of that magnitude. "Honey, how in the world did you get home?"

"I caught the bus," my dad slowly responded.

"You mean to tell me that the nurse on your job sent you home on the bus with this kind of blow to your head? I cannot for the life of me perceive someone being that insensitive and inhuman to send a man home with this kind of trauma. This is a severe head injury, and we have got to get you to the hospital for immediate medical attention."

"Kid, I'm going to be all right."

"No," she insisted. "You've got to go and get this looked at because you may even need stitches."

"Okay, okay. If I am not better by morning, I will consider going to the hospital." Later that evening, his friend, Simon, stopped by to see how my dad was doing, but he was asleep. My mom asked him if he knew how it had happened, and he told her the exact same thing that my dad had told her. He said that he rushed down where my dad was, and he and some of the other employees got him to medical. Simon and my mom both briefly discussed how insensitive the company was to send him home by bus with a blow to the head as he had sustained. He stood to leave and told her to make sure that she told my dad that he had stopped by to see him.

I was so young and did not realize the depth of the seriousness of my dad's condition, but I knew that it was not good. Just as day was breaking, my dad had to be rushed to the hospital because of the excruciating pain in his head and the constant bleeding. My dad was a big strong man that had suffered other minor blows to his head and had an incredible tolerance for pain, but this was different. He definitely needed immediate medical attention. My mom called his friend that he played the guitar with at the church and asked if he would come quickly and take him to the hospital. Before my dad left, he secretly told all of my brothers that if anything should happen to him to take good care of their mother and their little sister. He went in the closet in the hallway and took out the case with his guitar in it, and gave it to my brother, Jimmy, and told him to cherish it. My brother, Jimmy, had started playing on my dad's guitar; and you could tell that he was developing a passion for it just like his dad. He was learning incredibly fast. We were all young and as disturbed as children would be, and we were all going through the terrible motions—or should I say emotions—about our dad having to go to the hospital. I was sitting on my hideaway bed when my dad slowly walked over to me and kissed me on my forehead with tears in his eyes. "You do a good job today with your George Washington project and don't forget to take your dollar and a quarter." He told me to be a good girl and that he would be back real soon. I remember succinctly telling him that he had promised me when I was three years old that he would never leave me. I told him that he had crossed his heart and hoped to die that he would never leave me again like he did before in Arkansas. "I'm not leaving you, baby girl. I've just got to go and get this head of mine fixed and I'll be back."

"You promise, Daddy?"

"Yea, baby, I promise. I cross my heart and hope to . . . live."

When my mom and dad left for the hospital, I was so sad from the shock of what was going on. I lay back down on my hideaway bed and covered up my head. I could hear my brothers talking in their bedroom as they were getting ready for school. I felt so alone. Normally, I would have been up by then and having coffee with my dad. The house was void without him, and that familiar aroma was conspicuously missing. I knew that he must have been in a lot of pain to go without his coffee. I just wanted my daddy to hurry and get his head fixed and come home.

As I continued to process the abrupt turn of events in my life, I suddenly remembered that it was George Washington's birthday. I had to get up and get dressed and get ready for my presentation at school. My class was so excited about the skit that we were having that morning; and somehow, through the course of our activities, I managed to get my mind off my dad long enough to concentrate on my speech that I had to give about the cherry tree and also the dollar and the quarter that I had for show and tell that my dad had given me with George Washington's picture on it. For a brief time, I forgot about the pain that I had left at home, and I had the best time in the world. I was the only one that thought to bring a dollar and a quarter. My teacher was so incredibly impressed that she sent a congratulatory note home with me to give to my parents. They were going to be so very proud of me and especially my daddy when he got out of the hospital. It was a good day after all.

When my dad arrived at the hospital, he told the doctor that he was at work and had bent down to pick up some iron, and he felt a crushing pain in his head, and everything went black after that. He said that a huge heavy piece of iron had fallen from the upper level and hit him in the head. In order for the doctors to determine the extent of the injury, they asked my dad a series of questions such as if he had a headache, dizziness, or any noticeable cognitive deficits.

He told them that he had symptoms in each of those areas. He also said that he had lost consciousness initially, but that the horrendous headaches had continued. The doctor removed my dad's bandages and just from mere observation told my mom that the extent of the damage could only be assessed with an x-ray. This was in the '50s, and the computed tomography (CT) scan had not been invented as of yet. The test results showed that his skull was fractured, and that there was incessant bleeding that had caused blood clots between the skull and the brain. Since his skull was fractured, there were fragments that had been driven into his brain that could lead to an infection. A team of specialists were called in to evaluate his condition, and they laid all of the cards on the table. They advised immediate surgery, but they left it totally up to my mom and dad. They did add that he had sustained a profound head injury, and that he had a fifty-fifty chance of surviving the surgery. They candidly told her that if they decided against surgery that he could suffer epileptic seizures and permanent mental and physical disabilities—and still might not survive. His doctor left the room and gave my mom and dad a few minutes to ponder this ultimatum.

My dad looked at my mom and said, "Well, Kid, I'm going to leave it up to you."

"Honey, the doctors said that you have a fifty-fifty chance of surviving the surgery. I'm scared, honey, but you're in so much pain and there are blood clots. Surgery may be the only way that you will get better. I want you to have a quality life, so I think that I would have the surgery if I were you."

"Kid, you have never been wrong yet," my dad said as he held her hand. "That's exactly what I will do." They shaved my dad's head and prepped him for surgery, and my dad told my mom what a wonderful wife that she had been.

"What do you mean *have been*? Stop talking in past tense."

"Kid, I'm scared. I just hope that everything turns out all right."

"It's going to be fine, you just wait and see," my mom reassured him. The nurse had given my dad an injection to induce drowsiness and to help him relax just before taking him into surgery. He was kind of giddy and teasing my mom about the time that she was swinging her axe.

"Kid, I sure would not ever want you to be as angry with me as you were with that craps table and that moonshine stand, especially with an axe in your hand." My mom managed to smile just for him, but she knew that it was the medication. They held hands tightly, and she bent over to kiss him just before they rolled him away to surgery.

Although there were specialists that were giving advice and overseeing the delicate operation, the surgery was actually performed by practicing interns because we did not have insurance. I am of the persuasion that the determining factors for those young amateur surgeons experimenting in such a serious delicate operation were because he was a colored man and did not have insurance. That rips away at my heart even now, and my imagination runs away that my dad's life was in the hands of some unskilled beginners performing on him as if he was a medical mannequin. I reiterate that the surgeons were amateurs, and amateurs carry out a task for experience and pleasure rather than payment. But that was life in the '50s, and in all actuality, the system hasn't changed. Today the people that have substandard health coverage are yet robbed of quality medical care. If you should happen to have a need to go to the emergency room, the first question that you are asked at the desk is what company you are insured with. That seems to take preeminence over everything else. The surgeon informed my mother that my dad could be in surgery from two to four hours barring any complication.

It was a long frightening wait, and there was a nurse that periodically kept my mom updated on the progress of the surgery. What seemed like an eternity had gone by when one of my dad's surgeons stepped out of those double doors, pulling his mask from his face. My dad's surgery was over, and he was in the intensive care recovery room. "You can see him shortly for a few minutes," the doctor informed her, "but please be cautiously optimistic because he is in a grave, critical condition, and it's going to be touch and go for the next twenty-four hours. He will be in and out of sleep, and we are keeping our fingers crossed that he does not go into a coma." My mom sighed with relief that the worst part was over as she walked to my dad's recovery room.

She moved quietly into my dad's room and sat down by his bed. The room was very cold. As she waited for him to wake up again, their entire life together flashed before her. She reminisced about that hot, smoldering day when she was coming down the hill from the well with that heavy bucket of water. He was such a handsome man, carrying his guitar over his shoulder and that red bandana tied around his head. Even with a splitting headache from being up all night at the juke joint, he was a sight for sore eyes. She thought about the wonderful nights that they had spent together in rhapsody, sharing love and their dreams and aspirations. She could not help but remember even the pain that she had experienced from his insatiable desire to stray and play. He just could not resist the allure of the mysterious women that showered him with flirtations, seductions, and advancements that made him feel that he could make those same sounds of ecstasy with them as he made on his sweet guitar. *I guess men will be men*, she forgivingly thought to herself. *Maybe that's why he had that strong biological urge to knock on the woman's door down the road from our old house in Clear Lake*, she thought.

While sitting there, she not only thought about the gain that they had joyously shared, but she also reflected on the pain. But as the saying goes . . . no pain, no gain. Casting him aside or castigating him because of his waywardness would have been as wrong as throwing out the baby with the bathwater. The dirty water is what is contaminated, not the baby. Because she was loving, understanding, and patient with him and brought out the best in him, he eventually became the man that he was created to be. The zenith of their life together was when he walked down the aisle to the altar that Sunday morning and accepted Christ as his personal savior. That was worth all of the lonely weekends that she had spent wondering which one of the multiplicity of women he was loving. He was a changed man. He had been such a strong, robust, hard-working man, and he looked so vulnerable lying there with tubes everywhere. *Lord, please let my husband be all right. I beg you, God. My children need their father and I need my husband and God* . . . Before my mom could continue her prayer, my dad slowly opened his eyes, and through the blurriness and pain, he managed to focus on her.

"Honey, you made it . . . Your surgery is all over, and you are going to be all right." My dad looked at her in a way that she would remember the rest of her life. All she could see in his eyes was pain. He was attempting to speak, but his condition was so grave that he was not able to. It has been said that a picture is worth a thousand words, but in this case, a look would be worth a thousand words. The nurse came in the room to check my dad's vitals, and she tried to conceal her concerns because it was quite evident that his condition was rapidly making a turn for the worse.

"Please do something," my mom said over and over. "Please, please do something."

The nurse quickly ran out of the room to get the doctor while my dad's life was swiftly slipping away like the sand in an hourglass. A coma was inevitable, but before he slipped into it, he spoke to my mom through his pain-filled eyes. He gave her a look that was deep, helpless, and meaningful. The look that he gave to the real love of his life—the kid, the young girl at the well—seemed to have been saying:

> For all those times you stood by me
>
> For all the truth that you made me see
>
> For all the joy that you brought to my life
>
> For all the wrong that you made right
>
> For every dream you made come true
>
> For all the love I found in you
>
> I'll be forever thankful baby
>
> You're the one who held me up
>
> Never let me fall
>
> You're the one who saw me through
>
> Through it all
>
> I'm everything I am
>
> Because you loved me
>
> You were my strength when I was weak
>
> You were my voice when I couldn't speak
>
> You were my eyes when I couldn't see
>
> You saw the best there was in me
>
> Lifted me up when I couldn't reach
>
> You gave me faith because you believed
>
> I'm everything I am
>
> Because you loved me
>
> You gave me wings and made me fly
>
> You touched my hand and I touched the sky
>
> I lost my faith, you gave it back to me
>
> You said no star was out of reach
>
> You stood by me and I stood tall

I had your love I had it all

I'm grateful for each day you gave me

Maybe I don't know that much

But I know this much is true

I was blessed because I was loved by you

I'm everything I am

Because you loved me

You were always there for me

The tender wing that carried me

A light in the dark shining your love into my life

You've been my inspiration

Through my lies you were the truth

My world was a better place because of you

I'm everything I am because you loved me

The look that spoke those words with so much meaning—within a few hours, without any struggle or resistance—had turned into an empty glaze. His eyes remained fastened on her, but they were empty . . . And my mom gently closed his eyes. She sobbed uncontrollably, but to no avail because death is cruel and unrelenting.

It was around time for school to dismiss when a girl from my church named Bertha Johnson came to my room and told my teacher that she was there to walk me home. I wondered why she was doing that because she had never walked me home before, however, she was one of the older girls at the church and I felt excited and proud that she just wanted to be with me. I told her about my cherry tree speech and my dollar and a quarter for show and tell. I also showed her the note that my teacher had given me to show my mom and dad for my excellent presentation. We stopped at the corner store, and she bought me a bag of potato chips for doing such a fine job. I was a little chatterbox all the way home.

When we got to my street, I saw cars parked everywhere around my house. Bertha and I walked up my sidewalk; and when I opened the door, the house was filled with people. It was almost like they were there for a big festive party, but ironically, no one was happy. I wondered why all of the solemn faces for what appeared to have been a time of celebration. I looked for my mom, and when I saw her face, I knew that something terrible had happened. Her eyes were bloodshot, and she just looked at me. I remember one of the mothers from the church rushing over and lovingly hugging me and telling me that everything was going to be all right and that God never makes a mistake. I was trying to make some sense out of this madness and confusion. I went over to my mom and asked her why she had been crying, and why all of these people were at our house. The answer that she gave me seemed to have stopped my heart from beating. *My daddy is what? Gone to heaven?*

I have been telling you to fasten your seatbelts, and now I've got to fasten mine securely around me. This was over four decades ago, and I can still feel the turbulence and the bumpy ride from the pain. Death is so cruel and unrelenting. My dad died on George Washington's birthday. He died just as the president did, unexpectedly and peacefully. My daddy was the best part of my waking up. Pardon me while I step away from my computer until I regain my composure.

I was only eight years old, and I didn't fully understand the concept of death, but I had come to realize from my granddad's death that it was irreversible. Even so, I was in denial and was hoping that my dad would get better and come back to me. It is difficult sharing this part of my life with you, but it is important that I not keep silent on my tragedies as well as my triumphs. This is my life, and telling your life story is more effective and has more of an impact on others than merely philosophizing.

Lessons are learned through hard times and it is for us to share with others what life has taught us. It is imperative that we have the rain in order to appreciate the sun. This was a rainy day in my life, and it really felt as if it was raining all over the world. It was a major emotional disruption. Death! There is no compromising, stalling, pleading, and no negotiating. Immortality had turned a deaf ear to the cry of my hurting mother and her fatherless five children. There was denial, shock, guilt, and anger that crowded my mind. I went through the why me and the why him and the why now, which is all a part of the grieving process. Understanding is key, because once that was in place I could handle it a little better without going insane. I had to understand that death was a part of life. There is no way to escape it, and everyone will have an equal opportunity to experience it. That does not take away the pain, but it helps you come to grips with reality.

The hospital administrators asked my mom which funeral home she preferred, and her choice was Haynes Funeral Chapel. Again, because they had no insurance my dad was buried in the least expensive casket that was paid for by the county. The funeral service itself was a blur to my recollection, and I guess I just went through the motions. But what I do remember vividly is that he was buried in what they called the potter's field. I did not fully comprehend at the time, but the potter's field was not a place to be proud of. As a matter of fact, it was a piece of deserted land that was never manicured, where they buried people that were paupers or unknown. To be more explicit, it was a place for the impoverished or extremely poor person who was eligible or depended on the aid from public welfare funds or charity. It was for families that could not afford tombstones or any other type of grave markings, so a six-foot hole was dug and the casket was dumped into the ground, and the weeds would grow over it and make it their home. The snow would fall in the winter and softly cover it, and the location would never be found again. They actually became nameless. I was still very young and did not become cognizant of how embarrassing, humiliating, and demeaning being buried in the potter's field was until years later. The repercussion was devastating.

It was after the dinner gathering, the crowds, the telegrams, the cards, and the phone calls ceased that it finally sunk in that this was not a dream. The reality of it all stared me in the face. There was no aroma of coffee in the mornings to awaken me. I knew that my daddy had left me again, but this time it was forever. I was disappointed and angry because he promised me when I was three years old that he would never leave me again. As a matter of fact, he crossed his heart and hoped to . . . die.

One thing that got my mom and all of us through this tumultuous time was our faith in God, but even with that it was most difficult. Her recovery was slow, but because of her children she had to plow through her sorrow and bravely continue where my dad left off. For a long time, she blamed herself for his death because he had left the decision to have surgery up to her. The consolation and support from her family and friends encouraged her with words that she had done what she thought was best and that there was no need to feel remorse. However, guilt and blame are major parts of the recovering process.

I remember so well the first night that I rolled my hideaway bed out when it was bedtime. I procrastinated as long as I could because I dreaded the inevitable. I was scared to death, and I asked my mom if I could keep the light on in the living room all night. I was fine until it became dark. There was a feeling of anxiety and apprehension that was caused by the seemingly presence or nearness of danger. Clearly, it probably was all imaginative, but it was real enough to cause my heart to beat rapidly. Even with the light on I was afraid—not of my dad returning to harm me—but I was afraid of the boogey man. Imagine the irrational feeling of being traumatized by something that had no specific appearance, but is just an amorphous embodiment of terror. Please do not make light of this because in the mind of a child this is real. Parents (not mine of course) often use the boogey man as a scare tactic when the child has misbehaved, but I had done nothing wrong and the boogey man was after me. There must have been a mistake in identity. I covered my head up with my blanket and counted to five, but it did not alleviate the fear that consumed me. I was petrified of what might have been lurking under my bed, in the closets, scratching at the window, and at the back door, especially when Sisco would bark. I begged my mom to let me sleep with her, and she eventually consented. It's amazing, but I was never afraid of sleeping in the living room until after my daddy died. I always felt safe and secure, and the thought of something going bump in the night never occurred to me. There is an incredible feeling of safety and ultimate security when the father is present. He is the one that insures the safety of his family at the close of the day and answers the knock at the door after dark. And besides all of the other major responsibilities that are incumbent upon the father, no one can change a light bulb and kill spiders like your daddy. My dad was amazing, and he would lay his coat down over a puddle of water so that I would not get my feet wet if he deemed it necessary. He loved his baby girl. But now things were different, and fear was something that seemed to have tried to smother me. I needed someone to watch over me. I had not developed mentally enough to understand the extent of the need that I had for protection, but as I matured I clearly understood. Children need a protector, especially girls. It is something innate that God placed in us to desire the covering of our daddy as we grow up, and then later, the covering of our husband. We are the weaker vessel. Let me clarify that we are not weaker intellectually, neither are men superior intellectually, but they are the gatekeepers of the home and they provide vital protection for the family physically, socially, emotionally, and financially. My mom later admitted that she was just as afraid as I was. Not of the boogey man, but there was an overwhelming fear that she had from just being left alone to cope with all of the responsibilities that providing for a family entailed. She needed someone to watch over her as well.

My dad's death was one of those storms that I gave reference to in the first chapter of this book. His untimely death was sudden and unexpected, just as most storms are. I wish there could have been some warning . . . some indication or sign that something this devastating was going to happen so that I could have been better prepared and emotionally braced myself. But how does one really prepare for death? When I was a little girl outside playing and having a wonderful time, my mom would go to the window and look up at the sky and notice it turning dark in the middle of the day. She also could hear the wind starting to howl. She would call us and warn us to hurry and come in because it was getting ready to storm. I can make the declaration that there is nothing worse than getting caught in a storm. You can be caught in a traffic jam or by a long slow train when you are already late for an important mandatory meeting, or even get caught speeding by the powers that be, but that is nothing in comparison to being caught by a storm. The dark clouds and the strong winds prompted my mom to prepare to seek shelter for us, but there was absolutely no indication of my dad's impending demise.

What exactly is a storm? Well, a storm is an atmospheric disturbance that is characterized by an uncontrollable wind that can travel at the speed of 100 to 250 miles per hour. To make bad matters worse, a storm can be accompanied with blinding rain, thunder, lightning, snow, and hail as large as golf balls. There are several types of storms, which are typhoon twisters, tornadoes, and hurricanes just to name a few. A storm can do some irrevocable damage. They can toss a car around like a piece of paper. They can uproot trees that have been planted for thousands of years and completely demolish houses and skyscrapers. Storms are notorious for claiming the lives of 80 percent of their victims when they first strike because of the lack of preparation and insufficient shelter. None of us were prepared to mentally run for shelter at the time of my dad's death. The pain was severe, and I wanted to lose heart and faint and maybe even die from the grief, but there was something within that sustained me. In spite of the pugnacious winds, and in between the questions and the anger that inundated me I felt confident that when this storm subsided that I would yet be standing and unharmed. The pressure and the tight squeeze of life teach you that. Pressure empowers you with resilience, fortitude, and courage to victoriously roll with the punches of life (even the below-the-belt ones) and stand.

My daddy was my life—he was the best part of my waking up—and there were times that I felt as though I had been knocked down and out for the count, but I was like the palm tree in Florida after it encounters a storm. The ferocious winds cause them to bend all the way to the ground but they seldom break or up root because of their elasticity and their depth. . Although they have fewer roots than many other trees, their roots grow down deep. The roots are searching for two things: a rock and water. When it finds a rock, the roots wrap around the rock, giving them stability, and the water keeps them flourishing. A palm tree is made durable to stand the inevitable inclement weather and so was I. This is an important and interesting parallel. God creates things in nature that we can understand and use as a point of reference to reflect on when we go through challenges in life. At this point in my life my heart was overwhelmed. I felt as if I was on the brink of a cliff but I wrapped what little faith I had left around that rock which is Jesus and the waters of his love immersed me. I hated every minute of the pain from my dad's death, but it was instrumental in crafting me into something beautifully valuable. There is nothing strikingly beautiful or attractive about a palm tree. When I went to Florida a few years ago, I took special note of them. They reminded me of telephone poles in that they grew straight up and taller and distinctive from the other trees. They stood out, but not necessarily because of their beauty. And another interesting and most significant characteristic of the palm tree is that they will not and cannot be repressed. Repress means to stop, hinder, deter, block, impede, or prevent the development of something or someone. Nothing can stop their growth. You can place a heavy stone slab over the spot where a palm tree is sprouting to grow and the result is amazing. It will literally lift the stone up or grow around it and continue its course upward.

I, like the palm tree, am not easily repressed or swerved from the path of my destiny. I refuse to be hindered by the difficulties and unexpected storms that can beset my life. If it is impossible to remove an obstacle from my pathway, I will go around it, go over it, or if necessary, go through it by any means necessary to get to where I am predestined to be. Another interesting thing about the palm tree is you can cut it, but you can't kill it. The nutrients that most trees require in order to survive can be found just below the bark, so when you cut them they die. But not the palm tree; it thrives even under attack. Tropical storms can blow most trees away, but not the palm tree. It is resilient. It bends all the way to the ground and then when the storm is over, it straightens up again and stands at attention, actually stronger.

I mentioned that when the impetuous and tumultuous winds blow, many times the palm trees bend all the way to the ground from the fierceness of the storm. At that point in my young life, I can say that I was level with the ground emotionally. I was under major psychological attack. Mornings were the hardest for me because I missed the bonding time with my dad before he went to work. The first time that I washed the dishes after his death, I opened the cabinet to put them away and my eyes fell on the cup that we drank our coffee out of. I actually became nauseated. After I regained my strength, I held the cup and stared at it for what seemed like hours. I eventually threw the cup away (out of sight out of mind), and I thought that I would be somewhat relieved of the memories and the mental anguish, but that did not alleviate the deep agonizing and tormenting pain. I had to deal with my dad's death and the withdrawal from coffee simultaneously. I was experiencing well-defined symptoms of withdrawal. Caffeine is a stimulant and is not recommended for children. My mother was correct when she tried to discourage my dad from giving me coffee as it could potentially lessen my desire to consume milk, along with other negative effects. Have you ever heard someone say that they can't get started in the morning without that cup of coffee? A review and analysis of the effects of sudden caffeine abstinence claims that the withdrawal symptoms experienced are proof positive of physical dependence. Although my consumption was moderate, it was nonetheless affective, considering my age and biological tolerance. The list of symptoms is exhaustive, i.e. headache, decreased alertness, lethargy, irritability, etc., and also it is argued that the pleasurable aroma and social aspects of coffee are also addictive. Studies show that the onset of withdrawal symptoms typically begins twelve to twenty-four hours after abstinence, the duration ranging from two to nine days. This is a considerable amount of time that makes it easy to understand why people (children especially) would have a difficult time omitting caffeine from their diet. Experts have recommended that anyone looking to decrease and totally abstain from caffeine should do it slowly. Stopping abruptly can result in unpleasant side effects. The remainder of this chapter will be about the devastating side effects that coffee has had on my life, also the proclivities that I encountered due to the broken promise that my dad made . . . he said that he would *never* leave me. The aroma of coffee and sipping it with my daddy was the best part of waking up.

President Eisenhower had promised that if he was elected he would go to Korea and end the war. Well, he kept his word. Over thirty-five thousand Americans had lost their lives, and consequently, my mother lost her job because she made ammunition for that war at the Kingsbury plant. There is a saying that goes when it rains it pours. When my mom lost her job, it seemed as though the clouds were going to block the sun from shining on us forever. She had the house payment to make and all of the other expenses to meet, with no source of income. We also had fallen victim to the insensitivity of the bureaucracy that did not understand that we had just lost our major source of income at the abrupt death of my dad. My mom applied for Social Security. This process was tedious and consisted of a lot of red tape. She was promised that it would eventually be granted, but that it would probably take awhile. They recommended that she apply for emergency assistance from the welfare department until she was able to receive Social Security. Fortunately, we were accepted right away. I still remember that thick peanut butter that came in a big gray can with oil floating on the top and the powdered milk that had to be mixed with water before we drank it. The system was not as lenient as it is today. You could not own anything that they considered to be extravagant such as a car, diamonds, or even a television. There was a case worker that was assigned to everyone, and they closely monitored your purchases on a monthly basis and also made unannounced visits. All of the children in our neighborhood had a television, and my mom eventually saved up enough money to purchase us one so that we could have some entertainment once we finished our homework. It was a Motorola black-and-white set of course. She bought a stand for it to sit on with wheels so that when the caseworker came, we could quickly roll it into one of the bedrooms until she left.

We were too young to be cognizant of the degrading bureaucracy of the system, but my mom was well aware that its primary purpose was to demean the recipients and enrich the administrators. Even the questionnaire suggested that you had to be incompetent and impoverished and also prove that you were unable to work or that your spouse was unable to work. You had to be convincing. But I am of the persuasion that if you can successfully convince your social worker that you are incapable of working, you might eventually convince yourself of the same thing. It appears that it is designed to hold you hostage and stifle your quest for economic independence, thus you become solely dependent upon the system. It can keep you emotionally and psychologically down so long that getting up won't even cross your mind. My mother detested being on welfare, but when you look into the faces of five hungry children you do what is necessary for their survival. Within a few months, our Social Security benefits were approved and my mom said farewell to welfare. My mom was quite a woman, phenomenally.

While growing up in the South, my mom was only permitted to attend school during inclement weather, so consequently she only went as far as the fifth grade. Education was always something that she was adamant about, but picking cotton was an issue that was not negotiable and took precedence over everything as far as the white man was concerned. Her academic skills were limited to say the least, so she had to resort to day work, which consisted of cleaning white people's houses. Because of her meticulous style of cleaning, the word quickly spread in their aristocratic neighborhood, and she eventually had enough work that kept her busy five days a week. My mom cleaned the houses of white people as if they were her own. She cleaned their houses like Michelangelo painted the sunsets. Much thought, passion, professionalism, and energy went into each work day. There was not a speck of dirt left anywhere. There was not a wrinkle left on the clothes that she had to iron. Their breakfasts and lunches were delectably prepared by her to perfection, but sadly she was never invited to dine with them. On rare occasions, they tried to camouflage their discriminatory behavior by offering her the leftovers, but she had to eat in a separate room after they had completed their meals. The pay was fifty cents an hour, which was minuscule, but her immaculate performance did not reflect it. Her tired hands and sore knees were a testament to her diligence, integrity, and commitment. After the end of every long, hard, and unjustly—compensated day when they closed the door behind her, the only debris that still remained in their spic and span clean house was the filth of human abuse, injustice, racial discrimination, and the arrogance of superiority that was deeply embedded in the hearts and minds of the inhabitants. I was proud of my mom. Whenever my teachers or anyone else would ask what my mother did for a living, I responded with a smidge of arrogance that my mom was a domestic engineer. She worked hard and struggled to make ends meet, but she did not make enough to do it. A second job was inevitable.

She applied for a job at a nursing home and was immediately hired. My mom worked from nine in the morning until four in the evening and from ten at night until six the next morning. To say that she was exhausted between jobs would be a gross understatement, but her rigorous schedule was not an option because she had five hungry mouths to feed. I was a lonely girl. I missed my daddy terribly, and I needed my mom immensely. My life was in a whirlwind of unanswered questions, but there was always a small voice that echoed in my soul giving me an answer that this too shall pass. But in the meantime, I needed *someone to watch over me*. My brothers were busy with their friends, and because my mom was not at home, my girlfriends parents would not allow them to come over and play with me because of the lack of adult supervision. I was lonely. I found myself singing. I have been extraordinarily blessed with an incredible gift, and that is what I lost myself in that brought me comfort and satisfaction. I cannot even imagine my life without a song after the death of my dad. My mom eventually purchased an old, secondhand upright piano for me to dabble with to entertain myself, and that is how I spent my evenings after I finished my homework . . . singing and playing the piano. I was born with the passion and talent of singing, and I taught myself how to play the piano well enough to get compensation for it eventually.

I mentioned in the first chapter that my mom poured integrity, resilience, and the meaning of good character into me, which resulted into a good foundation. She did not have much quantity time to accomplish this, but she spent quality time. Hindsight gives me an appreciation of her due diligence, and it paid off as you will discover before my story ends. I would not be the woman that I am today without the unyielding teachings and the role model that my mom was to me. My debt to her is beyond measure.

I will never forget the summer of the same year that my dad died, there was a revival at my church. It is humanly impossible to remember being born and it is humanly impossible to forget being born again. I remember vividly, after the guest evangelist concluded his sermon, he asked if there was anyone that wanted to accept Christ as their personal Savior. With tears streaming down my face, I raised my hand. Many might have thought that I was rather young to make such a commitment, but I was always very serious about God. I would be remiss if I didn't admit to some mischievous misbehaving after that wonderful experience because after all, I was only a child, but the seed was planted and I assure you that God, along with my mom's chastening, kept it watered and the seed grew exponentially. That spiritual encounter kept me grounded through my fatherless, tumultuous adolescent years.

It was almost a year that had passed when my mom began hearing a rumor that my dad was not accidentally injured on his job. She was only able to gather bits and pieces, and she knew that there was only one person that could give her a firsthand account of what had actually transpired and that was Simon, my dad's friend. It seems to be a fact that when gossip involves you, you are the last to hear it. Simon had seen my mom waiting for the bus after she had gotten off from work on many occasions and had offered her a ride, but she always refused. My mother was devoutly religious and did not want to become a victim of whispers and scandal and neither did she want to place herself in a compromising position. She was a beautiful young woman, and men were coming out of the woodwork to befriend her, but I will attest that she always carried herself in such a way that any daughter could model after. One day Simon offered her a ride and she accepted. Her reason was to ask him what really had happened that day of my dad's accident. She mentioned to him about the rumors that she had been hearing. He appeared shocked and reassured her that he had witnessed the entire thing and that it was, in fact, an accident. He made some subtle overtures about wanting to keep her company when she became lonely. She reminded him that he was a married man and that she was insulted. He smiled sheepishly and apologized. The ride home was quiet and uncomfortable. As time passed, my mom saw Simon often. Even while carrying heavy groceries, she refused his periodic offers to take her home. One evening she was walking from the bus stop near home and she heard a car horn blowing. Initially she ignored it, but it was quite persistent, and she stopped to see who it was and it was Simon. He pulled the car over and parked and motioned for my mom to get in because he needed to talk with her. The look on his face was serious and did not suggest any ulterior motives, so my mom got in the car. He sat there stoically without saying one word. He just stared at her while nervously gripping the steering wheel. When he noticed that she was becoming frightened, he reassured her that he had no intentions of harming her but that he just needed to talk. With a trembling voice, he asked my mom if she remembered the time that they lived in Blytheville and she walked in on my dad sitting on the woman's bed down the road from their house. Of course she remembered, but she was shocked that he knew about it. Before she answered, she asked him what the interrogation was all about. He was shaking, but he proceeded to tell her that she was not the only one that had caught them together, but that he had caught them together also, but only in the very act. He told my mom that my dad had taken the only woman that he had ever loved and ever wanted to marry. "Leroy was my best friend and he knew that I was madly in love with her, and he took her just because he could," Simon said as he seemed to have been reliving the resurrected pain. My mom was speechless. "Beatrice, my conscience is eating away at me and I have to tell you exactly what happened. I never forgave Leroy and I never got married. I have a common-law wife that I have lived with for years, but I never really loved her. When I heard that Leroy had moved to South Bend, I moved here shortly after. I found out that he was working at the metal company and I applied there and was hired. I guess you might say that I was obsessed with him and had become a stalker. One day, Leroy and I had a man-to-man talk about it on our lunch break, and he made light of sleeping with my woman. He said that men will be men, and that it really meant nothing to him. He mentioned that it had occurred so long ago that he scarcely remembered it. Beatrice, Leroy was a handsome man and had a lot of women. Why did he have to sleep with mine?" Simon told my mom that he was never able to get the image of my dad in the bed with his lover out of his mind. He secretly vowed to get him if it was the last thing that he did. One morning he saw my dad bending over to pick up something and from the upper level, Simon dropped a piece of heavy metal on his head that weighed enough to split his head open. After my mom regained her composure from this emotionally disturbing news, she thanked him for finally bringing some closure to this dreadful event. She told him that he would have been a ruthless, gutless maniac with no mental compass if he had never disclosed this secret. He asked my mom what her plans were as far as reporting this to the police, and after she thought about it, she told him that she would only share it with her children. She added that if reporting this crime would bring her husband back, she would not hesitate to do it. My mom's reasoning and wisdom transcends anyone that I have ever known. She made it succinctly clear that her decision was by no means based upon the desire to spare him from any justifiable punishment, but it was to protect her and her children from being publicly exposed to our father's improprieties. She told him that she also wanted to protect her dead husband. Even though my dad was somewhere in a plot of land where they buried people that were perceived as insurgent and having no intrinsic value to mankind, he still meant the world to her. She had an endless love for the wonderful man that he had become and wanted to protect him even after death. I guess that really gives credence to the fact that it doesn't really matter *where you lay your head* after you leave this world. Your value and worth are not predicated upon wealth, prestige, and fame. That is superficial. If you have integrity, character, and love for all mankind and your family, you are somebody—even in the potter's field.

My mom now had the awesome task of breaking this disturbing news to her children. Most of my brothers were in their teens by then, and my mom had multifaceted responsibilities of juggling two jobs, nurturing, reinforcing, attending to our physical as well as emotional needs, PTA meetings (schools definitely respond differently when they know that you take your children's education seriously), and administering discipline. My brothers were mischievous boys, and their focus was now vacillating between outrageous urges for girls and breaking windows. The absence of the father in the home, whether it be by abandonment, divorce, or death, can affect boys significantly because they need that authoritative figure to mentor them and guide them on their challenging journey to manhood. The father is the head, which is the command center. That is the order and the way that God planned it. Children need structure and limits, and the father spares the unfair burden of the mother parenting alone. The death of my dad disrupted the flow of parenting, but my mom often reminded my brothers and me not to concentrate on his absence, but her presence. That did not negate the fact that he was sorely needed, but we had to play the hand that life had dealt us as best as we could. It was difficult telling us that our father had been, in all actuality, murdered. She was candid with us and told us exactly what precipitated the murder. My brothers' emotions were almost uncontrollable and went from anger to rage. They plotted to kill Simon and they expressed to my mom how they were going to do it. They needed to vent. The wound from our past emotional trauma was slowly healing, but had now been profoundly ripped open again, and the excruciating pain went to the core of our existence, only this time it was compounded with murder. My mom was so consumed with being our psychoanalyst, psychologist, and psychiatrist until she broke down from exhaustion. She lost her emotional equilibrium. The voice of the little girl at the well was crying out from inside of this strong, phenomenal woman. She needed someone to console her. She had her sisters and brothers and church family, and they did what they could, but their words of consolation could not bring solace to her internal emotional pain. Their presence could not fill the emptiness, and their embraces could not satisfy the hunger. She was gracious to them but . . . she needed her husband. She tried to remain strong for her children. I caught her sobbing one day, and I put my little arms around her as a sensitive daughter would do and naïvely asked her what was wrong. In essence, this is what she said,

There is someone I'm longing to see
I sure wish that he
Could turn out to be
Someone to watch over me

I'm a lamb
That is lost in the woods

I know I could

Always be good

To Leroy who'd watch over me

Won't you tell him to put on some speed

And come back to me

Oh how I need

Someone to watch over me.

She desperately yearned for his determination, courage, strength, direction, provision, and love. She knew that Simon had the wrong perception of her husband. Contrary to what he thought, the new Leroy's ultimate fantasy had no longer been a night of passionate love-making with the most beautiful woman on the planet, but rather by the help of Christ and a loving Proverbs 31 wife, his priorities had shifted. He had become a faithful husband and father with a will, confidence, and strength to overcome any obstacle that was set before him.

All hell broke loose. My brothers promised my mom that they would not retaliate against Simon, but instead they acted out their anger by rebelling and associating with the wrong crowd. Boys are two or three times more likely to end up in jail as adults without the guidance and supervision of a father. They are also less likely to graduate because of low grade point averages. My brother Jimmy was the only one that refrained from juvenile delinquencies. You can count on one hand and probably have fingers left the amount of times that he gave my mother trouble. Instead, he vented out his anger and frustration in another manner. Because he was underage, he asked a neighbor to forge my mom's signature and he enlisted in the marines at the age of fourteen. Without a doubt, the marines is the toughest, most challenging branch of the service, both mentally and physically. Boot camp alone was strenuous enough to make a grown man cry, and he was only a child. God protected him in his inappropriate, nonsensical reasoning because his intentions were good. First of all, he wanted to escape from his painful environment, and then he wanted to earn money to send back home to assist my mom with the financial challenges that she was grappling with. She was determined not to lose the home that she and my dad had worked so hard to buy. My brother consistently sent her money every time that he received a check. In addition to that, he took advantage of the educational opportunities, and after four years of faithful service to his country he received an honorable discharge. That speaks volumes to his level of maturity, discipline, and determination. After he returned home from the service, he felt the need to continue his education, so he enrolled at Saints Junior College in Lexington, Mississippi. After two years, he graduated.

My other brothers had a psychological chip on their shoulders and felt that the world owed them something for robbing them of their dad, and they intended to be compensated for it by any means necessary. They felt indescribable anguish, and all but clinical madness. They were in and out of correctional facilities until they finally realized that although this world is not fair, it didn't owe them anything but an equal opportunity. They eventually came to the conclusion through trial and error that if they wanted to become men of distinction and purpose, they had to learn to distinguish the trash from the treasures, accept what they could not change, responsibly pick themselves up by their own bootstraps, and go forward with dignity. Sometimes we are guilty of spending more time looking out of the window instead of looking in the mirror. While looking out of the window, if you have no will power, you have the tendency to focus on people that have an erroneous view of life and you can ultimately become what you see. If you see bitterness, you become bitter, if you see hatred, you hate, and if you see killing, you kill. But when you look in the mirror, you should see an image staring back at you, telling you undeniably that you don't have to be a product of your environment, but that you can revolutionize it instead. As the late Michael Jackson said It starts with the man in the mirror. He has to change his ways. No message could be any clearer. There are two voices in life. One tells you that you can't, and the other tells you that you can. They are both right. Go figure.

Before I share with you my challenges that surfaced as the result of my dad's death, I would like to mention my brother Wilburd's oppositions. Wilburd had a kind heart and was easily persuaded to do wrong in order to be accepted. I believe that your selection of friends (peer pressure) is crucial because association brings about assimilation. Your choice of friends can impact your life either positively or negatively. For him, it was the latter.

One night, Wilburd was out joyriding with his best friend. They stopped at a gas station, and my brother's friend told him to wait in the car until he returned. What transpired after that has impacted and affected my brother's life until this very day. Wilburd was not aware that his friend had a gun and that his intentions were to rob the service station. The robbery went bad, and his friend ended up shooting and killing the owner. When he returned to the car he was emotionally distraught, and he told my brother that he had shot a man and that he thought he was dead. They sped off in the car and my brother vowed secrecy in order to protect his friend. They were only naïve teenagers and they both were products of troubled homes. This is not a justification, but merely an explanation. A few days had gone by without it being discovered, and they did not realize that the detectives were on their job. My brother's conscience was eating away at him, and one day Wilburd asked me hypothetically that if I would report someone that I knew had killed somebody. I was scared to death because I thought that he was referring to Simon (the man that killed my father) and I told him that I didn't think that I would. I did not realize the dangerous predicament that my brother was in. Within a week or so, his friend was arrested and charged with murder, and they arrested my brother as an accomplice. Even though my brother did not pull the trigger, in the eyes of the law he was just as guilty as his friend because he did not report it. They considered him an accessory-after-the-fact. His friend was sentenced to life in prison without parole. He was a teenager, and he remains in prison today. His opportunities for freedom and to exist in normalcy were frozen for the rest of his life. My brother's lawyer argued convincingly to the jury that his defendant was not aware that his friend's intention was to rob and murder, and he received a more lenient sentence of twenty-five years to life. This horrendous crime was committed by young colored boys in the '60s, and the man that was killed was a white family man. Needless to say, it made the front page of the *South Bend Tribune* paper. I cannot begin to tell you the hurt, embarrassment, shame, and disgrace that my mother and I suffered. But that is the consequence for being in the wrong place at the wrong time with the wrong person.

I told you at the beginning of this autobiography that life for me ain't been no crystal stairway. I have tasted the sweet thrill of victory, but I have also shaken hands with the agony of defeat. But my foundation, which precipitated integrity, tenacity, and character was my stabilizing force and has kept me grounded. I have my mom and my early religious convictions to thank for that. Check your seat belt and make certain that it is securely fastened because there will be some turbulence until we rise above the storm.

It has been decades since the gruesome murder of my dad, but I have come to the resolve that some things you never get over, but you just get through. It is a nightmare from which I am still trying to wake up. I will always be a daddy's girl. A girl gets the message from her dad that she is special, loved, beautiful, and valuable. She receives approval and validation from him, and if he is absent, those needs are transferred to someone else. Girls who face life without the first man in their lives struggle to develop a sense of their own self-worth and often confuse Eros love for the love of their father. Researchers suggest that girls may respond to father absences with personality changes that lead them to form early and unstable bonding with older men. Not for sexual reasons, but simply because of the craving for the father image to occupy that void. Little girls need the love of their mothers, but they are innately hardwired to be loved by their daddies.

There is also something else that warrants your consideration and that is children don't just look like their parents, but they also inherit their personality characteristics. If the father has internal drives to be promiscuous and is a risk taker and has difficulty maintaining emotional attachments, then his son, or perhaps even his daughter, will have similar passions, behaviors, and eventually, social disruptions. These are just facts in life that have to be dealt with intelligently and soberly without being judgmental. The window of opportunity for exploitation was wide open because I was always alone. I started developing by the age of twelve. I was innocently blossoming into a very attractive teenager. I carried myself in a mature way because of the plethora of emotional trauma that had impacted my life, and consequently older men gravitated to me. We never had a car, so I was always mesmerized by them. I remember my first very frightening experience was when my neighbor, Quincy—who was twenty-three at the time, and very nice and respectable I might add—purchased a brand new red convertible. He observed me watching him wash his car one evening and asked if I would like to take a spin after he finished. Of course I said yes, and he let the top down and away we went, taking in the warm breeze. I was bright-eyed and ecstatic. A cab was just about the only car that I had ever been in, so a convertible was almost too good to be true and over the top. It was a hot summer night and people were outside sitting on their porches and enjoying the weather. Everyone was admiringly watching us with envy as we cruised around in our neighborhood. When we got to one particular corner, he spotted one of his male friends, and he asked Quincy if he could join us and he said yes. He eventually picked up two other young men and they all sat in the back.

I was enjoying the ride, but I started noticing that we were no longer in the city and were headed toward the country. I was young, but I sensed that I was in a detrimental environment. He eventually stopped the car, and all of them got out. I heard them whispering, and then Quincy raised the hood with the pretense of having car trouble. I sat there alone, trembling, not having a clue as to what their intentions were. Within a few minutes, I heard Quincy say, "No, we can't do that. She is my neighbor, and she is a young naïve church girl. And not only that, her brothers are dangerous and her mother will kill me. I have got to get this girl back home." I do not believe that Quincy's idea to rape me was premeditated. As a matter of fact, I think that it was the furthest thing from my neighbor's mind when I first got into the car. But somehow he was swayed in his intentions. I came into the knowledge later that they intended to pull the train on me, which means that each of the men would take turns having sex with me. Why they would want to traumatize a young girl with that extent of abuse baffles me. Maybe it was because they had been abused themselves and consequently understood the terror of being the helpless victim from their own childhood experiences. Quite often, when the abused grow up they reverse the role and become the abuser. They are now in control. I was too young to rationalize their disorders. They might have had an anti-social or narcissistic personality disorder or may have been under the influence of drugs or alcohol or just angry or they may have misconstrued my motives and thought that my mere presence gave consent. I am clueless. I am just grateful that I was spared from that inhuman, humiliating act that might have caused irrevocable mental damage to me the rest of my life. I did not always have someone to physically watch over me, but God was always very present to protect me in my irrational choices. There is a saying that goes fool me once, shame on you; fool me twice, shame on me.

While growing up, my mom continuously reminded me that I was a special miracle and that she wanted me to make something great out of my life. She warned me that I should not let surface issues derail me and that I should not succumb to short-term thinking. She envisioned me being successful. Education was something that she did not have the opportunity to get, and she stressed that it was one of the keys that would unlock the door to my success. I said *one of the keys* because not having a degree in nuclear physics is no indication that you will ultimately become a failure in life. One of the richest, most successful persons that I know only has a high school diploma. His name is John Arnold and he holds two major patents; one is the software used by eBay and Amazon.com to track sales, and the other is the technology that allows your cell phone to connect to the internet. These patents have made him a millionaire twenty times over, and he barely graduated from high school. But this is the exception and not the rule. Education is crucial. I had a golden opportunity and she did not want me to squander it. I remember every morning getting up to go to school without my mom there to coax me. The alarm clock of self-discipline woke me up and alerted me that playing hooky was not an option, neither was it negotiable nor debatable. There was only one time that I struggled in going to school, and that was when my brother, Wilburd, was charged with accessory to murder of a white man. The day after it hit the newspaper, I went to school and the children where snickering and whispering. One of the boys in my class started making the sound of a gun with his mouth, and I ran out of my classroom in tears, and I did not return for the rest of the week. I was so hurt and embarrassed. One of the girls from my church stayed home with me, and we cried and played bingo all day just to get through the pain. Mentally, I felt as if I had almost been pushed over the edge. It was my foundation, resilience, tenacity, and just knowing deep inside that I was still somebody and that this too shall pass were the only things that kept me going. I can only imagine the agony that my mom was experiencing because she had to face the white people that she worked for, and she did not have the option of missing work because money was a rare commodity in our house.

Many times, I only had bread and mayonnaise or bread and butter with sugar sprinkled on top and sometimes welfare peanut butter and bread to eat when I came home for lunch. You had to drink water after eating that peanut butter or you would choke almost to death. Just a bit of humor. Sometimes the refrigerator and cabinets were bare, but I knew that my mom was doing the best that she could to make ends meet, and I did not complain. As a matter of fact, I used my vivid imagination and would tell my friends that I had hot dogs, tuna, or a ham sandwich when I returned to school. I can honestly say that although times were rough, God never let us starve. One specific evening, my mom had absolutely nothing to cook. I remember her getting out the pots and a skillet and putting them on the stove. She told me to get out the plates and silverware and set the table. Everything was all there except one key component—the food. My mom prayed and exercised her faith in that manner a multiplicity of times, and I promise you that within a few hours there was always either a knock on the door or the phone would ring, and it would be someone with enough food to last us for a week. There was one time that there was absolutely no food in the house and my mom was scraping pennies so that she could go to the corner store and buy something for her and me to eat. Out of the clear blue, I remembered that I had put the dollar and a quarter under my mattress that my dad had given me for my presentation on George Washington's birthday. I was suppose to have given it back to him when I returned from school, but that was the day that he was maliciously injured on his job and later died. I secretly hid it as a keepsake, and because of the following days of emotional trauma, I forgot that I had it. God moves in mysterious ways because when we were in dire need for it, I remembered. It was difficult for my mom to spend it once I told her the surrounding circumstances, but I spoke wisdom and said, "Mom, Dad is still watching over us and providing for us even from his grave." That evening's dinner was quite sentimental and special.

I had no sisters, so there were no hand-me-down pretty dresses to wear, and we were too poor to shop, so my mom would bring home bags of brand-name designer clothes that the wealthy people that she worked for had set outside for the Salvation Army to pick up. Fate would have it that they had daughters that just happened to have been my age and size, and my mom and I became the Salvation Army. When they discovered that my mom was bringing the clothes home, they lavishly gave her more. I wore them with pride—and my physical attributes accentuated them—and no one ever knew the difference. I was young and not cognizant of jealous people. The clothes that I wore as I got into my teens had begun to stir up an incredible atmosphere of envy in the church. I was already lonely and craving for love and friends, but instead I was criticized and ostracized even the more. Little did they know . . . my designer expensive clothes had been gently worn and recycled. A vicious rumor started that my mom was doing some clandestine things to make the money in order to purchase such extravagant clothes for me. They surmised that her being a domestic engineer couldn't possibly have afforded us with such extravagance. It eventually got back to me, and I was hurt, confused, and disappointed that church people could have such contentious, suspicious hearts and manufacture vicious, degrading lies. I was quite visible in the church because of my incredible talent to sing, and I was constantly in the forefront, which exacerbated the situation. Fortunately my foundation (integrity) and tenacity that my mom incessantly instilled in me kept me focused and allowed me to somehow keep my head in spite of others losing theirs, and I ignored the whispers. That was just the beginning of the plethora of persecutions that I encountered for just being me. It seemed as though I was inevitably just picked out to be picked on. I encouraged myself by saying that the best flowers are always picked . . . on. I have discovered that when greatness awaits you, there are things that you just have to suffer through. Ironically, those things help to condition, test, prove, and most significantly, empower you. You just have to know how to make the best out of a bad situation and how to take a licking and keep on ticking. I had to weave my way through the perplexities of the nightmares of anxiety and the misty flat of this poignant juncture. I knew deep down in my knower that what was to come was going to greater than what had been. A lemon is a pungent fruit, but you can make some wonderful delectable things out of it . . . lemonade would be one.

Something a bit melancholy and comical and perhaps even nonsensical to some, but nevertheless, I would like to share it with you as I proceed into my final chapters. One evening when my mom came home from work with one of those Salvation Army gift bags, I searched through it anxiously and excitedly, and besides the wonderful clothes, I also found a nice lacey slip and two pairs of fancy underpants. Many years ago, mothers that could afford it would buy expensive colorful panties for their girls that had the days of the week stitched on each pair. That was a luxury, I promise you, and a quantum leap from the cotton, tattered ones that I wore. In my desperate search in the bag, I only found a pair for Monday and Thursday. They were so fancy and I was proud to own just the two pairs, but I vowed that one day I was going to save up enough money to buy the complete set and have a pair for each day of the week, and I did. I sold lemonade in front of my house on hot summer days to do it . . . Where there is a will, there is a way.

I would be remiss not to mention a godsend who observed our sufferings and shared his bounty with us. There was a minister extraordinaire from

Milwaukee, Wisconsin, named pastor Charles Upchurch that my pastor, Bishop Davis, had taken under his wing to mentor. Through his frequent visits to South Bend, he heard me sing and my brother, Jimmy, play his guitar, and he fell in love with both of us. He became our godfather in every sense of the word. Because he was financially stable, he made sure that we had the necessities. There were times that he even paid my mom's past-due mortgages and my school tuitions. I went to several proms, and he purchased each gorgeous dress. I periodically spent my summer vacations in Milwaukee, visiting him and his lovely wife, Clara. They spoiled me to life. God was always there to provide that which was needed to sustain us.

One morning, the aroma of coffee awakened me, and for a fleeting moment I just knew that I heard my daddy in the kitchen making his Hills Brothers coffee. I could taste it. Lots of cream and a little sugar. I sat straight up on my hideaway bed. The mind is powerful because . . . it was only a dream. Dreaming is somewhat like a computer saving files to the hard drive. It is a mechanism that allows us to recapture what we have done, and it is also a result of series of images, ideas, thoughts, and emotions that we subconsciously desire to do. Psychoanalysts tell the cause of dreams as the suppressed desires of the dreamer. The day that I threw the cup away that my dad and I shared to drink our coffee out of was the day that I unconsciously began suppressing my desire for coffee. I did not have the aroma to haunt me because no one in my house drank coffee; however, I continued to have that same reoccurring dream. Dreamland is amazing because there are no limits and no boundaries. I anxiously looked forward to those nights when my dad and I would share coffee together. That was the *worst* part of waking up. I kept it to myself, because after all . . . it was only a dream.

Chapter 6

I'm a Survivor

I am not certain how Beyoncé came up with such a meaningful song "Survivor," but it speaks volumes and best depicts my relentless determination while growing up. To survive means to remain alive or exist despite being exposed to life-threatening danger. A survivor is someone with great powers of endurance who shows a will to live or a great determination to overcome, despite the hardships and traumas of life. When the Continental Connection Flight 3407 crashed near Buffalo, New York, doctors, surgeons, and specialists were asked to remain at the hospital even after their shift was over because they thought that the extra assistance would be needed. Why? Because they were expecting and anticipating survivors. Regretfully, and certainly through no intentional fault of the occupants, there were none. However, there was another plane, US Air Flight 1549, that struck at least one bird and had to emergency land in the chilly Hudson River. All 155 orderlies walked out of that plane and stood on the wings of what I would unequivocally call hope, and all survived. I emphatically say without apprehension that they stood on the wings of hope because there is no other explanation as to how 155 people could stand on the wings of an airplane and not sink without the miraculous power of our Creator intervening. The president of the United States—who was President Bush at the time—said that he was inspired by the skill and the heroism of the flight crew and the rescue teams. Enormous praise was heaped on the pilot, Chesley "Sully" B.

Sullenberger; and he emerged as a hero in the eyes of the passengers, family members, officials, and aviation experts. My hat is off to him as well because a pilot does not practice water landings, and the sheer expertise and choices that he demonstrated were amazing. However, it was God that was underneath, sustaining that plane, and I recognize that for those that do not. Enough said!

I, too, am a survivor. I am allergic to failure. I had to persevere and survive through the incredible crashes of my life. I had to survive through the pain from the senseless murder of my dad and other extenuating circumstances. My life was dark and void of color. I never thought that I would see color or light again, but that is how it is while you are driving through a tunnel. In order to survive, I had to look straight ahead, knowing that there would be light and color at the end. I suppose restricted sight, such as tunnel vision, is not always a negative, nor is peripheral vision always a positive. Side attractions can become distractions and cause you to lose focus of your purpose. I am most grateful for the gift that God gave me to sing. Life for me without a song would best be compared to Flight 3407 or an airplane that has run out of fuel or a poem that doesn't rhyme or even a clock that does not tell time. I have often wondered why a nightingale waits until night to sing, or a teakettle waits until the boiling point to produce that high-pitched wonderful song. Anyone can sing on a bright sunshiny day, but to sing when the sun has hidden itself behind the dark clouds of the perplexities of life is incredibly challenging, but quite effective. And the teakettle does not sing until it is up to its neck in hot boiling water. There is nothing that compares to that sound, but the combination of heat and pressure is what produces it. I compare my colorless life after the death of my dad with the nightingale and the boiling teakettle but I SURVIVED!

When I was fourteen years old, I was asked to sing at the McCormick Place in Chicago along with my church choir. I lead a song, and the audience responded with a standing ovation, tears, and a thunderous applause. There was an enormous amount of people that met me backstage and commented that there was something unusual and penetrating about my voice. That is because the singing emanated not only from my melodious vocal cords, but from the recesses of my soul out of excruciating pain, experience, and also incredible joy. I knew then that I had been extremely blessed with a gift, and that I would literally sing my way through life in order to survive. I sang in the rain. No one offers you an umbrella to stand under with them when you really need one. I also sang through the pain. That's when you are able to successfully hit your best notes.

I still marvel at how focused I was to get up every morning and go to school without supervision. I had every opportunity in the world to be delinquent and involve myself in deviant behavior, but that was not an option for me. The risk is there, but many single mothers are successful at raising confident, responsible girls who go through adolescence with just the normal concerns, and I am one of them. My mother continuously stressed the importance of education, and I did not want to disappoint her or myself. I know unequivocally that it was because of my foundation. Having someone to watch over you as you grow is crucial, but when you don't have that significant component, that's when your integrity and character keep you grounded and sustain you. Remember I said earlier that integrity and character are who you are when no one is looking? I had already been labeled and counted as a girl that would become a statistic because of unfavorable circumstances that had occurred in my family. In addition to that, people—particularly females—have a tendency to judge you and form false preconceived ideas and conjure up devious motives in terms of your intentions, especially if you are an attractive girl. I call them character assassinators that do not have a life. Your very presence creates an element of suspicion. They automatically assume that your looks prevent you from being intelligent, as if brains and beauty are diametrically opposed to one another. But you cannot judge a book by its cover. It's the content that determines the intrinsic value or worth of the book.

Please know that while growing up, I was not perfect . . . well almost. Children will be children, and I did have an extracurricular habit that I engaged in when my mom was not looking. I loved rock and roll and dancing. That was something that the Pentecostal persuasion was diametrically opposed to. There was a place called the recreation center that was two blocks from my house that had chaperoned dances for teenagers every Thursday night. When my mother would leave for her second job, I would finish my homework, get dressed, and add the finishing touch of Revlon lipstick—which was also forbidden—and away I would go. I had a favorite partner named Otis Davis that knew how to synchronize with me, and our moves were so captivating that everyone would disengage in their dancing and form a circle around Otis and me. On this particular night, we were getting our groove on and I heard someone say, "Jennifer, your mom is coming in the door with a switch as tall as me." A switch was a limb that was cut off a tree and vigorously applied to your behind by your mom or dad when you were disobedient. How in the world did my mom know that I was at the dance, and why wasn't she at work like she was supposed to have been? Well, I was totally embarrassed because she applied her "it" right there in the presence of all of my friends, and I ran all the way home with her on my trail, applying the switch whenever she was lucky enough to catch me. Little did I know that my neighbor James Quincy—yes, the one that took me for a ride in his convertible—had been watching me all the time and knew that I was sneaking off to the dance. He snitched on me. I never went back to the recreation center, but there was another time that I ventured off into some deviant behavior.

There was a teen dance at the YMCA that was sponsored by my junior high class and, surprisingly, my mother consented for me to go. There was an older, very handsome, and popular boy in high school (a senior) that attended my church named Bob Graham. He had a mad crush on me. I was much too young to date, so I thought that that would be a perfect time to sneak away with him. I told him where I would be, and the plan was that he would pick me up from the dance and have me back before the chaperone noticed that I was gone. Mrs. Witherspoon, who was my teacher just happened to have been one of the chaperones, and she saw me when I left. Needless to say, she immediately called my mom and told her that I had left, but fortunately Bob had me back before my mom could get a ride, and my teacher called her back to tell her that I had returned. Surprisingly, my mom did not spank me. I told her who I was with, and she was quite fond of the Graham family. She chastised me and put me on punishment, but that was worse than a spanking. It was an innocent adventure (on my part) in my estimation. He took me for ice cream and brought me right back, however, I'm certain that the next time or two he probably would have attempted other things. It just always seemed like I could never get away with anything like other girls. I always got caught. I hated Mrs. Witherspoon, who incidentally is now Dr. Witherspoon-Hall and currently resides in Ft. Wayne, Indiana. I made it known that I detested her for years. Last year, my husband and I saw her and her husband in Memphis, Tennessee at our COGIC convention and we had dinner together. I asked her to forgive me, and we laughed about it all evening. Ironically, there was always someone to watch over me even when I didn't necessarily need their observance. But, it was for my good.

When I was sixteen years old, I had to sing in Detroit, Michigan, at a National Youth Convention, and I must say that I did a bumper job with the Lord's help. After I finished singing, a handsome young man with hazel eyes named Ronald Fitzgerald introduced himself to me, and it was love at first sight for both of us. I was a senior, and he had graduated from high school and had plans to go into the navy. He lived in Gary, Indiana (the home of Michael Jackson), which was only about sixty-five miles from South Bend. My mom was pleased with me dating him because he was an exceptionally nice young churchman who just happened to have been the nephew of the bishop of Northern Indiana. Within a few months, he asked my mom if he could marry me, and although she thought that we were moving a bit fast, she gave us her blessings. On Christmas day, he presented me with an engagement ring. I was ecstatic. Our plans were for me to enroll in college after graduation, and we would get married after he got out of the navy in two years. I very proudly showed off my diamond to my classmates and especially to my friends at church. They knew Ronald very well because we fellowshipped with his church in Gary, and everyone thought that we were the perfect cute little couple. He enlisted in the navy and left for Norfolk, Virginia, and I busied myself with my last year of school, singing, and making wedding plans. Ron visited me as often as he could after he finished training, and we were very excited about getting married. Graduation day came and my mom was beaming with joy. To see me in my cap and gown and receive my diploma with honors was a dream come true for her. I persevered through some rough times and had to navigate through some treacherous waters, but I remained focused.

My brother, Jimmy, had gotten married and was living in Warren, Ohio, and since I had finished school, I wanted to go there and spend the summer with him and his wife. They were expecting their first baby, and I stayed there for three months until their baby (Kim) was born. While there, of course, I found a wonderful church to attend, which was the St. James COGIC. My brother had mentioned to someone that I had an amazing voice, and one Sunday they asked me to sing before the pastor preached. In the audience was a recording producer/artist from Motown that was visiting, and after church he introduced himself to me and complimented me on my singing. He asked me if I ever considered going secular because there was little money in singing gospel, and he said that with my talent, persona, and looks, I would be famous and wealthy in no time. As he was talking, I could just see my name in neon lights with lots of money and all of the other added fringe benefits that went along with it. I also imagined buying my mom a car that she so desperately needed and deserved. I told him that I was very much interested and that I was going home within a few days. He said that he was on his way to Chicago to perform in a show, and he asked if he could stop by on his way and discuss it further with my mom since I was so young. I explained to him that my mom was devoutly religious and that I would have to get her opinion and approval before accepting his offer.

I will never forget the evening that he stopped by. I had given my mom a heads up, and we both were expecting his visit. My mom listened to him very politely and attentively until he was finished and then she responded. First of all, she thanked him for recognizing the God-given talent that I had and then she told him her testimony about her desire to have a girl after having five boys consecutively. She told him that she prayed and that God miraculously turned me from a boy to a girl in her womb and that there was no way that she would give me permission to sing for anyone but him. I can still see the startled look on his face as he looked me up and down, obviously trying to fathom how such metamorphosis could have transpired. I can also still feel the blood that rushed to my face, turning it red from embarrassment. She noticed that he was uncomfortable, and she graciously added that although she disagreed with his proposition, the decision was ultimately up to me. That was wisdom personified. My mom was confident of that which she had poured into me from a little girl, and she trusted the criteria. When you train up a child in the way that they should go, even if they depart, they will return. In life I believe that everyone comes to a fork in the road. The decision that we make at that juncture can have a major impact on our lives forever. The room was silent, and he stood up to leave because he knew that my answer was going to be no. I have often wondered where I would be today had I said yes. My girlfriend, the incredible recording artist Deniece Williams, sang with me in the choir. Someone from the secular industry heard her dynamic voice, approached her, and made her an offer, but she said yes. Her life has vacillated from fame to misfortune ever since. To each his own.

My church, Saints Memorial COGIC, where I made my first solo debut at the age of three, was known for having the greatest choir in Northern Indiana and the surrounding areas as well. We had recorded an album and were very much in demand. We traveled extensively giving concerts, and on every fourth Sunday, we had a musical in the afternoon that was phenomenal. Our large church was always packed from wall to wall, and I just happened to have been one of the lead singers in the choir along with Johnnie Davis and Marcella Jones-Preston.

One Sunday evening after the musical, my girlfriend, Delores Stewart, and I were hungry; so we got in her car and went to McDonald's for a cheeseburger, fries, and of course, a Coke. I was exhausted from singing, so I asked her to go in and get it, and I would just wait in the car. She immediately said that if I didn't go with her that she was not going. I was starved, so I acquiesced. When we got in the line, there was a young man that had gotten his order and was standing around, obviously just to check out the girls because he immediately came up to me and asked where I had been with my fine self all of his life. I ignored him because I smelled liquor on his breath. He was persistent and continued to pursue me.

"South Bend is a small city. Why haven't I run into you at any of the clubs?" he asked.

I very flippantly answered, "'Cause I don't go to clubs, I go to church."

"Wow, so you're one of those church girls."

"Yes, I am."

"Well, I sure would like to go to church with you sometime, but it would not be to get to know God, baby. It's going to be so I can get with you. My name is Ron Hoston, and I sure would like to get to know you better."

As we were leaving, he followed us out to the car and asked for my phone number. I rattled off my number just to get rid of him. He wrote it down on the bag that his food was in. I honestly did not believe that he would call me; and furthermore, I really did not want him to because, after all, I was engaged to be married. When I walked in the door, my phone was ringing, and it was that Ron guy. I quickly told him that I was engaged and that I knew that he had noticed the ring on my finger. He joked about the diamond being so small that he would have needed a microscope to see it. For some reason, we both laughed. We talked for hours. It was something about him that captivated me. He asked if he could come over to see me, and I reminded him again that I was engaged and that my fiancé was in the navy. He was nevertheless persistent, and I could not bring myself to hang up on him. "I am not going to let you go until you say I can come over." I finally said yes, and I gave him a time to come when my mom would be home as a safety precaution. I found myself actually looking forward to his visit. I went out of my way to look beautiful. My mom did not understand why I was receiving a gentleman caller when I was in fact engaged, but she graciously went along with my decision. The doorbell rang, and when I opened the door, there stood a man that obviously had stopped by the liquor store and drank too much before he got to my house. I was reluctant to introduce him to my mom in that condition, but since he was there and really meant nothing special to me, I proceed with the introduction. I felt pity for him because he was trying extremely hard to be on his best behavior while under the influence of alcohol. He wasn't drunk but just tipsy. My mom said something like it's nice to meet you, and she cunningly smiled while making direct, disapproving eye contact with him. From the look that she gave me after meeting him, I knew that she had smelled his breath and would have a plenty to say after he was gone.

She left us alone, and initially I felt awkward and uneasy, but there was something about him that caused me to relax, and we actually had a wonderful time getting to know each other. He had spent two years in the navy and traveled to Italy, Greece, Spain, Jerusalem, and India. He had a plan for his life, and that was to go back to school and become an electrical engineer. I was impressed because he knew where he wanted to go. If you don't know where you want to go, any road can take you. Clearly, he was an experienced intelligent man and extremely easy on the eye. When he stood to leave, he held both of my hands and told me that his search was over, and that he wanted to spend the rest of his life with me. I perceived that it was just the liquor talking and I laughed, but he didn't. His aggressiveness frightened me, and I refused to see him in person again; however, we continued our extensive conversations on the phone every night.

A month had gone by, and it was time for our fourth Sunday musical again. I called Ron and invited him to church to hear me sing, and he said that he would be there with bells on. Everyone at my church knew that I was engaged, so I had not breathed a word that I was attracted to someone else. I was sitting in the choir stand when he walked in the church and took a seat near the back. My heart skipped a beat. One of the girls in the choir whispered to me, "Look who is coming to church. That is my neighbor, Ron Hoston, and I wonder which girl that drunk is coming to see?" I shrugged my shoulders, suggesting that I didn't know, but I was offended because I was beginning to like him a lot. He left right after the musical was over, and I was relieved. I rushed home in hopes that my phone would ring, and it did. He explained that he did not wait around because he did not want to arouse any suspicion or jeopardize my reputation in any way. He was a gentleman of the highest caliber.

He complimented me on my singing; but he said that the jumping, hollering, and shouting that the people were doing was a bit ridiculous and radical and that he thought it was a big joke. I explained to him the best that I could that the Pentecostal church was very emotional and spontaneous in their style of worship and that they were authentic. He jokingly asked me if I ever jumped and shouted like that and we both laughed hysterically. Before we hung up, he invited me to go with him to a party that one of his friends was giving at the Hyatt Hotel. I had lived a sheltered life of church and school, and the idea of going to the Hyatt to a party excited me. I had just gotten my first job, so I had a little money to buy myself a dress that was appropriate for the occasion. When Ron picked me up, he was pleasantly surprised to see me in a black fitted sleeveless dress with black sheer stockings and black suede high-heeled pumps. My hair was styled in a carefree pageboy with wispy, coquettish bangs just above my eyes—to emphasize them—and I applied candy-red lipstick as a finishing touch. He smiled and looked at me seemingly enthralled, and that was the beginning of a new adventurous life.

When we arrived at the party, there were several couples dancing, and other people were mingling and socializing. This was an elite group of professionals that lived on the upscale south and west sides of South Bend. Ron was in his element, but I was the new kid on the block. There was a buffet table that was sumptuously filled with all kinds of interesting-looking food. Ron noticed that I looked fascinated and a bit puzzled as to the array of food that was being served, and he politely familiarized me with the shrimp, lobster bisque, and crab legs, all of which I had never seen in my life. There were several salads and a large assortment of desserts. I was a novice and younger than anyone there, but everyone made me feel comfortable. Ron's friend, the host, was a teacher in the South Bend city school district, and he periodically threw these catered, lavish, extravagant parties in hopes that his estranged wife would eventually come. The ambiance was mesmerizing and created an atmosphere of elegance and a festive time. After dinner, Ron escorted me over to the bar; and the bartender poured him his favorite drink, Chivas Regal, which is one of the finest Scotch whiskeys in the world. You could tell that he was familiar with Ron's preference. I watched him down several drinks and smoke a half of a pack of cigarettes before he convinced me to try my first drink. How did I react? With a frown initially because of the burning, tingling sensation, and then good golly miss molly . . . A relaxed "I can get use to this" smile came over my face. Suddenly the people that I thought were laughing too loud and behaving rather rambunctiously were simply just having a good time. I always felt that anything that interfered with the normal workings of the mind and numbed your senses or clouded your perception was harmful, but I was beginning to have a different opinion.

I started juggling the party life with church. I was in hopes that the staunch members of the congregation had not noticed, but I later found out that they were very much aware. Some were gracious and understood that I was a young wounded girl that life had tossed around like a piece of paper and had been bombarded with life's complexities and desperately needed some guidance and love. But then there were those self-righteous persons that already had a contentious axe to grind and were elated to finally have a valid reason to perpetuate their scandalous jabber. So-called religious people really know how to shoot the already wounded. It does take a village to involve themselves in the rearing of our youth, but not when the village is drunk with jealousy and has a dwarfed mentality and lacks sensitivity, integrity, and maturity themselves. That might strike a nerve for some of you, but this too shall pass. Over the years I have been able to emerge out of my bitterness and resentfulness toward religious stone-throwers and forgive, but it wasn't easy. I had to dismiss it mentally, because when you sow a thought, you reap an action; sow an action, reap a habit; sow a habit, reap a character; sow a character, reap a destiny. My destiny was more important than becoming side-tracked with nonsensical productivity. My mom taught me well. I loved singing and I never missed a Sunday and neither did Ron.

Being that South Bend was such a small town, the talk was noisy and quickly spread like wildfire that we were seeing each other. The word eventually got back to Ron, my fiancé. Isn't it ironic that they both had the same name and both were navy men? When my fiancé came home for a weekend, I was not aware that he had been informed that I had been seeing someone else, and he managed to suppress his anger and intentions and kept his composure when he came over to see me.

We went out for what I thought was going to be a nice candlelight dinner, but instead he parked his car down the street from my house and slammed the gear into park. I had to brace my body to avoid hurting myself on the dashboard. The first words that came out of his mouth were, "I want my d---- ring back right this d---minute." I had never heard him cuss before—after all, he was a church boy—but it certainly had not taken him long to learn the sailor's limited vocabulary. I was startled; but seeing him again, especially in his navy uniform, reminded me of how good-looking he was and how much in love with him I thought I was. I asked him very innocently and sheepishly what was wrong, and he told me that he had heard about Ron Hoston and that I had humiliated and embarrassed him, and all he wanted was his ring back.

I instantly turned my charm and passion on and began kissing him and told him that it was a lie. He was slowly responding to my advances, but then suddenly he pushed me away as if he had had a flashback and threatened to hurt me if I didn't give his ring back. From the look of detestable fury in his eyes, I knew that he was serious. I slowly pulled off the ring, and there was nothing left on my finger except the imprint of what wasn't to be.

When I returned home, I told my mom what had happened, and she reminded me that she had warned me that it was unethical and dangerous to date someone after I had promised myself to another. Within a few weeks, I told her that Ron Hoston had proposed to me and that he was going to call her to set up a special time to talk with her to get her blessings. Her exact words to me were "I think that you are moving too fast, and furthermore, if you marry that drunk I will not attend the wedding." She ended her lecture by saying, "Jennifer, that is not the man for you. Remember you are my special miracle baby, and your destiny is to become a bishop's wife not a drunk's." She told me that she did not want me to go through the pain and suffering that she had gone through with my dad, and she begged me to break off the relationship.

Ron and I began seeing each other even more so. He took me to his house to meet his mom and dad and little sister, Tracie. His dad was anxious to meet me, and afterward he gave Ron a thumbs up and soon began calling me his favorite gorgeous daughter-in-law-to-be. He later affectionately nicknamed me Jeannie Bo Beanie and called me that for the rest of his life, even on his death bed. Ron and I continued to party together, and our weekends consisted of drinking sociably—and eventually I began smoking. Ron smoked two packs a day, and it was nothing for us to go through two packs of cigarettes at the nightclubs in one sitting. My life had always been sheltered and always centered around church, and that was all I talked about even at the clubs. The more inebriated I became, the louder I talked about my love for God and singing. I even felt the presence and the power of God to the point of tears while under the influence of liquor. Although we partied, he always picked me up on

Sundays, and we went to church together. You can say that I had a cigarette and liquor in my right hand and a hymnbook in my left.

Ron had never mentioned it to me, but he had begun to enjoy my preaching to him about God as much as my singing. One Sunday morning, he called to ask what time I wanted him to pick me up for church, and I told him that I had a hangover from that Saturday night and that I wasn't going. I never missed church *ever*, but I was sicker than a dog. He literally begged me to go to church. He said that he was going to stop taking me out on Saturdays if I couldn't get up on Sundays for church. He told me that crackers with a little honey poured on top would make me feel better. I followed his advice, and believe it or not, it worked. I hurriedly showered and dressed in my white blouse and black skirt (our choir uniform for that Sunday) because I was having the time of my life and had no intentions of stopping. I was just in time to march in with the choir.

As my pastor was preaching, I noticed that Ron had stopped making goo-goo eyes at me in the choir stand and had become deeply engrossed in the sermon. I will never forget the topic: where will you spend eternity? The Pentecostal preacher has a way of skillfully exegeting the scriptures and pounding his fist on the podium to emphasize his point. They start very calm and methodical, but by the time they get to the climax, they have preached you into a frenzy. As he brought his sermon to a crescendo he said, "Don't let it be said too late. You have to choose the Lord today. My sisters and brothers, do it today because tomorrow will never come. It's always today and if you procrastinate it very well may be too late." At the end of his thought-provoking and conscience-awakening sermon, the choir stood to sing "It's Almost Midnight" while the pastor was making the call to discipleship.

Ron was convicted and pricked in his heart and stood up and walked down front to the altar. I couldn't believe my eyes. The audience exploded with a thunderous applause. My mom had tears of joy streaming down her face. Everyone was happy except me. I should say, rather, that I had mixed emotions. I loved God and had accepted him as my personal Savior when I was eight years old, but when I met Ron Hoston, he showed me a new life and my eyes had become opened to a whole new world. I had become entrenched with habits that I was not ready to break. I enjoyed dancing in the nightclubs and drinking. I was smoking a pack of cigarettes a week, and on the weekends, we would smoke at least two packs together. I preferred drinking above eating and had gone from a size six to a four. It was rumored that I was ill with tuberculosis, which was prevalent then. I maintained my beauty, but my weight was diminishing. Cigarettes can increase your metabolic rate and deaden your taste buds, which explains the extreme weight loss. Alcohol actually suppressed my appetite as well. I was hooked on both of them. I had found something that took the place of coffee that numbed my senses and made me forget my pain. I was not ready to quit. I had been bitten.

My advice to you is if you don't want the devil to bite your forbidden fruit, stay out of his orchard. After the choir finished singing, everyone was in a celebratory mood. Ron was rubbing his hands together and shouting, "Glory Hallelujah." All of those things that he had laughed about and thought were preposterous he was now doing himself. He told me that he had silently said to himself, "God if you are real, let me feel you right now"; and from his response, you knew that he had had a visitation from the Holy Spirit. He said that he felt something like a bolt of lightning hit him from his head to his toes. I reluctantly went down to the altar and embraced him, but when we hugged, I felt the presence of God, and I wept and instantly renewed my commitment. When we left church, he took me to his parent's house for Sunday dinner. He kept saying over and over on the ride home that he had never felt such joy and peace in all of his life.

When we pulled into the driveway, he turned the car off and reached into his glove compartment where he had two cartons of cigarettes that he had purchased for the week. I was expecting him to smoke a cigarette as he usually did, but he didn't. Instead, he carried the cartons inside. You could smell the welcoming aroma coming out of the kitchen of the pot roast with potatoes, carrots, and onions and the smothered cabbage that was cooked with smoked turkey necks. His mom had also made my two favorite desserts: her delicious lemon Jell-O cake with glazed lemon icing drizzled on top and the "next best thing to Robert Redford." Incidentally, they both are to die for. It was a typical relaxed Sunday afternoon, and his dad and some of his buddies—including his pretentious friend, Trout—were watching the ballgame and drinking beer and whiskey.

As soon as Ron stepped into the living room, he announced unabashedly loud and clear that he had accepted Christ as his personal Savoir. The room went silent. Ron walked over to his dad and handed both cartons of cigarettes to him and told him that he could have them because he doesn't smoke anymore. His mother was setting the table and stopped dead in her tracks. They could not fathom him doing something that drastic overnight. But God had radically changed him, and he did it suddenly. His dad finally spoke and jokingly said, "I guess this means that you have stopped drinking too." Without hesitation or reservation Ron said, "Yes, Dad, that is exactly what it means."

This was an unbelievable, unimaginable transformation that had instantly taken place. Drinking and smoking were as common for Ron and his family as it is for a cat to meow. Ron drank socially every day of his life. His mother was on prescribed tranquillizers because of the anxiety that she suffered for fear that he would either kill himself or someone else while driving under the influence. His dad had a lock on the liquor cabinet because that was the only way that he was certain to have some left for himself. Ron embraced his dad in tears and told him that he could unlock the cabinet and throw away the key because he would never take another drink as long as he lived. From that day (over thirty years ago) to this one, neither he nor I have taken another drink of alcohol or smoked another cigarette.

There is a session called hypnotherapy that is quick and uncomplicated and has successfully helped countless people to stop smoking. There is also a twelve-step program of Alcoholic Anonymous (disempowering) where you have to stand up in front of everybody and make the absurd statement: "Hi, my name is . . . and I am an alcoholic." Although both of these options are indeed helpful, many times the participants find their success temporary at best. Most substance abuse specialists believe that your addiction is caused by a chemical imbalance in the brain or a learned behavior that must be treated with cognitive behavioral therapy or an antidepressant. Well, I'm here to tell you that there is a better and less expensive program and solution, and that program is called a one-step encounter with Jesus Christ. Not to say that we were not tempted after we accepted Christ, but Ron and I developed a symbiotic relationship. This is a term that is commonly used in biology to explain the relationship between two entities that need each other to prosper and survive. The bumblebee and the flower would be a perfect example. The bumblebee extracts the flower's pollen for protein and energy. While collecting these sources, they inadvertently brush pollen from one flower to another and that ensures the flower's reproduction process. The bumblebee needs the flower and the flower needs the bumblebee. Ron needed me and I needed Ron, and it was imperative that we kept that in mind so that our relationship would not be jeopardized and put at risk. Even today we maintain that principle.

When we walked into my house that Sunday night, my mom hugged us both and said, "Now we can have a wedding." Ron said something that shocked both my mom and I, and that was "Not so fast, not so fast." And then he proceeded by saying, "First of all, I want to tell you, Mrs. Thomas, that I have found a young lady that has become my best friend, and I am definitely ready to take our relationship to the next level. I would like to marry your daughter. I understand the seriousness of this big step, and that this is your baby girl, your only girl. And with that in mind, I promise that I will cherish her and take care of her as long as I live. I have fallen in love with your daughter, and I admire and respect her. She is different from the other girls that I have dated. She introduced me to Jesus, and that is the best thing that has ever happened to me. Mrs. Thomas, I respectfully ask your blessings." My mom was overwhelmed with joy and expressed it in the way that the Pentecostals do, and then she calmed down and said, "You have my blessings, son."

Ron did not elaborate to my mom as to how I was different from the *many* other girls that he had dated, but he later shared it with me. I think that it is worth mentioning that many times he would bring me home after partying, but when he left, he would not go home himself. At this point, I am going to be cautiously explicit and direct. I was warned by my mom and brainwashed at an early age by my brothers that good girls do not fall for the line "if you love me you will." Instead, they reversed it by saying, "If he loves you, he won't insist."

I was an eyewitness to my brothers' shenanigans when our mom was working the night shift. They had different girls on different nights that came over to our house. I was always very observant (borderline nosey), and I noticed that the nice respectable girls at the church that they really had a crush on were never invited. I learned an astounding and beneficial truth, and that was just because a boy sleeps with you does not mean that he loves you, and most of the time it doesn't even mean that he likes you. When their hot, sizzling sex was over, it generally meant that the girls were out of sight and out of mind until the next time. My brothers warned me incessantly to do as they say and not as they do.

Boys will only do what you let them. Do you blame them? That would be like blaming the bear for wanting to sleep all winter. That's what bears do. Someone asked a man why he climbed Mt. Everest and he responded, "Because it was there." Because of my foundation and the character that my mom poured into me, I was never easily exploited, hoodwinked, or deluded. Because of that, I felt safeguarded and knew that I didn't have to march to the tune of just any and every drummer. In other words, you had to get up much earlier than I did to beguile me. Please don't misunderstand and confuse me to be a little Jesus junior. There were times that I didn't want to be a puritanical angel, but making Ron wait seemed to have been a rewarding, satisfying game that I was persistently engaged in. I promise you that it was probably as frustrating for me as it was for him, but nevertheless, a girl has to do what a girl has to do.

There is a slang term that would best describe why Ron wasn't going home after he dropped me off, and I trust that you will not find it offensive. The term is he had to make a booty call. Are you okay? Great, that means that I can proceed. A booty call is a telephone call or other communication or visitation that is made with the sole intent of engaging in sex or other forms of sexual release with the person being contacted. In many instances, a booty call is made when the prospect of a traditional, respectful, romantic date is unlikely. This term is especially used to describe initiations that are made from either gender of a recently terminated relationship who may have lingering emotions and feelings of a need for physical connection *without feeling compelled to continue dating that person.* This call generally takes place *late in the evening, after midnight, or in the predawn hours, thus making it obvious that the express purpose is for sex only, and it is without commitments, liabilities, or responsibilities.*

Originally, black males were associated with this term; but like everything else that originates or is associated with us, it is now used by persons of all ethnicities and it is not gender-specific. The telephone was traditionally used, but due to technological advancements over the last decade, there are now chat rooms, YouTube, e-mail, text messaging, Twitter, Facebook, MySpace, and a most recent one, sex-text. Dating websites have also created a forum for a convenient online booty call. At this moment in history, when abstinence is thought to be archaic or antiquated, I have to concur wholeheartedly with the philosophy of Steve Harvey's new book, *Act Like a Lady, Think Like a Man.* Thanks, Steve, for accepting the challenge to declare that even in this sex-saturated culture, it is more advantageous and still a class act for girls to hold on to their "cookies" until the wedding night. I say more advantageous because you will have less emotional distress, distrust, regret, shame, guilt, and emptiness—not to mention sexually-transmitted diseases and unwanted pregnancies. My mother always told me that when a boy is pursuing me that I should "climb up high in the tree of modesty, self-determination, preparation, and pride, and make that boy climb after you." Girlfriend, we hold the key, so there is no need or room for desperation. Men have and always will love cookies whether they be macadamias, chocolate chip, peanut butter, or oatmeal raisin. They are not going anywhere unless *He's Just Not That into You.* And even if he isn't that into you, you still do not have to condescend and resort to desperation. There is one waiting in the wings that is tailor-made for you and will appreciate your modest demeanor.

Ron gave me an engagement ring on my birthday, July 2, and we set the date for the wedding. There was so much to do before October 22, and hopefully we had enough time to do it in. After jumping up and down and staring at my ring, I contacted my girlfriend, my maid of honor, and told her that we had work to do. A wedding is the biggest most involved ritual that your fiancé and you can put together, and you need all of the assistance that you can get. Deciding on a budget, participants, invitations, gown, photographer, location, and reception was all an overwhelming process that can frazzle you out; but with the help of my mom, church family, friends, and Ron, it looked as if we were going to make it.

It was September on a brisk Saturday afternoon, one of those dreary days when the sun had decided not to show its face at all. I stood looking out of my window, daydreaming about my exciting future, and suddenly my attention was diverted and captivated by the foliage. The leaves seemed to have finally made up their mind to release the summer, and they had begun gradually losing their vibrant green color and were turning yellow, red, purple, and orange. I wondered, *Where did those beautiful colors come from?* It has been said that those colors were there all of the time, but only manifest themselves when the green fades from the lack of light, and then the leaves start their dying process. How could dying be so colorful? I noticed that there were brown leaves that had already succumbed to Mother Nature and had fallen to the ground. I suppose they were dead, but there was still something amazingly beautiful about them. The light from the summer sun (photosynthesis) creates the rich green color, and in the autumn, the leaves do not get as much light, so they gradually turn. The awesomeness of God's splendor can enthrall you. I vividly remember inhaling and exhaling and lying down for a quick power nap. I can't tell you how long I had been asleep when I felt my dad kiss me on my forehead as I lay on my hideaway bed.

"Wake up, baby girl," I heard him whisper as he went into the kitchen to fix his bacon and eggs and a delicious pot of Hills Brothers coffee. "Hurry, I don't have much time," he said while looking at me out of those big beautiful eyes that he gave me. I jumped up out of my bed and ran in the kitchen and sat on his lap. He had saved a half of a cup of coffee for me. I looked over into the cup and, surprisingly, it did not have that rich caramel creamy look, but instead it was black. I tasted it and it was bitter. There was no sugar added.

"Daddy, you forgot to put lots of cream and a little sugar in our coffee."

"No, I didn't, baby girl. I saved that for you to do. You are a young lady now, and how you drink your coffee should be a matter of choice to suit your own individual taste. Baby girl, I never told you this, but I always drank my coffee strong, robust, and black—without sugar—until the day that you were born. I could hardly wait until you were old enough so that I could share my coffee with you, but I knew that you could not drink it like that so I put lots of cream in it so that you could get the nourishment to grow strong, and I added just a little sugar to make it sweet to epitomize you, but not enough to give you a tummy ache. I did that just for you."

"Oh, Daddy, I love you so much."

"I love you too, baby girl."

"Daddy?"

"Yes, baby girl."

"What about those grounds that always settled in the bottom?"

"Oh those. Remember I told you not to swallow them?"

"I remember, Daddy, but just between you and me, the coffee was soooooo good that I swallowed a few of them." We laughed so hard, and then I asked, "Daddy, where did the grounds come from and why were they in your cup?"

"Baby girl, the grounds managed to escape through the filter during the brewing process of the coffee. You see, sometimes, right in the midst of the joyous times in life, unfortunate things slip in. Things can happen to us that are unforeseen and unplanned, but we have to work around them, concentrate on the good, and continue to survive. We cannot allow a few grounds to prevent us from enjoying the best part. You see, the grounds are where that delicious, dominating flavor and irresistible aroma come from. There would be no coffee without the grounds. It's just like life . . . There would be no flavor in our character if we just experienced the cream and sugar of life, but it's the dark grounds of disappointment, despair, discouragement, discomfort, and even death . . ."

"Daddy . . . Daddy . . . ," my voice echoed in the distance. He turned and slowly walked away, disappearing into a deep foggy mist as if I were not calling him.

The pounding of my heart awakened me, and I sat straight up on my hideaway bed and looked toward the kitchen, but it was empty. The mind is so powerful because . . . It was only a dream. Have you ever awakened from a beautiful dream much too soon? I woke up before I could ask my daddy, "*Is there any coffee in heaven?*" Just like coffee, life can really grind away at you, but that is how we get the flavor and the aroma to develop integrity, tenacity, discipline, and patience. If you have never experienced the grounds of life be thankful, but don't get too comfortable because they will surely come. I am not a pessimist, but a realist. What a metaphor. Without the rain, the flowers wouldn't grow. Without the wind, we wouldn't have a gentle breeze.

I believe that most dreams are trying to provide an extremely valuable service to the dreamer, particularly if the dreams are recurring. I am convinced that they are, in fact, a signal that there is an issue at hand that needs your attention. I was so caught up into the euphoria of planning my wedding that I had forgotten an essential service that I needed. I had not asked anyone to give me away. That dream had reminded me that the one that was there to witness my miraculous birth would not be there to share with me the most important event in my life—the bliss of my wedding day. I am certain that I had mentally suppressed it. I immediately placed a call to my godfather, and just as always, he was there to make my day.

There is so much time, energy, and absurd and sometimes incongruent amounts of money that go into planning a wedding. It's a major event. Everything has to be impeccably and meticulously in place because one slip up or one thing that falls through the crack can cause the bride, who is already tensed, uneasy, and a bundle of nerves, to anguish as if that was an indication or a sign that perhaps she is making the biggest mistake of her life. I'm speaking from experience because there was a last minute crisis pertaining to the flowers just a few hours from the time of my wedding that sent me on an emotional tailspin, and I cried uncontrollably and wanted to call the whole thing off. I snapped at everyone in sight. It's called the wedding "jitters." We must always keep in mind that the wedding, although important, is only an event. An event is an organized occasion, an important occurrence, especially one that is particularly significant, interesting, exhilarating, or unusual—such as a social function, sports competition, and yes, even a wedding. But those are only events, and they are soon over. But an accomplishment takes it to another level. Accomplishment is the after-result of the event. It's the achievement, the fulfillment, the remarkable, successful completion. It's the final calculated score or the grade awarded to someone after a *job* well done. It's the final outcome. Studies prove that over fifty percent of all marriages end in divorce. I believe that marriages would have a better success rate if more time was spent in getting the necessary counseling on how to skillfully and lovingly handle future incidentals. This determines the success of the accomplishment, which is far more important than the here and now of the event.

After the bride's gorgeous, Chantilly-laced dress that is embellished with pearls is dry-cleaned and stored away, and after the black tuxedo and bowtie that the groom wore is returned back to the rental store, there are two individuals who have come from different families with different sets of values and different expectations concerning marriage standing at the threshold of a new life together. Both the bride and the groom have been influenced by negative and positive experiences within their own childhood homes. Because of this, each has a predetermined idea about how conflicts should be resolved, the value of money management, which church to attend (religion), children, intimacy (totally different than sex), and sex, and not necessarily in that order. Open communication is crucial, and I recommend that a considerable amount of time be spent in premarital counseling with your spiritual advisor or another professional.

Major disagreements will inevitably occur, usually a few weeks later (sometimes the day after the wedding, and in my case, the day of the wedding), when you discover that you have radically different views on non-negotiable issues. That is when the glue of love and good counseling is the cohesiveness that holds you together. There are going to be some rainy days ahead and some chronic disappointments, challenges, and conflicts, and a counselor offers a friendly reminder and gives you basic instructions on how to deal with the inevitable. Baggage that was previously overlooked or denied will become obviously prevalent after the honeymoon. Love is blind until the novelty wears off. The little things that he thought were cute that you did prior to the event will no longer be thought of as attractive. The sacred words *will you love, honor, and cherish, for better or worse, richer or poorer, in sickness and in health* have the tendency to glide right over the bride's lovely French-rolled hair that is ornately nestled under a fabulous tiara spilling with feathers and jewels, and those sacred words fly over the grooms freshly meticulously-cut hair because they both are mesmerized by the event and oblivious to what they are saying "I do" to. The event is quickly over within an hour, but the accomplishment is until death do you part.

Our wedding day finally came. The stage was set for the unforgettable that I had been waiting for with great anticipation. My godfather looked so handsome and smiled at me reassuringly as I placed my arm in his. I glanced down the aisle that seemed endless. My flower girl had scattered exotic orchids that lead the way to the most handsome man on the planet. I heard my pastor Bishop C.E. Bennett say, "Dearly beloved, we are gathered together in the sight of God and these witnesses . . ." I drifted into a trance, which is a decreased awareness of the things around you. Have you ever driven from one destination to another and not remembered very much about what you experienced when driving? Research has concluded that daydreaming is the result of the brain mulling over important and relevant things when your current environment ceases to capture your attention. When you daydream, there are blips of thoughts that pop up on the screen of your mind, generating feelings, images, and voices. It is a fantasy dream while awake, especially of the fulfillment of aspirations, hopes, and wishes. I heard my pastor say, "Who gives this woman to be married to this man?" I know that my godfather responded, "I do," but I didn't hear him because subconsciously my daddy had exchanged places with him. I was now holding my daddy's arm, and he whispered these words to me while looking deep into my eyes . . .

> My seed has blossomed into a lovely flower
> Let this day become one of your greatest hours
> I made so many plans as you would grow
> I had hopes and dreams how I could make it so
> I tried to cherish every minute
> And sharing my coffee with you is one way that I spent it
>
> I hope that I took enough time on my way
> To give you my heart at the start of each day
> My death was sudden but there is no doubt
> That it is truly divine how you have turned out
> I know that I'm not really here but my spirit is with pride
> As I gladly present you to Ron as his bride

I was immediately brought back into my surroundings as he disappeared into eternity, but he left a piece of heaven with me, his blessings. Although my godfather was proudly standing beside me with incredible love and support, it was my daddy that gave me away. What a magic moment.

I will never forget our first small three-and-a-half-room apartment. Ron and I purchased some plastic chairs and a few beanbags to go in the living room and some inexpensive bedroom furniture. Our kitchen was too small to accommodate a dinette set, so we bought some tray tables to eat off. It was not hard for me to adjust to this humble beginning because I remembered how my mom took pride in decorating the basement with dirt floors that we lived in when we moved from Clear Lake County, and I applied those same ingenuities and thrifty skills. I even purchased extra tray tables and proudly and unabashedly invited young people over from the church to dine with us. I mentioned earlier that Ron and I have a symbiotic relationship. We need each other to thrive and survive like the bumblebee needs the flower and the flower needs the bumblebee. With that in mind, I must share with you our first fight.

The first big fight that we had was serious enough to march into Judge Hatchet's divorce court. It was so serious that I don't remember what precipitated it. I think it was something major like not rolling the toothpaste from the bottom. We were in bed, which is definitely not a place to argue, and we both were equally engaged in an intense fellowship that was loud enough for the neighbors to hear. I kid you not, a storm suddenly aroused and it started lightning and thundering, and a bolt of lightning zigzagged downward in a fork-shaped pattern into our bedroom window. We actually witnessed it with our eyes, and it came close enough for us to touch it. I jumped into Ron's arms faster than right now. The storm subsided, and we resumed our fight. How quickly we forget. Someone asked if lightning can strike in the same place twice. Ron and I can answer that question with an emphatic yes! While a storm is in progress, there is nothing to stop a positive charge from collecting in the exact same place it did before. In the heat of our fight, a bolt of lightning once again zigzagged downward in a fork-shaped pattern into our bedroom window, but this time it touched our bodies, and we experienced a shock. I jumped into Ron's arms and we embraced each other tightly, and I began to cry. We knew that it was divinely orchestrated.

All couples, particularly newlyweds, will have a "let's get ready to rumble" time. It's healthy and the making up is wonderful, but over time you learn to pick your battles. The lesson that I learned from that experience was that I had been blessed with an incredibly kind, loving, and intelligent man with aspirations and attainable goals in his view. I learned that my purpose as his wife was to enrich his existence by cheerfully and energetically helping him achieve them by tackling the challenges that we would face with wisdom, patience, femininity, faith, and dignity. I knew from that terrifying experience that my top priority was to create an atmosphere of peace in the home. I remembered that I was a miracle baby and that the man I was to marry would be destined for greatness. I certainly did not want to be the culprit that would hinder him from being respected at the gate with the elders. There was a lesson that Ron learned as well and that was to deal with me as the weaker vessel. Not weaker in terms of my mental capacity because Ron married a strong, intelligent, dignified, multitalented, multifaceted, phenomenal woman in my own right. I guess those are enough superlatives and adjectives. But women are weaker in terms of timorousness. We require gentle and loving responses. We are like fine china, easily broken, and might I add, expensive as well. We are also sensitive, easily hurt and offended by our husbands, and require that they deal with us accordingly. A work in progress, but we both were. That's why I say that we have a symbiotic relationship, because we needed each other to develop and bring these things into fruition. What we could accomplish together is far greater than what we could accomplish apart.

Ron and I had another thunder-and-lightning experience before we were married. We were necking in the car when a bolt of lightning struck. We were not aware that the car had been electrically charged by ions until we kissed each other and we could actually taste it. We were both wondering within ourselves what the other had been eating, and neither I nor he said anything until the taste became unbearably obvious. We also were experiencing tinges of electrical shock when we touched. We were unquestionably insanely in love, but had no clue that it could affect you in that manner. Ron finally realized that it was the result of the thunder and lightning. We both learned something from that experience as well, but I opt to leave your inquiring minds in a quandary.

It has been said that we are all creatures of habit. Our habits, whether good or bad, identify and define us. I was not aware that Ron was struggling with his drinking habit. Habits generally bring you pleasure and thus they are hard to break, but when you make up your mind to break them you generally replace it with another. This is not a bad thing if the substitute is not detrimental. Ron and I had been married a few months when I came home one afternoon from grocery shopping and an eye-catching glass apparatus was sitting on the kitchen counter. I asked him what it was and he said that he had purchased a coffeemaker so that he could brew his own coffee at home. Ron had been drinking six to eight cups of coffee while at work. Actually, it had become one of his most important meals during the day. It was a stimuli. He would drink sodas when he came home in the evenings because we did not have a coffeemaker. I had not been around any coffee or coffee drinkers since my daddy died. I did not realize the devastating effect that it would have on me until he made the first pot. He was so excited and enjoyed the aesthetics of making his first pot of coffee at home, just as a little boy assembling his new electric train set on Christmas morning. He was one of the designated coffeemakers at work because he had acquired a level of expertise and particular skill in the preparation and comprehensive understanding of how to make the perfect coffee. He boasted about knowing the secret, that since the drink is ninety-nine percent water, you could ruin it by using terrible tasting H_2O. He began this process with fresh cool water because he said that there was little point in investing in a nice coffeemaker and some rich aromatic coffee beans if the water wasn't right. I observed it closely, and you could actually compare it to watching a lesson in physics. There were two containers that were fastened together by an airtight seal. The upper container held the ground coffee and the lower container held the water. As the water reached the brewing temperature, the increasing pressure of the hot air in the pot forced the water through a tube into the cool upper container. The hot water mixed with the grounds and slowly, there it was . . . déjà vu.

That familiar aroma began filling the air, permeating every room in our little apartment. The heat was removed from the lower container and the pressure normalized. The black substance flowed back into the lower container through a filter screen. The process stopped, and there stood a pot of fresh-brewed coffee. Ron looked at me and proudly smiled like a little boy that had just watched his electric 200-piece train set successfully pull six cars around an over/under figure-eight track with a bridge, railroad crossing, stacks of signs, people, animals, and all of the other bells and whistles, including a working headlight. There was such a sweet innocence about him that was almost intimidating. We are creatures of habit, and Ron had found one that gave him a pleasurable warm feeling just as the Chivas Regal did, but without the hangover. It was euphoric for him. Euphoria is an immense, gigantic, colossal sense of well-being. I watched him slowly pour himself a cup, and then he asked me if I would like to join him. I responded, "No, thank you," rather emphatically, without even thinking. I felt nauseous and angry and believe it or not, I was jealous. I had a flashback of me sitting on my daddy's lap drinking coffee from his cup . . . lots of cream and a little sugar. I waited for Ron to add the necessary condiments of cream and sugar, but he proceeded to drink it black. Déjà vu . . . just the way my daddy drank his before I was born.

The pain was deeply embedded, and I was not cognizant of the extent of it until I witnessed my husband thoroughly enjoying something that I thought was meant for my dad and me alone. I felt so vulnerable and helpless as those memories began to resurrect. In my psychology class, we had to do a paper on the process of problem-solving, and the first critical step to solving a problem is to first define or acknowledge that one exists. Subsequently, rather than facing this problem, I had camouflaged and suppressed it because of the pain from the memories. That's like putting a Band-Aid on a car's blinking oil light and ignoring it in hopes that it will just correct itself. The day that my dad died, I cut all of the anguishing strings and mentally dug a hole in the recesses of my consciousness and buried all of my connections with coffee. But the seed of bittersweet nostalgia that I had buried in the soil of love for my daddy had germinated and taken root in my soul, and over the years it had sprouted and grew exponentially. I could not tolerate the smell of coffee, and I had an incessant resentment for anyone that I witnessed enjoying its distinguished taste. They say that time heals—and it does—but first you have to seek an antidote.

I functioned very well physically, but I was struggling emotionally. Your mental state is inextricably linked to your physical state, so if you do not seek a solution, there will soon be physical telltale signs. My major mistake was not communicating this delicate issue that was taking its toll on me with my symbiotic partner. I was too embarrassed to share with him my struggles with coffee, just as I had been too embarrassed to share with him, or anyone else for that matter, that I was once a boy that was miraculously turned into a girl in my mother's womb. Then, to add insult to injury, I never told him or anyone else that my daddy had been murdered, but rather, I felt more comfortable just saying that he had died accidentally to avoid opening Pandora's box. That's a tremendous amount of mental pressure to function under. Ron and I have been married for over thirty years, and I kept most of these secrets from him until I decided to write this book four years ago. Becoming ambivalent and not readily seeking a solution that would best counteract the effects of my problems was in fact the cause of my mental gridlock. I had shared with him jokingly about my miraculous birth numerous times, but only in the context that it was probably a figment of my mom's imagination. I had never heard of anything like that happening to anyone in this world, and I did not want to be labeled as weird. I feared the innuendos, implications, and perhaps the indirect suggestions that I might encounter. There were several issues that were of significant concern that I had been holding on to, but the real culprit was coffee.

About six years after Ron and I were married, I began experiencing sudden episodes of intense fear that caused a shortness of breath, rapid heartbeat, hyperventilation, and a feeling that I was losing control. I felt as if I was having a heart attack or even dying. The best way that I can explain it is it was a feeling of fight-or-flight and my body reacted instinctively, but nothing or no one was around to jeopardize my well-being. It came without warning when I was driving the car, at church, at the mall, sound asleep, or in the middle of a business meeting. I hid it as long as I could, but eventually it began to affect my quality of life, and I had to share it with Ron. We made an appointment with our family physician, Dr. Jared Krackov—who incidentally is the greatest ever—and after hearing my symptoms, he diagnosed me as suffering from panic disorder. He told us that it was difficult to pinpoint the cause, but a few of the things that could play a role would be significant stress, undergoing a traumatic event such as a sudden death of a loved one, or perhaps genetics. He asked me if anyone on my mother's side or my father's side had this condition. I gave him an emphatic no, but as I sat there, I was reminded that I knew absolutely none of my relatives on my father's side. My dad left home when he was in his teens because of unfavorable and irreconcilable differences with his dad. He had nothing but his guitar on his back, and he never returned. He earned his living by chopping cotton and playing his guitar in the honkytonks. The opportunity to go to school for most coloreds during those times was rare, so consequently, reading and writing were something that he never learned to do. My dad signed his name on legal documents by making an X. Traveling from place to place and state to state he lost contact with his family, and because he was illiterate, he just did not pursue it. I am certain that embarrassment was a contributing factor. Sometimes you can drift so far until it's hard to find your way back. I vividly remember one night my mom and I reminiscing as we went through some old pictures, and we ran across my dad's obituary. I was too young to notice it at the funeral, but that night it hit me like a ton of bricks that the obituary had excluded the names of his side of the family. As a matter of fact, there was no one at his funeral from his side of the family. I asked my mom why, and she reminded me that she was only thirteen years old when she married my dad and that there were a multiplicity of things that she did not know about him and did not even think to ask. Some things he was just secretive about, and other things he would share on rare occasions. He always proudly told her that he had a beautiful sister named Vanessa that I looked exactly like, including her sandy-colored hair.

Not knowing any of my relatives on my father's side weighed heavily on me emotionally, but I had suppressed it as well. Every time I met a Thomas, or someone that strikingly resembled my dad or my brothers and me, there was always a question in my mind. Are they or are they not related to me? I actually have family members in this world that I am not aware of. One of which could be you, so be nice to me. Modern technology, such as the internet, libraries, and funeral homes afford us accessibility and have a plethora of information that allows us to find out whatever we would like to know. Writing this book has awakened my quest to know who I am on my daddy's side. He was such an incredible man that I think I finally would like to know more about him. I said *think* because tracing your family tree can be frightening. Some things are better left unknown (too much information), especially if they are going to stir up more difficult emotions. Slavery did some crazy things to our ancestors, and discovering it could really dismantle my personal image, but I guess self-discovery would be part of my objective. I do know for a fact that I am part Indian and whatever else only God knows.

I was processing a lot as I sat in the doctor's office gripping Ron's hand. Ron looked puzzled, as if to say, *what could possibly be stressing her to the point of a panic disorder?* I knew that the main risk factors were my anxiety about coffee, and then not knowing my family on my dad's side, also the murder of my dad and surrounding circumstances that I had refused to share with my partner for life. My doctor told us that we had done the right thing by seeking out professional help for evaluation because he was able to rule out any life-threatening issues. He said that his goal for treatment would be to eliminate all of my panic attack symptoms. He prescribed an antidepressant that was safe and had a low risk of side effects. It was recommended that I stick with the treatment plan by taking the entire prescription, even though I felt better, in order to prevent a relapse. He also suggested that I practice relaxation and stress-management techniques such as yoga, meditation, or any hobbies that I found enjoyable. Ron and I looked at each other and simultaneously said *singing*! We rushed to get the prescription filled, and I felt an immediate sense of well-being after the first dosage. It was very effective. One morning after I had taken a pill, I remember looking at the bottle and I saw in big letters, *no refill*. I panicked! I knew that because the medication was habit-forming and might cause physical dependence was the reason that my physician would not recommend prolonged usage. One of the worst things about panic attacks is the intense fear that you will have another panic attack. I always sang with depth, sincerity, and meaning and intensity, but after this experience, I took it to another level. Singing became the air that I breathed. Our life was moving very fast because within a few months, Ron was divinely called into the ministry. This was amazing and very convenient because whenever I felt a panic attack, he would say a little prayer for me and instantaneously I felt relief. My singing and his continued prayer got me through some rough times until I felt comfortable and confident enough to share all of my secrets with my partner for life. I mentioned that when solving a problem, the initial critical step is to first define or acknowledge that one exists. In other words, you have to face it to fix it. Suppressing and denying was the worst thing that I could have ever done, and it wreaked havoc on my emotional well-being. I must say that circumstances forced me into telling him about all of my dilemmas, especially about *coffee*.

Coffee has always been a popular beverage that people enjoy. The caffeine in coffee metabolizes into sugar and gives people that surge or boost that they need in the mornings as a stimulus or a pick-me-upper. It is a drink that people indulge in while doing paperwork, with dessert, during intense board meetings, at social gatherings, before a meal, after a meal, to stay awake while driving, studying for an exam, or just a quiet evening alone out on the terrace. Even at work, when it is time for a break it is called a coffee break. Why not a ginger ale break? It seems as though everyone has to have some coffee pumping through their veins, and they will find the time and the occasion to make it happen. Within the last ten years, coffee has become a phase that has skyrocketed. Coffee has become an epidemic. Everywhere I looked here were Starbucks sprouting up all over to bring the good coffee experience to the American mass market. It started in Seattle as a single store, and that single store became a second, then a third, and before long, it had become a demand phenomenon. It was rapidly becoming the third place to frequent after home and work. There were long lines that wrapped around the corner, with people anxiously waiting to experience customized coffee that once was simply served either black or with cream and sugar. But now there are a variety of styles, flavors, and presentations that have become a work of art. The menu has become bewilderingly complicated, with a multiplicity of choices—hot or cold—such as cappuccino, frappuccino, latte, espresso, decaf mocha grande, vanilla crème, and smoothies that are served with whip cream, marshmallows, and sprinkles, almost interrupting the wonderful experience. They have hired trained baristas who have the skill, expertise, and passion for blending the best coffee while entertaining the thirsty ones. McDonald's has also joined the band wagon, and is now promoting coffee as much as they promote their famous quarter pounder with cheese. The competition was getting fierce, so they offered theirs with quality at a lower price. I was struggling immensely as coffee bombarded my space. You could find a Starbucks at every shopping mall, airport, and Barnes and Noble—which offers you the opportunity to sit down and read a book while sipping on your favorite flavor. Then there were coffee shops sprouting that prefer to remain small and intimate, with a club-like atmosphere with linger-all-day sofas. Coffee has gotten ubiquitous and complex and has saturated every commercial corner in every town. There was no escape.

Everywhere I looked I was having a mental head-on collision with coffee. I had to face it. I woke up one morning in a cold sweat. My heart was pounding and my body was trembling uncontrollably. I had not had a panic attack for years, but as I said earlier, you cannot put a Band-Aid on a red blinking oil light in your car and ignore the problem in hopes that it will just go away. The antidepressants had been just a Band-Aid, which served as a temporary fix. It only took the edge off depression. I woke Ron up, and he held me in his arms and said a prayer for me. That was the night that I revealed to him what I had been concealing ever since we had been married. Coffee was the primary culprit for my anxiety. Coffee was everywhere, reminding me of my last day with my daddy. There were other issues that I had to face, but sometimes when you address the main problem, it can have a trickledown effect and eradicate the others that have been affected. For example, if you have cardiovascular disease, the trickledown effect will be that it will interfere with the functioning of your lungs because of the lack of oxygen, and it will also interfere with the proper functioning of your kidneys and your liver. The culprit is the diseased heart. Fix the heart and the other issues will no doubt be corrected.

When I look back, in retrospect I know unequivocally that my dad's sudden death affected me so devastatingly because he was brutally and senselessly murdered, and the man that did it was never held accountable. There were so many questions that I had while struggling to grow into the woman that he would be most proud of. I felt that I had been robbed and cheated out of the most important person in a girl's life, her daddy. Fathers, more than anyone else, set the perimeters for their daughters' lives. He is the determining factor for his little girl growing up into a confident, well-adjusted woman and no one can fill that role like a girl's daddy. Girls take cues from the father in practically everything from the time that they come into the world until he marches with her down the aisle, and even long after. He stands between her and a toxic world and guards her against low self-esteem, academic failure, eating disorders, promiscuity, unwed pregnancy, drug and alcohol abuse, and the list goes on. They are the ones that place healthy restrictions on you and enforce them, even while you are kicking and screaming the entire time. They have tough love. My daddy was my hero, and he was snatched away from me without a warning and for reasons that lacked purpose, mental perception, or comprehension. My psyche kept mentally returning to the scene of the crime and thus wanting me to do my own internal investigation. I had to let it go.

The sentimental remembrance that I have of my dad was the short time that we spent together every morning without fail before he went to work, eight years to be exact, drinking that delicious Hills Brothers coffee from his cup . . . a lot of cream and a little sugar. I did not get the opportunity to do much more, and that is the reason that coffee has impacted my life in such an incredible way. The aroma was so distinct and stimulating and the taste was so incredibly smooth and satisfying, and I associated that experience with the bonding time that I spent on my daddy's lap. I felt that no one had the right to enjoy that satisfying experience since I couldn't. I had to let it go.

I have discovered that, in spite of the agonizing pain, problems give us unimaginable potential for growth. The moment we make a conscientious decision to face and admit our problems—rather than suppressing them and allowing them to mentally weigh us down—is the moment that we are on the road to recovery. I had to stop pointing my finger outwardly at Simon for murdering my dad; I had to forget about the jealousy that was inflicted upon me from my critics for just being me, the haters, and the self-righteous stone-throwers, and I had to slowly turn that finger 180 degrees and point inwardly. It was up to me to get over the overwhelming feelings of despair and hopelessness and depression. I also had to forgive my daddy for breaking his promise. When we were reunited after he left suddenly for Indiana, he crossed his heart and hoped to die that he would never leave me again. But a promise is a present commitment about future behavior. As much as he would have desired, my daddy could not control the future. I had to forgive him as well. Talking to my symbiotic partner for life, the other beat of my heart, and disclosing all that I had concealed for years was like coming out of a deep black dungeon of agony and emerging into a bright white light of victory. An incredible wave of tranquility and serenity engulfed my soul, and forgiveness escaped through the openings of my consciousness. I experienced calmness in its rawest form. I had found something that I felt had eluded me all of my life. And it's like a breath of fresh air being able to tell the world that I truly believe that I was once a boy and turned into a girl through miraculous divine intervention in my mother's womb.

I have had to come to grips with the fact that regardless of who my dad was or his descendants are will not change who I am. I am Leroy Thomas's miracle baby girl, and I am a strong, amazing survivor. Ron has played an intricate part in my becoming an incredible woman. His patience and understanding has been incessantly consistent. He was both velvet and steel as I unraveled to him my struggles. He counseled me that a problem is only a problem when you perceive it as one. He emphatically suggested that I start looking at them as opportunities for growth and enhancement and not let surface issues derail me. Through the times that I grappled and wrestled resolutely with the opposing forces in my mind, I needed him to hold me and then other times I needed him to scold me. There were times I needed him to walk away from my stubborn will to nourish my past, and sometimes I needed him to run. My mind has taken a paradigm shift and has gone from one fundamental view point to another. Many times, human beings have the propensity to attach themselves to people that think exactly the way that they do because it brings some level of comfort, but what if their reasoning is diametrically opposed to the right solution or resolve? Rather than experiencing a paradigm shift, they will ultimately find themselves in a paradigm paralysis. That is, a person that fails to change his or her beliefs and assumptions after new information that they have received shows that a change is needed. Change is a matter if choice. The pieces to my puzzled life have fallen into place.

How blessed can one woman be to have such an amazing man to love her unconditionally and give her permission to be herself authentically?

My life has come full circle. My mother told the midwife after she delivered me on that scorching hot summer afternoon that she was going to name me Jennifer because one day I was going to be a bishop's wife. Wow! That's incredible, because in February of 2008, Ron was consecrated as bishop of the New York Central Jurisdiction COGIC. Bishop Charles E. Blake, presiding bishop of the COGIC was the chief consecrator. It was a long time coming, but that prophecy finally came into fruition. That makes me really believe her other testimony that I was a boy and was miraculously turned into a girl in her womb after she prayed. There . . . I've said it again.

It has been quite an interesting journey since that long cramped up ride from Clear Lake County to where I am today. I mentioned in the first chapter that while traveling on the highway you will see many road signs along the way, such as detours, danger up ahead, slow down, construction up ahead, road bumps, proceed with caution, slippery when wet, rest stops, traffic emerging, expect delays, and exits. I must say that I have encountered every one of those signs on my road to destiny. The signs are there for my observation, my preservation, and for my safe destination. I have not always observed them, which has oftentimes caused a delay, or allow me to say, extended stay, but there is another road sign that says *don't park here*. In spite of the boisterous waves and the tumultuous, howling winds of life, I have refused to park. Harriet Tubman instructed the slaves, and my mom gave directives to those two strange men . . . keep going, don't stop. I have irrevocably adapted that same disposition. It's my foundation that has given me that determination, tenacity, resilience, exuberance, courage, fortitude, and faith to persevere and fulfill my purpose. It becomes easier to face life's ups and downs when you know and understand your purpose.

If you take a person that has never witnessed a football game and set him in a stadium, he would be puzzled as to why those men have on funny-looking uniforms and head gear, and why they are running, tackling the opponents, and kicking a ball. But once he understands that the purpose is for one team to carry the ball the length of the field ten yards at a time for a touchdown and that the opponent's purpose is to prevent it, then he has a clearer understanding. I am proof personified that you can stay the course in spite of the oppositions when you know your purpose. I style my life as a game of football. Football is the only game of sports that starts off with a coin toss, and then there is the kick off. Life tossed the coin for me in Clear Lake County and the kickoff was that long, cramped up ride from Arkansas to South Bend, Indiana. Along the way, there has been a multiplicity of obstacles to prevent me from getting to the end zone. I call it pass interference. I have experienced the tackling and the unnecessary roughness, holding, facemask, and you name it. Any hurdle just to deter, stop, block, or hinder me from reaching my goal. It was painful, but "no pain, no yard gain" for a touchdown. My purpose in life is to know, grow, and show. I *know* who I am and I have *grown* exponentially from where I was, and now I can *show* others how to successfully make great exploits as they fairly play the game of life.

This book opened up with me riding in a cramped up car emigrating from Blytheville, Arkansas, to South Bend, Indiana. I was antsy, anxious, and bewildered because I felt that my daddy had abandoned me. I was so young and shortsighted, and only saw the need to be with him for the security, comfort, and love that a daddy has for his only little girl—and the coffee, of course. But the most significant thing that I imminently needed and had begun learning was the value of building a good foundation—which is tenacity, resilience, elasticity, exuberance, courage, fortitude, integrity, and patience. These are the prerequisites that will best prepare you to deal with the tough times of life.

I mentioned patience last because that is what I needed most on that long ride, and that is one of the essential things that has sustained me until now. You see, when I was finally reunited with my daddy, he crossed his heart and hoped to die that he would never leave me again. But as I said before, a promise is a current commitment for a future endeavor. We have no control over the future. As fate would have it, he inevitably broke his promise and left me again. I know that he will never return to me, but this time I will have to go to him. Just as I had to patiently wait in that car to get to a place that I had never been before to be with my daddy, I'm in that same predicament once again. South Bend was an amazing place because my daddy was there, and now he is in heaven. It's got to be an amazing place. I did not have a clue how long it would take to get to Indiana, and it's déjà vu because I haven't the slightest inkling how long it will be before I get to heaven. While traveling, you have the propensity to take on the disposition of impatience. Here I am, waiting again.

I have come to the resolve and accepted the fact that I will never get over the intimate times that I spent bonding with my daddy drinking coffee from his cup. That was the best part of waking up. It's that intoxicating aroma and that distinct soothing taste and the intimate memories that are indelibly embedded in the recesses of my consciousness. I will always remember the last cup of coffee that my daddy and I shared on George Washington's birthday, and how Simon rudely interrupted our precious time together. Coffee has been around for over one thousand years and it looks as if it isn't going anywhere; over 122 million people drink coffee a day. I've got to deal with it. It's my husband's favorite beverage and I'm finally okay with that. A cup of coffee is an excellent way to relax for a moment after a long day at the office or to catch up with friends and have a chat. We entertain occasionally, and the first thing that Ron does is get the coffeemaker out. He is very aware of my sensitivity, so the coffee-making is his job, unambiguously. I'm dealing with it. Every time we dined out at a restaurant, it would affect me when our server would ask me if I would like coffee, so now I turn my cup down into the saucer to eliminate the anxiety. Some things you never quite get over; you just have to learn how to get through it and SURVIVE! I have not had a cup of coffee since my daddy died and I know that I will never drink coffee again until I drink it out of his cup in heaven.

Many people perceive that heaven is a figment of the imagination, or simply an opinion that is based upon incomplete facts or reasoning that is predicated upon risky information. But I firmly believe the Bible to be the absolute, infallible, inspired word of God and it succinctly states in St. John 14:2-3 that

> In my Father's house (heaven) are many mansions. If it were not so I would have told you. I go to prepare a place for you. And if I go and prepare a place for you, I will come again and receive you unto Myself; that where I am, there you may be also.

Every good father should want to prepare a place of rest and a sanctuary of comfort for his children. I will always remember that little two-bedroom house that my daddy had built for us so that we would have a place of comfort, security, and safety. It was a far cry from a mansion, but it was nonetheless extraordinary because he prepared it and he was there with us. Now my daddy has a mansion. Can you imagine that an illiterate man that was buried in a potter's field—a plot of land where they buried people that were perceived as insurgent and having no intrinsic value to mankind—now has a mansion prepared for him? What a dichotomy. An impoverished man living in a mansion. My dad could not afford the exquisite furnishings and the elegant décor to accentuate our humble dwelling, but now he can bask in splendor. Writing this book has sparked an incredible quest about heaven. I guess it is normal to want to find out all of the information that you can about a place that you plan to spend eternity in one day. Before my husband and I moved to Rochester, New York, we did an inquiry on the job opportunities, cost of living, housing, schools, climate, and the churches. Why? Because we were immigrating there. The source of information that convinced us that it would be a good move was predominately by word of mouth, which is the best and the most effective form of marketing there is. The reason is because it was verbal recommendations and positive approval from satisfied occupants. However, heaven is a bit different because I am not aware of anyone that I can text, e-mail, or personally ascertain any information from that is a satisfied occupant, so the Bible has to be my reliable source. In fact, the only things that we know for certain about heaven are the things that are mentioned in the Bible. I cannot, by a single act of my intellect, come remotely close to describing heaven and give it justice because it is indescribably incomprehensible. But through my clouded vision and limited knowledge, I will do my best.

First and foremost, there will be no sun there, because the Son of God himself will provide magnificent illumination. All self-imposed obstacles will be removed, and consequently, there will be uninterrupted eternal peace. Revelation 21: 1-27 gives a description of heaven and it is compared to a mansion in St. John 14:2-3. I have never visited the White House to meet the president or London to see the queen, but I've heard of the opulence. But comparatively speaking, *heaven* is beyond the *stratosphere*. In other words, no comparison. There are twelve gates there, and each individual gate is comprised of breathtaking pearls. The walls inside the mansion are made out of jasper and accentuated with exquisite sapphire, emeralds, amethyst, topaz, and other precious stones. The entire external walls that surround the mansion are made out of pure gold, and instead of the streets being paved with asphalt, they are paved with solid gold, like transparent glass. There is a crystal river that flows from the throne of God, and each side is lined with trees that bear delicious fruit all year round. According to an NBC poll, nine out of ten people believe in heaven. I did not participate in that particular poll, but count me in because I, too, am a believer. But even if I wasn't, I would still consider the possibility, just in case there is. It's better to be safe than sorry. I have already called ahead and reserved my mansion to avoid the last minute hassle.

I've enumerated some of the things that would best constitute heaven as a mansion, but those would not be my primary reasons for my insatiable longing. It is not the opulence, because I played on a dirt floor and I slept on a hideaway bed, and that was heaven to me. You see, it is not the provision that makes it heaven; it is the person that provided it. My daddy provided it, and that was the epitome of heaven. Spending eternity with Jesus is going to be heaven, not the opulence. The opulence is the amazing fringe benefit, but my heavenly Father is the provider. He is the wonderful final Authority that will constitute it as heaven. And with my daddy being there, that just takes it to another level. I mentioned in my description of heaven that there will be trees on both sides of the crystal sea that yields fruit year round, but I have never read in the Bible where there will be something to drink. In the Old Testament, it was an act of courtesy to offer a nice drink to quench the thirst of a tired, distant traveler when they arrived at your home. My daddy loved coffee and I have always wondered if there will be any coffee in heaven to quench his thirst. It's been a long time since I sat on his lap and sipped that delicious Hills Brothers coffee out of his cup, with lots of cream and a little sugar. I don't think that a request for coffee would be asking too much, and I am expressing my petition right now. Matthew 7:7 says, "Ask and it shall be given unto you." And Philippians 4:19 says, "And my God shall supply all of our need according to his riches in glory by Christ."

These verses tell us that God will supply our need by a distinct and sumptuous measure if we would but ask. This means that every need is adequately covered because he does it according to his riches. If he can supply us with many mansions, gates of pearls, walls of jasper that are embellished with exquisite precious stones, walls of pure gold, and streets paved with gold like transparent glass, and year-round fruit, I believe unequivocally that he can supply some Hills Brothers coffee with lots of cream and a little sugar. That will be for me because my daddy prefers drinking his black. I am a daddy's girl. No apologies necessary. I only have eyes for him, and

> If my eyes could take just one last glance
> If I could have one final chance
> I'd search the world over and over again
> For the biggest cup so our mornings wouldn't end
> I'd give most anything
> To have coffee with my daddy again
>
> This is all I ever dream
> Just a little sugar and lots of cream
> I never thought that he would be taken from me
> But on George Washington's birthday
> It happened suddenly
> Every night as I lay on my hideaway bed
> This nebulous question filled my head . . .

Will there be any coffee in heaven? I say a resounding yes, and that is my final answer!

Quotes: ■ He's just not that into you - Greg Behrendt
         ■ Life for me ain't been no crystal stairway - Langston Hughes
         ■ We only have a minute - Dr. Benjamin Mays
         ■ There is so much bad in the best of us - Martin Luther King
         ■ To err is human - Alexander Poe
         ■ Sow a thought - John Stott

Songs: ■ Someone to watch over me - George Gershwin
         ■ Will you still love me tomorrow - The Shirelles
         ■ Because you loved me - Celine Dion
         ■ I believe I can fly - R. Kelly

References

         ■ Bible - King James Version
         ■ Wikipedia, the free encyclopedia
         ■ Legal consultant Loretta Courtney, esq.
         ■ Special enlightening moments with my mom

CPSIA information can be obtained at www.ICGtesting.com
Printed in the USA
BVOW07s1626251113

337287BV00002B/82/P